CUSTOM WOODWORKING

American Style
Shaker, Mission
& Country Projects

CONVERSION CHART

WEIGHT EQUIVALENTS
(ounces and pounds / grams and kilograms)

US	METRIC
¼ oz	7 g
½ oz	14 g
¾ oz	21 g
1 oz	28 g
8 oz (½ lb)	227 g
12 oz (¾ lb)	340 g
16 oz (1 lb)	454 g
35 oz (2.2 lb)	1 kg

CONVERSION FORMULA
ounces x 28.35 = grams
1000 grams = 1 kilogram

TEMPERATURE EQUIVALENTS
(fahrenheit / celsius)

US		METRIC
0° F	(freezer temperature)	-18° C
32° F	(water freezes)	0° C
98.6° F	(normal body temp.)	37° C
180° F	(water simmers)*	82° C
212° F	(water boils)*	100° C

*at sea level

CONVERSION FORMULA
degrees fahrenheit minus 32, divided by 1.8
= degrees celsius

LINEAR EQUIVALENTS
(inches and feet / centimetres and metres)

US	METRIC
¼ in	0.64 cm
½ in	1.27 cm
1 in	2.54 cm
6 in	15.24 cm
12 in (1 foot)	30.48 cm
1 ft^2	929.03 cm^2
39½ in	1.00 m
1 yd	91.44 cm
1 yd^2	0.84 m^2

CONVERSION FORMULA
inches x 2.54 = centimetres
100 centimetres = 1 metre

VOLUME EQUIVALENTS
(fluid ounces / millilitres and litres)

US	METRIC
1 tbsp (½ fl oz)	15 ml
½ cup (4 fl oz)	120 ml
1 cup (8 fl oz)	240 ml
1 quart (32 fl oz)	960 ml
1 quart + 3 tbsps	1 l
1 gal (128 fl oz)	3.8 l
1 in^3	16.39 cm
1 ft^3	0.0283 m
1 yd^3	0.765 m

CONVERSION FORMULA
fluid ounces x 30 = millilitres
1000 millilitres = 1 litre

American Style

Shaker, Mission
& Country Projects

CONTENTS	# American Style
CUSTOM WOODWORKING	Shaker, Mission & Country Projects

SHAKER PROJECTS 6

Shaker Step Stool 8

Lots of Shaker touches are found in this small project. There are two versions, one made with hand-cut dovetails, the other with butt joints.

Shaker Hall Table 14

Simple lines hide the challenges that make this table rewarding to build. And the whole project can be done with a table saw and a router.

Rocking Chair 26

Its Shaker heritage has been updated with some modern techniques. And there's an old skill that may be new to you: weaving a seat.

Shaker-Style Footstool 43

It doesn't take long to build this footstool to match the rocking chair. The two projects share many of the same techniques.

MISSION PROJECTS 46

Hall Clothes Tree 48

A special interlocking design brings this hall tree together with a distinctive look. It also makes it strong and stable, without a massive "trunk."

Shaker Step Stool

Oak Sofa Table...54

Everything you'd expect in a Mission-style sofa table is featured in this project, including quartersawn oak, square spindles, and mortise and tenon joinery.

Glass-Top Coffee Table.................................62

Made of quartersawn oak, this traditional coffee table is enhanced with a beveled glass top. There's also an option for a solid wood top.

Mission Bookcase..72

Built with machinery and handwork, this cherry bookcase features through mortise and tenon joinery. It can be built with or without the glass doors.

COUNTRY PROJECTS 88

Coat and Glove Rack.....................................90

Hang coats and mittens or cups and linens on this rack featuring storage behind its door. An optional finish turns it into an "instant antique."

High-Back Bench...96

This bench can be built with or without storage under the seat, with your choice of designs in the back and finished with stain or milk paint.

Jelly Cupboard...106

Back when jelly was made at home, a simple cupboard like this stored the finished product. This version offers several options to "dress it up."

Dovetail Chest..114

Hand-cut dovetails provide strength and beauty. For a different look, try the frame and panel version. Both offer lots of storage and a pull-out tray.

Sources..126

Index..127

Oak Sofa Table

High-Back Bench

SHAKER PROJECTS

The Shakers developed a uniquely American style of furniture. By removing unnecessary ornamentation, the Shakers kept their designs simple and functional, yet always in perfect proportion. The true Shaker look is clean and elegant, with every feature serving a purpose and with nothing wasted.

The first two projects are perfect examples of the Shaker ideal of function without decoration. The step stool's hand-cut dovetails lend strength where it's needed, yet display workmanlike detail. The hall table achieves its lightness and grace by its legs cut with simple tapers.

On the matching rocking chair and footstool, you'll find an interesting way to make your own dowels. Then, when the woodworking is done, you can try your hand at another Shaker craft, weaving seats with traditional webbing.

Shaker Step Stool   8

Shop Tip: Filling Gaps. 9
Designer's Notebook: Country Step Stool 12

Shaker Hall Table   14

Shop Tip: Tight-Fit Shoulders 17
Joinery: Locked Rabbet Joint 20
Designer's Notebook: Lamp Table 21
Shop Jig: Leg Tapering Jig 22
Technique: Tapering on the Jointer 24

Rocking Chair   26

Shop Tip: Shaping Leg Bottoms. 30
Technique: Routing Tenons on Dowels 31
Technique: Notching Round Stock 35
Technique: Making Your Own Dowels 37
Technique: Weaving a Shaker Seat 38
Designer's Notebook: Alternate Weaving Patterns. 42

Shaker-Style Footstool   43

Shaker Step Stool

Made from cherry with hand-cut dovetails, this step stool has lots of Shaker touches in a small project. Or you can try your hand at our optional country version made of pine and using butt joints.

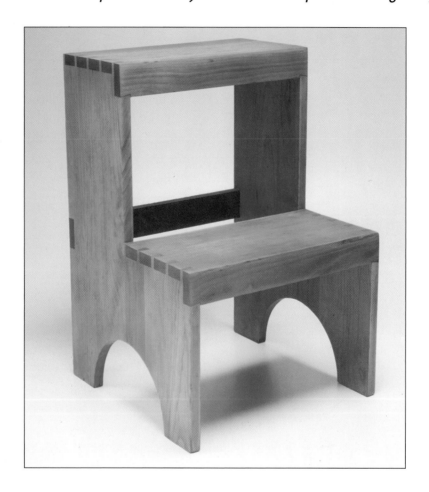

Shaker furniture is famous for its basic, uncluttered style, as well as its unquestioned utility. The step stool shown here is a classic example of Shaker design at its best. It's simple furniture that works.

DOVETAILS. The only decoration (if it can be called that) is the beauty of the wood and the dovetail joints.

And when you look closely, you'll see there are two types of dovetails. First, the treads of the steps are joined to the legs with traditional through-dovetails. Then, you'll see the braces at the front of each step (and also across the back) are secured to the legs with a variation

of this joint. Here, a half-dovetail joint adds a nice touch of craftsmanship. (If you've never cut dovetails by hand or need to brush up your technique, step-by-step instructions begin on page 120.)

ALTERNATE STYLE AND JOINT. With a few minor changes, the step stool can be built as a country-style stool. This version is put together primarily with butt joints and screws. Instructions for building this option are given in the Designer's Notebook on page 12.

MATERIALS. The step stool in the photo was made from cherry. I chose cherry for this project mostly because it's tight-grained so it's an excellent

wood to work with hand tools. Also, the Shakers would likely have used cherry for this project. But just about any $3/4$"-thick hardwood would be suitable.

FINISH. The stool shown above was finished with Danish oil, which is a mixture of tung oil or linseed oil and varnish. This provides a finish that's durable, but easy to touch up as the step stool gets scuffed from use.

There is also an unexpected benefit to choosing this finish. It provided a way to fill some of the slight imperfections you may have in the fit of the dovetails. To learn more about this, see the Shop Tip on the next page.

EXPLODED VIEW

OVERALL DIMENSIONS:
15W x 14D x 21H

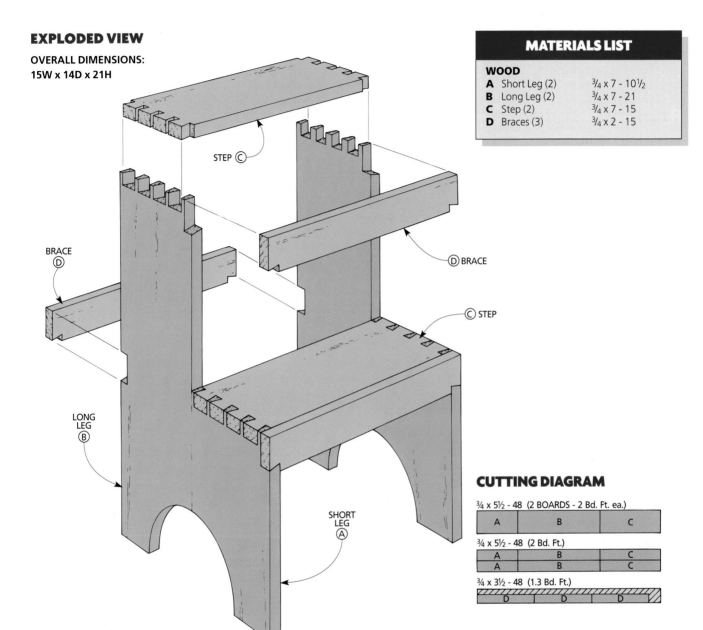

STEP ⓒ

BRACE
ⓓ

ⓓ BRACE

ⓒ STEP

LONG
LEG
ⓑ

SHORT
LEG
ⓐ

MATERIALS LIST

WOOD

A	Short Leg (2)	¾ x 7 - 10½
B	Long Leg (2)	¾ x 7 - 21
C	Step (2)	¾ x 7 - 15
D	Braces (3)	¾ x 2 - 15

CUTTING DIAGRAM

¾ x 5½ - 48 (2 BOARDS - 2 Bd. Ft. ea.)

A	B	C

¾ x 5½ - 48 (2 Bd. Ft.)

A	B	C
A	B	C

¾ x 3½ - 48 (1.3 Bd. Ft.)

D	D	D

SHOP TIP . . . . *Filling Gaps*

Very few woodworkers can cut perfect dovetails every time. There are bound to be small voids no matter how hard you try. The trick is to fill these voids so they blend into the rest of the joint.

One solution is to apply a liberal amount of a Danish oil. Then while it's still wet, sand with 220 grit silicon carbide sandpaper.

While you sand, you'll create a slurry of sawdust and oil. As it accumulates, work this slurry into the gaps in the joint. Keep sanding until there's enough to fill the voids between the pins and tails.

The mixture will dry very hard, and it matches the end grain of the pins and tails almost perfectly.

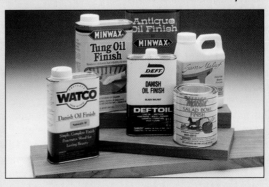

LAYOUT

It's easiest to start this project by thinking of the legs as four separate pieces. There are two short legs (A) for the front and two long legs (B) for the back *(Fig. 1)*. Later, a short and long leg are joined together to form each "stair-step" leg *(Fig. 3)*. So I started by laying out the cuts to make the four legs and two steps (C).

GLUE UP. First, I cut two pieces for each leg, one 5" wide and one 2½" wide. These are edge-glued together *(Fig. 1)*. (These pieces can be different widths as long as the glued up blank is a bit wider than 7".)

After the glue was dry, I planed the blanks flat. Make sure they're an even thickness, especially at the ends (where the dovetails will be cut).

After each blank was planed, I cut off one end square with the edges (leaving the other end rough, and a little long for now). Then I ripped them all down to the final width of 7".

DOVETAILS

The next step is to lay out the cuts for the dovetails in the legs and steps.

Since the tails can be made fairly wide, they're strong enough to support a person's weight. So the joints should be laid out with the tails on the steps and the pins on the legs.

Once I'd decided on the placement of the pins and tails, I figured their size *(Fig. 2)*. The tails are five times wider than the pins to provide the strength needed on the steps.

However, there is one more thing to allow for when laying out the joint. Even though the width of each board is 7", the dovetails are laid out across a width of only 6¼". The extra ¾" on the front edge of each board allows for the thickness of the brace (added later).

PINS. The pins are laid out so the narrowest part is on the outside (face side) of each leg (Top View in *Fig. 2*). Then a bevel gauge is set to a 1:5 angle to mark the angles on the end of each board (Top View in *Fig. 2*).

After marking the cut lines, cut the pins as with any other dovetail joint — except the half pin on the front edge of each piece is left extra wide to allow for the notch for the brace *(Fig. 3)*.

GLUE UP LEGS. Before marking the cut lines for the tails, I glued a short leg

to each long leg to form the stair-step legs *(Fig. 3)*.

Although this makes laying out the tails a bit awkward *(Fig. 4)*, there is a reason. If you glue the legs together first, you can plane this assembly, evening out any variation at the glue-joint line. Since you'll have to plane the whole surface, the thickness of the pins will change. When the pins are at their final thickness, then they can be used to lay out the tails. When marking the tails, make sure the steps are lined up with the *back* edge of the leg.

FINAL FITTING. Once the pins and tails are cut, go ahead and tap the joints together. The joints should be tight, and the assembled stool should be square.

Once everything fits, the bottom of the legs can be cut off square. Finally, to keep the stool from rocking on an uneven floor, a 4"-radius half-circle is cut on the bottom of each leg.

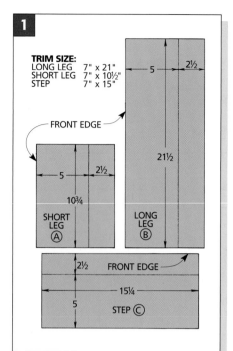

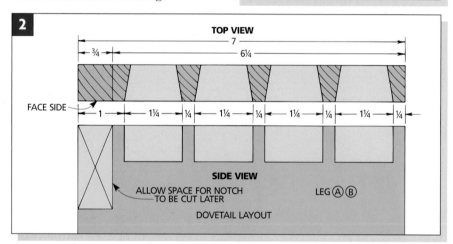

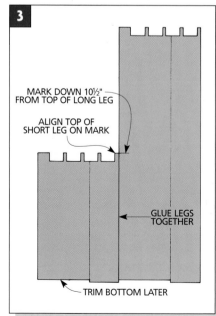

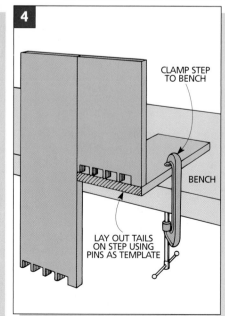

BRACES

Before gluing the legs and steps together, the braces (D) must be cut. There are three braces: one on the back to prevent racking and two at the front to reinforce the steps.

HALF-TAIL. All three braces are joined to the legs with half-dovetail joints. This amounts to a large half-pin notch in the front edge of each leg, and a matching half-tail on each end of the braces. I found it easiest to cut the half-tail first, then use it to lay out the notches.

To cut the half-tail, mark a 1:5 angle on only one end of each brace. This line starts ¼" up from the bottom edge *(Fig. 10a)*. Then mark a shoulder line equal to the thickness of the leg. Cut down the shoulder line with a dovetail saw and remove the waste with a chisel.

Before marking the shoulder line on the other end of each brace, first dry-assemble the legs with the steps. Then make sure the shoulder-to-shoulder measurement on the brace is equal to the distance between the legs *(Fig. 5)*. Now you can mark the angle and cut out the V-notch.

HALF-PINS. Once the half-tails are cut, hold the ends of the brace against the front legs to mark the cut lines for the half-pin notches *(Fig. 6)*. I used a dovetail saw to saw down both cut lines.

The half-pin notch on the back is cut a bit differently. After marking the cut lines (so they're even with the front brace), I made the two shoulder cuts to the depth of the notch *(Fig. 8)*. Then I removed most of the waste with a coping saw, and cleaned up the cut with a chisel.

After the notches are cut, trim the front edges of the steps to final width *(Fig. 9)*.

GLUE UP & FINISHING

After dry-assembling the stool to check the fit and for square, I glued everything together. I positioned the clamps on top of the tails to pull the joints tight. A piece of scrap under the legs provided a clamping surface across the half-circle cut-out.

Although it was nice to use hand tools for most of this project, I cheated a bit and used a belt sander to bring the pins flush with the surface of the steps.

FINISH. Finally, I finished the step stool with a Danish oil. ■

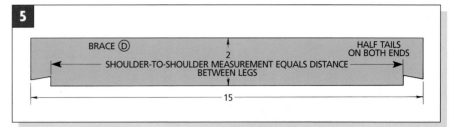

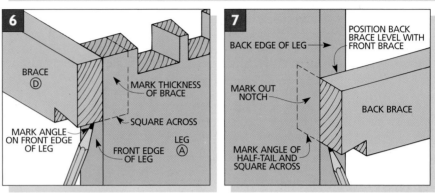

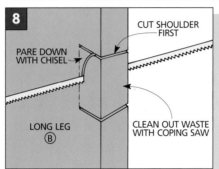

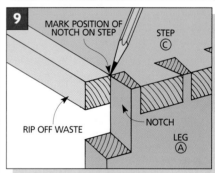

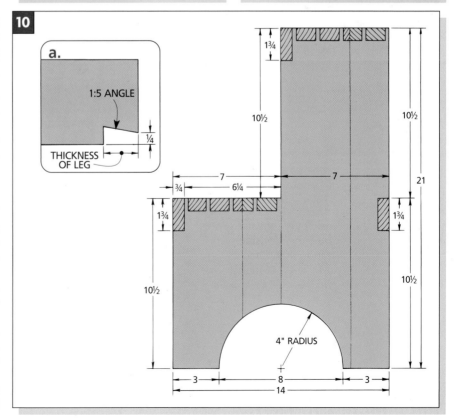

DESIGNER'S NOTEBOOK

This country version of the step stool uses screws and butt joints instead of dovetails. For a real country look, try making it from pine and finishing it with milk paint.

CONSTRUCTION NOTES:

■ Start by gluing up four panels a little long for the two short legs (A) and two long legs (B) (see drawing below). When the glue is dry, cut the panels to finished length. (The legs are not glued together to form the stairsteps until after some cuts are made in each piece.)

■ Next, cut $2\frac{1}{4}$"-wide notches in each panel for the braces. One way to cut these is with a dado blade on the table saw. A tall auxiliary fence fastened to your miter gauge will help keep the pieces steady during the cut.

■ To lay out a $\frac{3}{4}$"-wide notch for the bottom step in the long leg (B), set a short leg (A) next to a long leg with their bottom ends flush. The top of the short leg indicates the bottom of the step notch. Cut the notch $\frac{1}{4}$" deep.

■ Now lay out the location of the heart cutout in each of the long legs.

COUNTRY STEP STOOL

MATERIALS LIST

CHANGED PARTS		HARDWARE SUPPLIES
A Short Legs (2)	$\frac{3}{4}$ x 7 - $9\frac{3}{4}$	(12) No. 8 x 1" Fh screws
B Long Legs (2)	$\frac{3}{4}$ x 7 - $20\frac{1}{4}$	(8) No. 8 x $1\frac{1}{2}$" Fh screws
C Steps (2)	$\frac{3}{4}$ x 8 - 16	(1) $\frac{3}{8}$" dowel, 12" long
D Braces (3)	$\frac{3}{4}$ x $2\frac{1}{4}$ - 15	

(dimensioned drawing of LONG LEG (B) and SHORT LEG (A) with measurements: 7, $\frac{3}{4}$, $2\frac{1}{4}$, $5\frac{7}{8}$, $5\frac{8}{8}$, C, 2, DRILL TWO $1\frac{1}{4}$" HOLES, 7, $\frac{3}{4}$, $20\frac{1}{4}$, $2\frac{1}{4}$, $\frac{1}{4}$, $\frac{3}{4}$, SHORT LEG (A), $2\frac{1}{4}$, $\frac{3}{4}$, LONG LEG (B), 1" HOLE, $7\frac{1}{2}$, $3\frac{1}{2}$, $9\frac{3}{4}$, 3, $1\frac{1}{2}$, 3, 14)

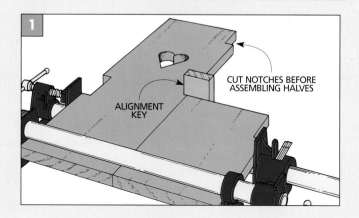

1

CUT NOTCHES BEFORE ASSEMBLING HALVES

ALIGNMENT KEY

(A diamond shape can be cut instead of the heart by using the pattern on page 99. Just reduce the scale of the pattern to one square equals one-half inch and use a radius of $2^1/_{16}$".)

■ To cut the heart, simply drill a $1^1/_4$"-dia. hole on either side of the panel's centerline. Then use a jig saw to cut along a line connecting the outside of each circle to the centerline. Use sandpaper to ease the edges of the cut-out and smooth any rough spots.

■ Finally, glue the short and long legs together *(Fig. 1)*. An alignment key made from scrap will help keep the short leg flush with the step notch.

■ When the leg assemblies are dry, lay out the stool's feet. To do this, first locate and drill the 1"-dia. holes at the top. Then cut out the remaining waste using a jig saw.

■ Next, cut three braces (D) $2^1/_4$" wide and 15" long from $3/_4$" stock *(Fig. 2)*.

■ To lay out the arc on each of the braces *(Fig. 2)*, refer to the Shop Tip on page 65.

Note: The shoulder of the arc is slightly wider than the leg ($^{13}/_{16}$"). Later, this shoulder is sanded down, helping the brace blend into the leg.

■ Through the end of each brace, drill $3/_{16}$"-dia. shank holes with $3/_8$"-dia. counterbores $3/_8$" deep *(Fig. 2)*.

■ To assemble the framework, first position the braces against the legs and drill pilot holes into the legs. Then glue and screw the braces to the legs *(Fig. 3)*.

■ Next, fill each counterbore by gluing in a length of $3/_8$"-dia. dowel.

■ With the framework assembled, the panels for the steps (C) can be glued up and cut to size *(Fig. 4)*.

■ A hand-hold in the top step makes the step stool easier to carry. Lay out the hand-hold as shown in *Fig. 4*. To cut it out, first drill a 1"-dia. hole at each end and then cut out the waste between them with a jig saw *(Fig. 5)*.

■ To ease the edges of the steps and the hand-hold, use a $3/_8$" roundover bit to rout a bullnose profile. To do this, set the bit $5/_{16}$" below the router base and make a pass on each face *(Fig. 4a)*.

■ Next, cut notches in the bottom step that match up with the notches in the back legs *(Fig. 6)*. To do this, center the bottom step on the frame and mark the positions of the notches. Then cut the notches $1/_4$" deep using a dado blade.

■ Now you can fasten the steps to the legs. Simply center a step on the frame. (There should be a $1/_2$" overhang on all sides.) Then drill counterbores, shank holes and pilot holes as you did for the braces. Finally, glue the steps to the braces and screw them to the legs using No. 8 x $1^1/_2$" Fh woodscrews *(Fig. 7)*.

■ Fill the counterbores on the steps with dowel plugs, then cut and sand them flush.

■ Finally, ease any sharp edges with sandpaper, then apply a finish. For a finish that stands up to lots of use, try polyurethane. For a more traditional country look, see the Finishing box about milk paint beginning on page 104.

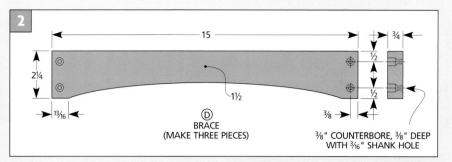

2

15 · $3/_4$ · $1/_2$ · $1/_2$ · $2^1/_4$ · $1^1/_2$ · $^{13}/_{16}$ · $3/_8$

Ⓓ
BRACE
(MAKE THREE PIECES)

$3/_8$" COUNTERBORE, $3/_8$" DEEP
WITH $3/_{16}$" SHANK HOLE

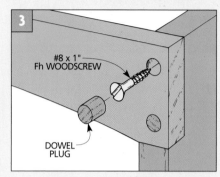

3

#8 x 1"
Fh WOODSCREW

DOWEL
PLUG

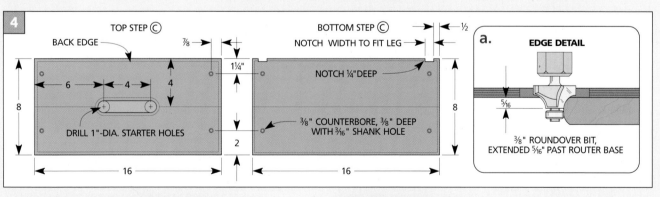

4

TOP STEP Ⓒ
BACK EDGE · $7/_8$ · $1^1/_4$" · 4 · 6 · 4 · 8
DRILL 1"-DIA. STARTER HOLES · 16

BOTTOM STEP Ⓒ · $1/_2$
NOTCH WIDTH TO FIT LEG
NOTCH $1/_4$"DEEP
$3/_8$" COUNTERBORE, $3/_8$" DEEP
WITH $3/_{16}$" SHANK HOLE · 8 · 2 · 16

a.
EDGE DETAIL
$5/_{16}$
$3/_8$" ROUNDOVER BIT,
EXTENDED $5/_{16}$" PAST ROUTER BASE

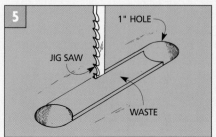

5

1" HOLE
JIG SAW
WASTE

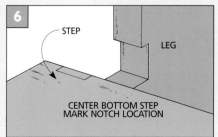

6

STEP
LEG
CENTER BOTTOM STEP
MARK NOTCH LOCATION

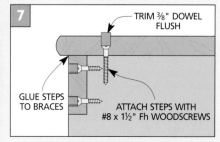

7

TRIM $3/_8$" DOWEL
FLUSH
GLUE STEPS
TO BRACES
ATTACH STEPS WITH
#8 x $1^1/_2$" Fh WOODSCREWS

Shaker Hall Table

The simple lines of this table hide the woodworking techniques that make it so rewarding to build. Even though there's a variety of joinery, it can all be cut on the table saw and router table.

This hall table is probably the most traditional Shaker project in this book. The tapered legs, a hallmark of Shaker design, lead up to the straight, uncluttered lines of the table.

The legs have a square taper that's cut on a table saw. It's a simple technique that's made even easier with a jig we show you how to build beginning on page 22. There's also a way to taper the legs on the jointer. Instructions for doing this begin on page 24.

JOINERY. The legs are joined to the front and side aprons with traditional mortise and tenon joints. If you haven't tried this type of joinery, it's not as diffi-

cult as it sounds. It can all be done on a router table (for the mortises) and a table saw (for the tenons).

DRAWERS. For the drawers, I used two variations of a locked rabbet joint. As its name implies, it locks the sides of the drawer to the drawer front and back. This makes it quite strong so the drawers can take years of use. This joint is also cut entirely on the table saw.

FINISH. I built this table out of cherry. One of the keys to success when finishing cherry is patience. It takes time for the wood to reach the rich red color that cherry is known for.

When it comes from the lumber-

yard, cherry is usually a light pink or salmon color. There's no need to stain it to get the dark color. As soon as the finish is applied, the wood will darken somewhat. With time (about six months) and continued exposure to sunlight, it will turn a rich, dark red. It's well worth the wait.

LAMP TABLE. In the Designer's Notebook on page 21, we show how you can make a lamp table companion piece (or two) by simply shortening the length of the table. And since the construction is so similar, it's easy to cut the parts for the lamp table while you're set up to cut pieces for the hall table.

EXPLODED VIEW

OVERALL DIMENSIONS:
42W x 14½D x 29H

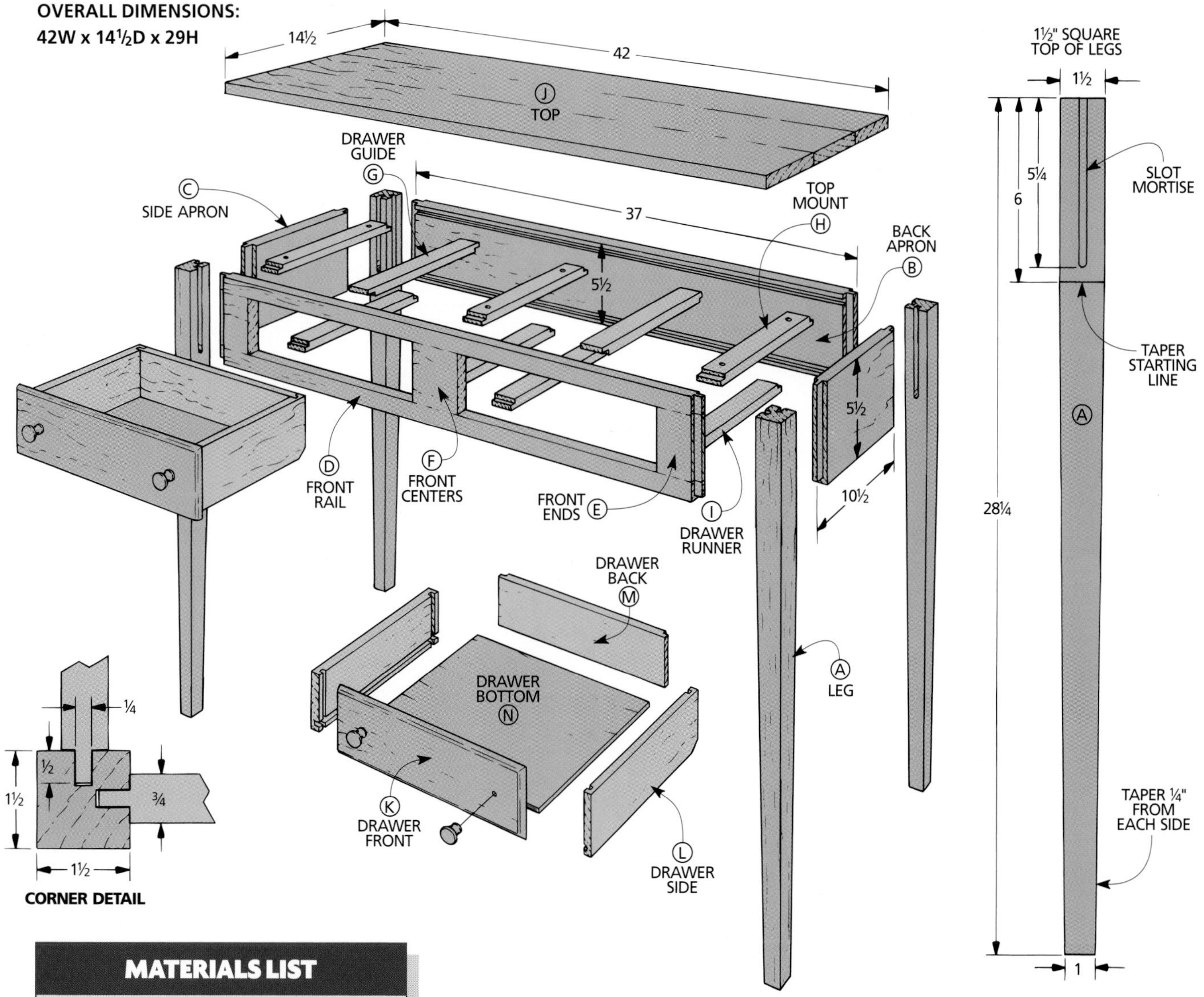

14½
42
J
TOP
DRAWER GUIDE
G
37
C
SIDE APRON
TOP MOUNT
H
BACK APRON
B
5½
5½
10½
D
FRONT RAIL
F
FRONT CENTERS
FRONT ENDS
E
I
DRAWER RUNNER
DRAWER BACK
M
DRAWER BOTTOM
N
K
DRAWER FRONT
L
DRAWER SIDE
A
LEG
¼
½
1½
¾
1½
1½" SQUARE TOP OF LEGS
1½
5¼
6
SLOT MORTISE
TAPER STARTING LINE
A
28¼
TAPER ¼" FROM EACH SIDE
1

CORNER DETAIL

MATERIALS LIST

TABLE		
A	Legs (4)	1½ x 1½ - 28¼
B	Back Apron (1)	¾ x 5½ - 37
C	Side Aprons (2)	¾ x 5½ - 10½
D	Front Rails (2)	¾ x 1 - 37
E	Front Ends (2)	¾ x 3½ - 2¾
F	Front Center (1)	¾ x 3½ - 3½
G	Drawer Guides (2)	¾ x 1½ - 10¾
H	Top Mounts (3)	¾ x 1½ - 10¾
I	Drawer Runners (4)	¾ x 1½ - 10¾
J	Top (1)	¾ x 14½ - 42
DRAWERS		
K	Fronts (2)	¾ x 4³⁄₁₆ - 14¹¹⁄₁₆
L	Sides (4)	½ x 3⁷⁄₁₆ - 10¾
M	Backs (2)	½ x 2¹⁵⁄₁₆ - 13⁷⁄₁₆
N	Bottoms (2)	¼ ply - 10⅝ x 13⁷⁄₁₆

HARDWARE SUPPLIES
(2) No. 6 x ¾" Rh woodscrews
(6) No. 8 x 1¼" Rh woodscrews
(6) ³⁄₁₆" flat washers
(18) ¾" brads
(4) ⅝" brads
(4) 1"-dia. cherry knobs w/ screws

CUTTING DIAGRAM

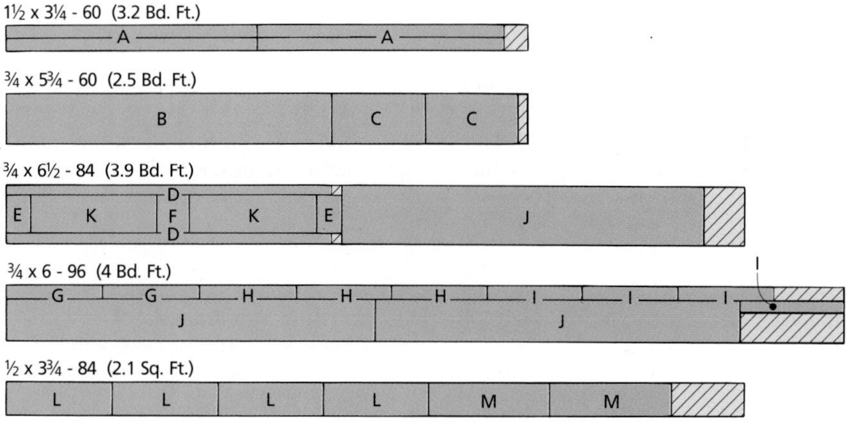

1½ x 3¼ - 60 (3.2 Bd. Ft.)
A
A
¾ x 5¾ - 60 (2.5 Bd. Ft.)
B
C
C
¾ x 6½ - 84 (3.9 Bd. Ft.)
E
K
D
F
D
K
E
J
¾ x 6 - 96 (4 Bd. Ft.)
G
G
H
H
H
I
I
I
I
J
J
½ x 3¾ - 84 (2.1 Sq. Ft.)
L
L
L
L
M
M

NOTE: ALSO NEED ONE SHEET OF ¼" x 24" x 48" PLYWOOD FOR DRAWER BOTTOMS.

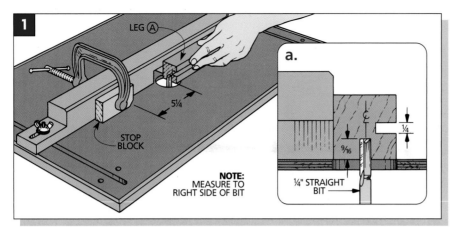

1

LEG (A)

5¼"

STOP BLOCK

NOTE: MEASURE TO RIGHT SIDE OF BIT

a.

¼"

9/16"

¼" STRAIGHT BIT

2

TAPER LEG

CLAMP LEG TO JIG

NOTE: SEE PAGES 22-23 TO BUILD TAPER JIG

a. BOTTOM VIEW

¼" · 1 · ¼"

¼"

1

¼"

1½

1½

3

PIPE CLAMPS

14

3½

14

2¾

2¾

(D)

(E)

(F)

(E)

FRONT APRON

NOTE: GRAIN DIRECTION RUNS SIDE-TO-SIDE

5½

1 · 3½ · 1

¾"

END VIEW

4

NOTE: GROOVE FRONT AND BACK APRONS

FRONT APRON

BACK APRON

(B)

a.

EQUALS THICKNESS OF CROSS MEMBER

SAW FENCE

JOINT LINE

½

5/16

DADO BLADE

LEGS

This project starts by making the tapered legs and cutting the mortises in each of them.

Begin by cutting four leg blanks (A) to 1½" square by 28¼" long (refer to the Exploded View on page 15).

MORTISES. After cutting the legs to size, mark two adjacent sides where the mortises will be cut. (It's best to cut the mortises before tapering the legs.) The mortises are easy to cut on a router table with a ¼" straight bit.

To set up the router table for the mortises, start by raising the bit 9/16" high *(Fig. 1a)*. Then move the fence until the bit is centered on the thickness of the leg.

The length of the mortise is set by clamping a stop block to the fence 5¼" from the *right* side of the bit *(Fig. 1)*. Now you can cut the mortises on two adjacent sides.

TAPERS. After the mortises are routed, the next step is to taper all four sides of each leg. To cut the tapers, I used a sliding platform jig on the table saw *(Fig. 2)*. (Instructions for building and using this jig begin on page 22. An alternate method of tapering the legs, using the jointer, is shown on page 24.)

Whatever method you use, the point is to cut a taper on each side of the leg that starts 6" from the top end and tapers down so the bottom end is 1" square. This means cutting ¼" off each side *(Fig. 2a)*.

APRONS

After the tapers are cut, the next step is to cut the front apron assembly. This consists of five pieces glued together to form two drawer openings *(Fig. 3)*.

FRONT APRON. To make the front apron, start by ripping the top and bottom rails (D) 1" wide by 37" long.

To make the three dividers for this front assembly, rip a blank 3½" wide. Then cut off two end dividers (E) 2¾" long, and a front center (F) 3½" long. (This ensures that the grain runs the same direction as the rails.)

ASSEMBLE FRONT APRON. After cutting all five pieces for the front apron, glue and clamp the dividers between the top and bottom rails *(Fig. 3)*. Make sure the center divider (F) is centered on the length, and the end dividers (E) are flush with the ends.

BACK AND SIDE APRONS. Next, cut the back apron (B) and side aprons (C). Start by ripping the stock for these pieces to a width of 5½". Then cut the three pieces to finished lengths of 10½" for the sides, and 37" for the back. (The back apron should be exactly as wide and as long as the front assembly.)

GROOVES. To support and guide the drawers, cross members (G, H, I) fit into ½"-wide grooves cut along the inside faces of the front and back aprons (refer to *Fig. 11* on page 18).

The positions of these grooves are critical. They have to be cut so that when the drawer runners (I) are mounted, they're flush with the top edge of the front apron's bottom rail (refer to *Fig. 11c* on page 18).

To set up the saw for this position, adjust the fence so the distance from the inside edge of the rail (the joint line shown in *Fig. 4a*) to the inside edge of the dado blade equals the thickness of the stock for the drawer runner. (This means you need to measure from the joint line, not the rip fence.) Then cut the grooves in the front and back aprons (*Fig. 4*).

TENONS. Now tenons can be cut on the ends of the aprons to fit the mortises in the legs. I cut them on the table saw (*Fig. 5*).

The ½"-long tenon is formed by cutting ½"-wide rabbets on both faces of the apron (*Fig. 5a*).

Note: The tenon is ¹⁄₁₆" less than the depth of the mortise to allow a little glue relief at the bottom of the mortise.

To cut the tenons, I used a ¾"-wide dado blade and moved a wooden auxiliary fence over the blade so only ½" was exposed (*Fig. 5*).

Sneak up on the final height of the blade by raising it and making a pass on both faces of a scrap piece until the tenon fits the mortise. Once set, cut rabbets on both ends of all four aprons to produce tenons centered on the thickness of the stock.

Note: To get a tight fit against the leg, I used a chisel to slightly undercut the shoulders of each tenon. (See the Shop Tip at the bottom of this page for more on this.)

NOTCH TENONS. So that the top of each apron will sit flush with the top of each leg, the bottom end of each tenon has to be notched (*Fig. 7*). Since the mortises are rounded on the bottom, I cut the tenon a trifle shorter so I didn't have to square up the bottom of the mortise. This means cutting a ³⁄₈" notch on the bottom of each tenon (*Fig. 6*).

END PIECES. To make assembly easier later, I glued a pair of legs to each side apron to produce two complete end units. But don't glue on the front or back aprons yet.

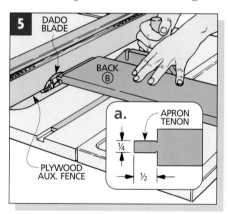

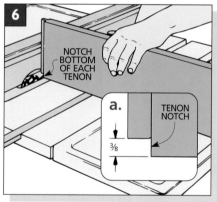

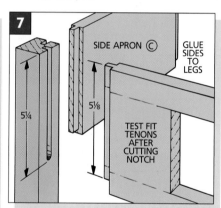

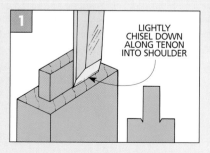
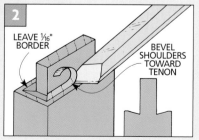
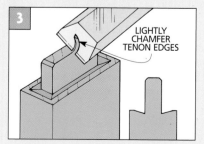

CROSS MEMBERS, TOP, & ASSEMBLY

Next, nine cross members are cut to fit between the front and back aprons. Two of these pieces mount above the drawers for drawer guides (G), three are top mounts (H) used to fasten down the table top, and four sit below the drawers as runners (I) *(Fig. 10)*.

CUT TO SIZE. First rip enough stock $1\frac{1}{2}$" wide to make the nine pieces. To determine their length, dry assemble the table. (It may be easiest to do this with the table upside down.) Measure the distance between the front and back aprons to get the shoulder-to-shoulder length of the cross members. Now add $\frac{1}{2}$" to this measurement to account for a $\frac{1}{4}$"-long tenon on each end.

After cutting the pieces to length, form the tenons by cutting a $\frac{1}{4}$"-wide by $\frac{1}{4}$"-deep rabbet at each end *(Fig. 8)*.

DRAWER GUIDES. The two drawer guides (G) each have a $\frac{1}{8}$"-wide groove cut down the center *(Fig. 9a)*. This groove guides a pin that's mounted on the back of the drawer. The pin helps keep the drawer straight as it's pulled out of the carcase.

TOP MOUNT PIECES. To allow the table top to expand and contract, I drilled oversized shank holes ($\frac{3}{8}$"-dia.) on the three top mounts (H) *(Fig. 11b)*. These holes are centered on the width and drilled $1\frac{1}{4}$" from each end on all three pieces.

TABLE TOP. Now glue up a blank for the table top (J). Then cut this blank to final size so it will overhang each of the side aprons by $1\frac{7}{8}$" and the front and back aprons by $1\frac{3}{8}$".

ASSEMBLY. After the parts are cut, dry-assemble the table and check it for square. If everything is okay, glue and clamp the front and back aprons to the leg units. Make sure the cross members are in position but *not* glued in.

There's one important thing to watch as you position the cross members. The rabbets face down on the drawer guides *(Fig. 11a)*, but up on the top mount *(Fig. 11b)*, and drawer runners *(Fig. 11c)*. Use $\frac{3}{4}$" brads to tack *only* the top mounts (H) in place. The other cross members will be secured after the drawers are added.

Now center the table top on the aprons and screw (don't glue) it down to the top mounts *(Fig. 11b)*. Use $\frac{3}{16}$" washers under the screw heads.

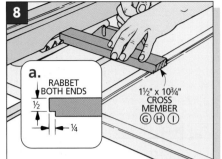

8

a.
RABBET BOTH ENDS
$\frac{1}{2}$
$\frac{1}{4}$

$1\frac{1}{2}$" x $10\frac{3}{4}$"
CROSS MEMBER
G H I

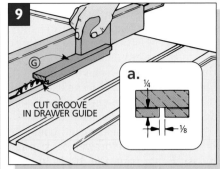

9

G
CUT GROOVE IN DRAWER GUIDE

a.
$\frac{1}{4}$
$\frac{1}{8}$

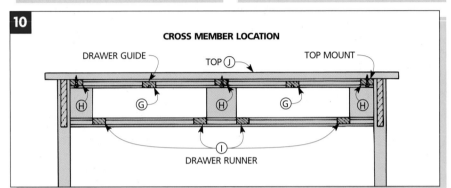

10

CROSS MEMBER LOCATION

DRAWER GUIDE   TOP J   TOP MOUNT

H   G   H   G   H

DRAWER RUNNER

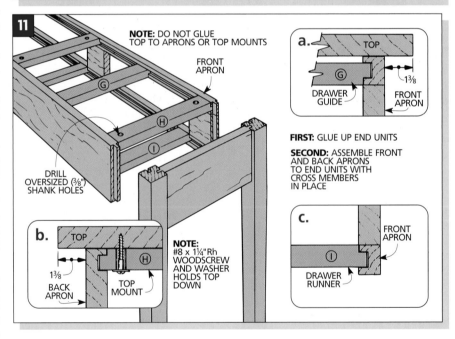

11

NOTE: DO NOT GLUE TOP TO APRONS OR TOP MOUNTS

FRONT APRON

G

H

I

DRILL OVERSIZED ($\frac{3}{8}$") SHANK HOLES

a.
TOP
G
$1\frac{3}{8}$
DRAWER GUIDE
FRONT APRON

FIRST: GLUE UP END UNITS

SECOND: ASSEMBLE FRONT AND BACK APRONS TO END UNITS WITH CROSS MEMBERS IN PLACE

b.
TOP
$1\frac{3}{8}$
BACK APRON
H
TOP MOUNT

NOTE: #8 x $1\frac{1}{4}$"Rh WOODSCREW AND WASHER HOLDS TOP DOWN

c.
FRONT APRON
I
DRAWER RUNNER

DRAWERS

Once the table is assembled, all that's left to build are the drawers. The first step in making the drawers is to cut the pieces for each drawer to size.

FRONTS. The drawer fronts (K) are cut from $\frac{3}{4}$"-thick stock. The length of each front is $\frac{11}{16}$" more than the width of the drawer opening. This allows for a $\frac{3}{8}$" lip on both ends ($\frac{3}{4}$" total), minus $\frac{1}{16}$" for clearance. As for the height of the drawer front, measure the height of

the opening, add $\frac{3}{4}$" for the lips, and subtract $\frac{1}{16}$" for clearance.

SIDES. The drawer sides (L) are cut from $\frac{1}{2}$"-thick stock. Cut them to width (height) to match the height of the drawer opening, minus $\frac{1}{16}$" for clearance. As for the length of the sides, measure the depth of the table (from the front of the drawer opening to the back apron). Then subtract about $\frac{1}{4}$" from this measurement.

BACK. The backs (M) are cut to rough width to match the drawer sides and to rough length to match the drawer front. (The backs are trimmed to final size later.)

LOCKED RABBET JOINT. After cutting the pieces to size, locked rabbet joints are cut to join the drawer sides to the fronts *(Fig. 13)*. See the Joinery box on the next page for details on doing this.

A variation of the locked rabbet joint is used to join the drawer back to the sides. First, trim the back to final length. To get this length, measure the distance from end to end of the tongues on the drawer front. Cut the back to equal this measurement.

To cut the locked rabbet joint, first cut rabbets on both ends of the back to leave $^1/_8$"-thick tongues *(Fig. 13)*. Then cut a dado in each drawer side to accept this tongue.

DRAWER BOTTOM. Before the drawer can be assembled, a $^1/_4$"-deep groove must be cut in the drawer front and sides for the plywood bottom (N). (No groove is needed in the back, since it rests on top of the drawer bottom.)

To locate the grooves, you need to measure from different points for the drawer front and the sides. On the drawer front, the top edge of this groove is located $^1/_2$" up from the bottom edge of the lip *(Fig. 14)*. On the drawer sides, it's $^1/_2$" from the bottom edge *(Fig. 15)*.

After the grooves are cut, dry-assemble the drawer and cut the drawer bottom to fit. Then trim the back to width so it rests on the plywood bottom.

COMPLETE DRAWERS. All the parts for the drawer are cut, but there are still a few details to take care of before the drawers are done.

First, round over the front edges of each drawer front with a $^1/_4$" roundover bit *(Fig. 12)*. Now glue each drawer together, making sure it's square.

When the glue was dry, I added a guide pin on the top edge of the back *(Fig. 12c)*. This pin is simply a No. 6 x $^3/_4$" brass screw that's screwed part way into the back. Then I cut off the head to leave a guide pin.

One other detail is to cut a slight chamfer on the bottom back edge of the drawer so it can be tilted into the opening *(Figs. 12b and 16)*.

Finally, for mounting the knobs, I drilled a $^1/_4$"-dia. hole $2^1/_8$" from each end of the drawer fronts *(Fig. 12a)*.

SECURE CROSS MEMBERS. To finish the table, the drawer guides and runners need to be secured. To do this, remove the top and drawers and drive $^3/_4$" brads into the tongues *(Fig. 16a)*. ■

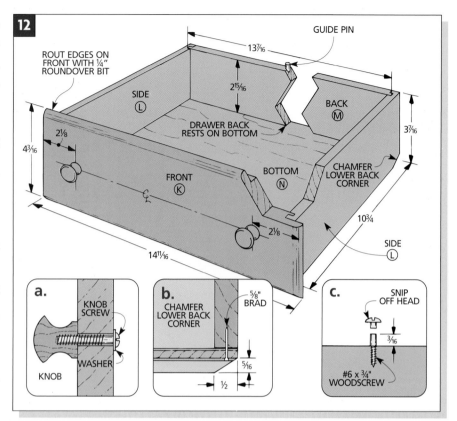

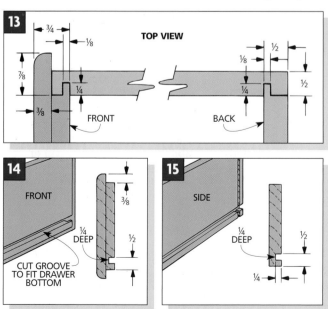

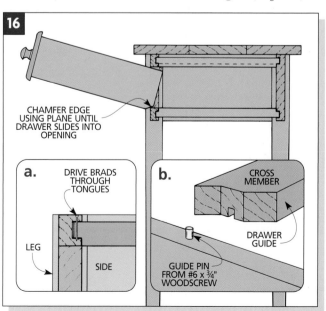

JOINERY ....Locked Rabbet Joint

There are probably a dozen joints that can be used to join the four corners of a drawer. One of the easiest (and strongest) is a locked rabbet. It doesn't require any fancy equipment. All that's needed is a table saw and a combination blade to cut a flat-bottomed groove.

The version of the joint shown here is for a drawer that has a lipped edge all the way around the drawer front.

RABBETS. The first step is to cut rabbets (lips) on the top and bottom edges of the drawer front (*Step 1*).

TONGUE. Then a tongue is cut on both ends of the drawer front. To do this, stand the drawer front on end and cut a groove on the end of the stock (*Step 2*). Then widen it to leave a ⅛"-wide tongue. (The ⅛" thickness of the tongue is based on the width of the kerf left by the saw blade.)

The tongue is completed by trimming it to a length of ¼" (*Step 3*).

DADO. To complete the other half of the joint, a ⅛"-wide dado is cut on the inside face of the drawer side (*Step 4*).

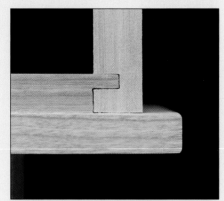

1 Cut the rabbets on the top and bottom edges. Set the blade ⅜" high and adjust the fence ⅜" from the outside of the blade. To complete the rabbet, set the fence ⅜" from the inside of the blade.

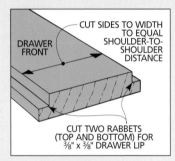

DRAWER FRONT

CUT SIDES TO WIDTH TO EQUAL SHOULDER-TO-SHOULDER DISTANCE

CUT TWO RABBETS (TOP AND BOTTOM) FOR ⅜" x ⅜" DRAWER LIP

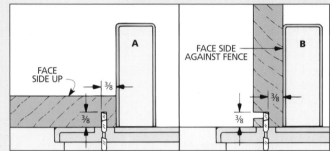

A — FACE SIDE UP — ⅜ / ⅜

B — FACE SIDE AGAINST FENCE — ⅜ / ⅜

2 To cut the tongue, set the blade height to ⅞". Then move the fence so the inside of the blade is on the shoulder of the rabbet. Make the first cut, and then move the fence away from the blade to leave a tongue the same width as the blade.

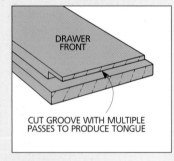

DRAWER FRONT

CUT GROOVE WITH MULTIPLE PASSES TO PRODUCE TONGUE

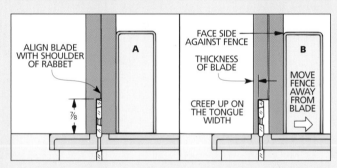

ALIGN BLADE WITH SHOULDER OF RABBET — A — ⅞

B — FACE SIDE AGAINST FENCE — THICKNESS OF BLADE — CREEP UP ON THE TONGUE WIDTH — MOVE FENCE AWAY FROM BLADE

3 To cut the tongue to length, raise the blade so it just clears the tongue. Next, screw or clamp a spacer to the fence for the lip to ride against. (This will help prevent the waste piece from kicking back.) Then adjust the fence to leave a ¼"-long tongue.

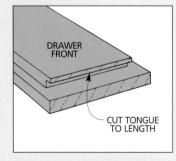

DRAWER FRONT

CUT TONGUE TO LENGTH

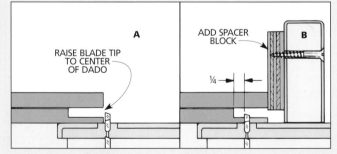

A — RAISE BLADE TIP TO CENTER OF DADO

B — ADD SPACER BLOCK — ¼

4 Now cut a dado in the drawer side to accept the tongue. Use the drawer front as a gauge. Raise the blade to a height equal to the length of the tongue. Then push the end of the side piece against the fence and cut the dado.

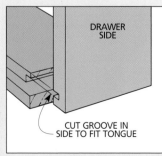

DRAWER SIDE

CUT GROOVE IN SIDE TO FIT TONGUE

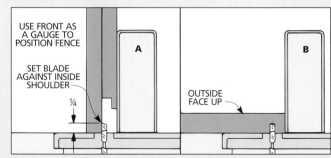

USE FRONT AS A GAUGE TO POSITION FENCE

SET BLADE AGAINST INSIDE SHOULDER — ¼

A

B — OUTSIDE FACE UP

DESIGNER'S NOTEBOOK

By simply shortening the length, the hall table becomes a lamp table with a single drawer. And because construction is so similar, it's easy to build this companion piece at the same time as the hall table.

CONSTRUCTION NOTES

■ The lamp table is built the same as the hall table. However, some pieces are cut shorter and there are fewer of other pieces (see the Materials List below).

■ The back apron (B) and front rails (D) are each cut to a finished length of $19\frac{1}{2}$" *(Fig. 1)*. The front center (F) is not needed in the front apron assembly.

■ Cut only one drawer guide (G), two top mounts (H), and two drawer runners (I). Cut rabbets at each end of all these pieces as was done for the hall table. Also cut the groove for the guide pin in the drawer runner.

■ The table top (J) is cut to a finished length of $24\frac{1}{2}$" *(Fig. 1)*.

■ With only one drawer, you'll need just one drawer front (K), two drawer sides (L), one drawer back (M) and one drawer bottom (N). The drawer uses the locked rabbet joint and is assembled the same as the drawers for the hall table.

■ After the drawer is assembled, mount a single knob centered on the face of the drawer front *(Fig. 1)*.

■ When assembling the table, the top mounts (H) set against the inside edges of the legs (Top View in *Fig. 1*).

LAMP TABLE

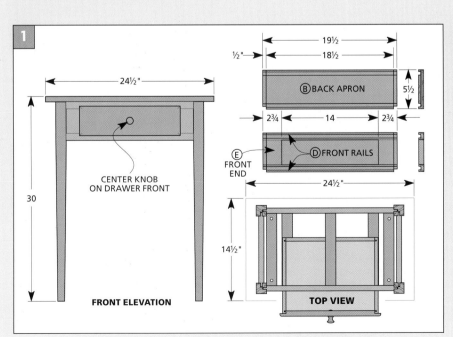

FRONT ELEVATION

TOP VIEW

CENTER KNOB ON DRAWER FRONT

MATERIALS LIST

CHANGED PARTS
B Back Apron (1) $\frac{3}{4}$ x $5\frac{1}{2}$ -$19\frac{1}{2}$
D Front Rails (2) $\frac{3}{4}$ x 1 - $19\frac{1}{2}$
J Top (1) $\frac{3}{4}$ x $14\frac{1}{2}$ - $24\frac{1}{2}$
Note: Only need 1 each of parts G, K, M, N.
Only need 2 each of parts H, I, L.
Do not need part F.

HARDWARE SUPPLIES
(Note change in quantities)
(1) No. 6 x $\frac{3}{4}$" Rh woodscrews
(4) No. 8 x $1\frac{1}{4}$" Rh woodscrews
(4) $\frac{3}{16}$" flat washers
(10) $\frac{3}{4}$" brads
(2) $\frac{5}{8}$" brads
(1) 1"-dia. cherry knob w/screw

When it was time to cut the tapers on the hall table legs, I was stumped at first. It was easy to make a jig to set the angle for the cuts on the first two sides of the legs. But then I'd have to take those angles into consideration when tapering the other two sides.

SLIDING PLATFORM

The jig I came up with is a sliding platform for the table saw. The great feature of this jig is that all you have to do is rotate the leg to taper the next side. The way the jig does this has to do with the centerpoint on the end of the leg. (More on how this works in a bit.)

For now, just mark the centerpoint on the bottom of the leg. To do this, draw lines on the bottom of the leg, connecting opposite corners *(Step 1)*. At the point where the lines cross, drill a $^1/_4$"-dia. hole with a brad point bit and push in a $^1/_4$"-dia. dowel.

PLATFORM. To build the jig, start with a piece of $^3/_4$" plywood about 9" wide for the platform (A). Cut it to a length of 31" *(Step 2)*.

RUNNER. Next, cut a groove in the bottom of the platform and add a hardwood runner (B) that will fit your miter gauge slot *(Step 2)*. To determine the location of the groove, measure from your saw blade to the miter gauge slot and add 1". Cut the groove, then glue and screw the runner in place.

Finally, place the runner in the slot of the saw and trim off one edge of the platform *(Step 3)*. This edge shows you *exactly* where the taper will be cut.

FENCES

The jig has two fences that help align the leg for each cut.

When a leg is mounted to the jig, the dowel slides into a hole in the rear fence *(Step 5)*. After one side is tapered, the leg is rotated 90° to cut the next side. The dowel realigns the piece on the edge of the jig. But one of the problems I had was getting the hole in the fence in exactly the right position. Then I discovered a trick — actually two tricks.

REAR FENCE. First, cut the rear fence (C) to a width (height) to match the thickness of the leg. Then draw an "X" on the fence to match the pattern on the end of the leg (Detail in *Step 4*). Drill a $^1/_4$" hole at the crosspoint.

The second trick has to do with mounting the fence to the platform. In order to get a $^1/_4$" taper on each side of the leg, the crosspoint on the rear fence has to be $^1/_4$" closer to the path of the blade. So all you do is shift the whole rear fence so it extends $^1/_4$" over the edge of the platform *(Step 4)*.

SIDE FENCE. A side fence (D) mounted on the platform helps hold the top end of the leg. To position this fence, place the leg on the platform with the dowel mounted in the rear fence *(Step 5)*. Then position the taper start line (near the top end of the leg) on the edge of the platform *(Step 6)*. Now draw a line along the back edge of the leg to indicate the position of the side fence. Then screw the fence in place *(Step 7)*.

HOLD-DOWN. To complete the jig, add a hold-down clamp. You can make this with a few scraps of wood (E, F) *(Step 8)*. However, I like the ease of using a quick-release clamp as shown in the photo. (See Sources, page 126.)

CUTTING TAPERS

To cut the tapers on the leg, mount the leg on the platform and push it through the blade *(Step 9)*. Then simply loosen the clamp, rotate the leg, and cut the next side.

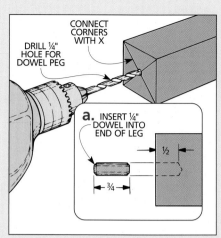

DRILL ¼" HOLE FOR DOWEL PEG

CONNECT CORNERS WITH X

a. INSERT ¼" DOWEL INTO END OF LEG

½

¾

1 To find the center of the bottom of the leg, connect the opposite corners with an "X". Drill a ½"-deep hole at this point and insert a ¾" length of dowel.

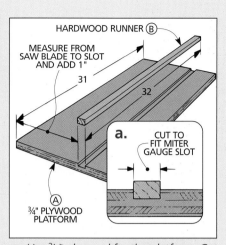

HARDWOOD RUNNER Ⓑ

MEASURE FROM SAW BLADE TO SLOT AND ADD 1"

31

32

a. CUT TO FIT MITER GAUGE SLOT

Ⓐ ¾" PLYWOOD PLATFORM

2 Use ¾" plywood for the platform. Cut a ¼"-deep groove in the bottom to hold a hardwood runner that fits your miter gauge slot.

SET GUIDE RUNNER IN SLOT AND CUT OFF WASTE

WASTE

3 Put the runner in the miter gauge slot and trim the side of the platform. This gives you a reference edge that shows exactly where the blade cuts.

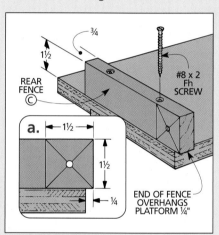

¾

1½

REAR FENCE Ⓒ

#8 x 2 Fh SCREW

a. 1½

1½

¼

END OF FENCE OVERHANGS PLATFORM ¼"

4 A rear fence the same width as the leg overhangs the edge ¼". Make an "X" on the end to match the "X" on the leg. Drill a ¼"-dia. hole at the crosspoint.

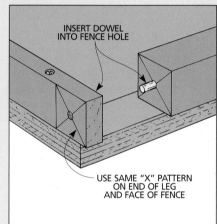

INSERT DOWEL INTO FENCE HOLE

USE SAME "X" PATTERN ON END OF LEG AND FACE OF FENCE

5 To position the side fence, first insert the dowel in the leg into the hole in the rear fence. (The dowel is trimmed off later to fill the hole in the leg.)

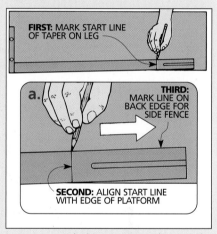

FIRST: MARK START LINE OF TAPER ON LEG

a. **THIRD:** MARK LINE ON BACK EDGE FOR SIDE FENCE

SECOND: ALIGN START LINE WITH EDGE OF PLATFORM

6 Next, mark the taper start line on the leg. Then place this line on the jig's edge. Mark the location of the leg's back edge onto the platform.

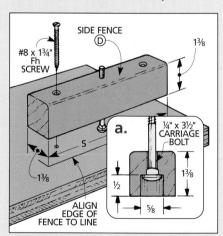

#8 x 1¾" Fh SCREW

SIDE FENCE Ⓓ

1⅜

a. ¼" x 3½" CARRIAGE BOLT

5

½

1⅜

1⅜

5⁄8

ALIGN EDGE OF FENCE TO LINE

7 The side fence is shorter than the leg thickness. Align it with the line and screw it in place. Add a carriage bolt for a shop-made hold-down (next step).

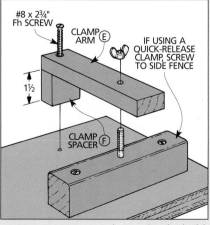

#8 x 2¾" Fh SCREW

CLAMP ARM Ⓔ

IF USING A QUICK-RELEASE CLAMP, SCREW TO SIDE FENCE

1½

CLAMP SPACER Ⓕ

8 Use scrap to make a simple hold-down clamp. Tightening the wing nut applies pressure. (If a quick-release clamp is used, the fence should be 1½" wide.)

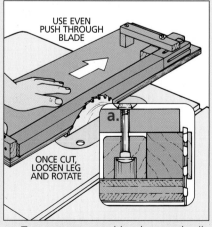

USE EVEN PUSH THROUGH BLADE

a. ONCE CUT, LOOSEN LEG AND ROTATE

9 To cut tapers, position leg on the jig and push the platform past the blade. Rotate the leg one-quarter turn to make next cut. Then repeat for other two cuts.

Usually, you think of using a jointer to get a straight edge from one end of a workpiece to the other. But how about using the jointer to cut tapers? After all, a taper *is* a straight edge. It's just that it doesn't run the full length of the piece.

Another reason the jointer is an ideal tool for cutting tapers is that the jointer produces a clean, crisp cut that needs little (if any) sanding. And unlike a table saw, tapering on the jointer doesn't require any special jigs or complicated layouts. All you need is some masking tape and a pencil.

PROCEDURE

When cutting a long taper, like on the hall table, you don't taper the entire leg. Instead, there's a flat at the top where the leg is joined to the apron.

Note: Complete any joinery on the leg before it's tapered.

LOWER WORKPIECE. The basic idea behind tapering on the jointer is simple. Instead of starting the cut at the end of the workpiece, it's lifted up and the flat portion of the leg is pushed forward, past the cutterhead. Then the leg is lowered onto the cutterhead to start the taper. The trick is knowing where to lower the workpiece to start the cut.

REFERENCE LINES. To do this, I make two reference lines. One marks the start of the taper on the leg *(Step 1)*. The other line indicates the front edge

of the jointer's outfeed table *(Step 2)*. When the two marks align, the workpiece is lowered onto the jointer.

SNIPE. Since the workpiece is coming down at an angle, the knives will create a dished cut (snipe) at the beginning of the cut. To prevent this, I wrap two layers of masking tape around the leg *(Step 3)*. This raises the workpiece above the cutterhead just enough to produce a smooth cut.

DEPTH OF CUT

Another thing to keep in mind is the depth of cut. This determines how many passes over the jointer you'll have to make to get the finished taper.

To plan the cut, start with the

amount of taper you want at the end of the leg and divide it by the depth of cut. For example, if your jointer is set for a $1/16$" cut, four passes will cut a $1/4$" taper.

But in practice, to allow for a cleanup pass, I adjust the infeed table so the cut is a hair ($1/64$") less. To do this, measure the gap between the infeed table and a straight stick laid across the outfeed table (see photo below).

CUTTERGUARD. Before making your first cut, it's a good idea to get a feel for opening the cutterguard with a workpiece. This takes some practice — with the jointer turned off. What I've found works best is to slightly raise the end of the workpiece off the table and use it to nudge the cutterguard open *(Step 4)*.

CUT TAPER

With the setup complete, it's time to make some test cuts before moving on to the real leg pieces.

Measuring the Depth of Cut. *Place a straight piece of scrap on the jointer's outfeed table. Then measure the gap between it and the infeed table.*

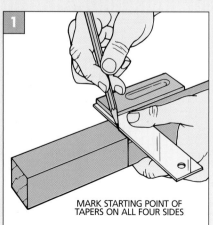

MARK STARTING POINT OF TAPERS ON ALL FOUR SIDES

Lay Out Tapers. *Using a try square, lay out the starting point of the tapers around all four sides of the leg.*

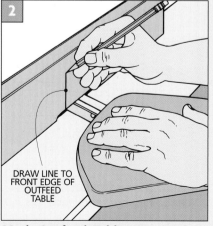

DRAW LINE TO FRONT EDGE OF OUTFEED TABLE

ALIGN EDGE OF TAPE WITH LINE

Mark Outfeed Table. *Now make a pencil mark on the jointer fence to indicate the front of the outfeed table.*

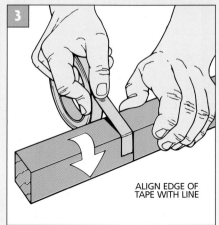

Add Tape. *To prevent the jointer knives from making a "dished" cut, wrap two layers of masking tape around the leg.*

TEST CUT. Once you get the feel of opening the cutterguard, check the setup by making a test cut. You should not have any snipe at the start or end of the cut.

Safety Note: Be sure to hook a push block over the end of the leg when you make the cut.

CUT TAPER. Now you're ready to taper the actual workpiece. Depending on the depth of cut, you'll need to make several passes on each side *(Step 5)*. And since it can be easy to lose track of the cutting sequence, I just label the cutting order right on the masking tape (see photo above).

When it's time to taper the fourth side of the leg, you'll have a tapered face facing the fence of the jointer. If you press this face against the fence, the start of the taper will be angled. To prevent this, press the untapered top of the leg against the fence during the cut. This will leave a gap between the tapered face and the fence.

CLEANUP PASS. After the taper is cut on each side, all that's left to complete the job is to make one cleanup pass on each side. The goal is to take as light a pass as possible, yet still cut the taper right up to the layout line.

To do this, remove the tape and raise the infeed table until the knives just graze the line at the start of the taper *(Step 6a)*.

Finally, instead of lowering the workpiece onto the cutterhead, make a full-length pass with the leg riding on the tapered side *(Step 6)*.

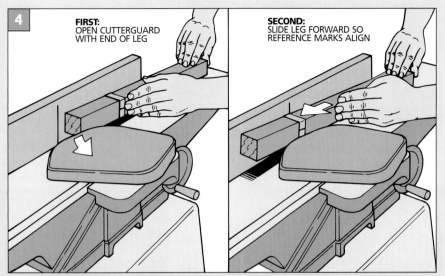

4 FIRST: OPEN CUTTERGUARD WITH END OF LEG

SECOND: SLIDE LEG FORWARD SO REFERENCE MARKS ALIGN

Position Leg. With the leg against the fence, raise the end slightly above the table. Now nudge the cutter guard open with the end of the leg and slide the workpiece forward until the reference mark on the leg aligns with the mark on the fence.

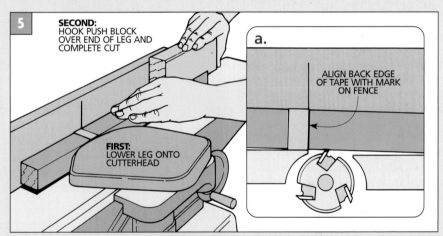

5 SECOND: HOOK PUSH BLOCK OVER END OF LEG AND COMPLETE CUT

a. ALIGN BACK EDGE OF TAPE WITH MARK ON FENCE

FIRST: LOWER LEG ONTO CUTTERHEAD

Begin Cut. When the back edge of the tape aligns with the mark on the fence, lower the leg down onto the cutterhead. Then hook a push block over the end of the leg and complete the cut.

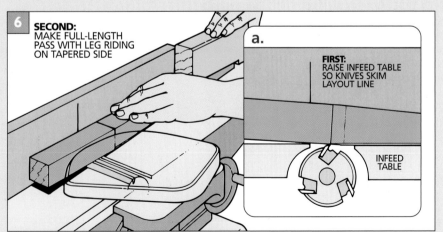

6 SECOND: MAKE FULL-LENGTH PASS WITH LEG RIDING ON TAPERED SIDE

a. **FIRST:** RAISE INFEED TABLE SO KNIVES SKIM LAYOUT LINE

INFEED TABLE

Cleanup Pass. After the taper is cut, remove the tape. Then center the layout line on the workpiece across the opening in the jointer table. After raising the infeed table until the knives just graze the line, make a full-length pass.

Rocking Chair

While the heritage of this chair is distinctly Shaker, it's been updated with some modern techniques. And there's also one very old technique that may be new to you — weaving the seat and back.

This rocker looks just like an old-fashioned Shaker rocker. But while some of the clean lines and graceful curves are borrowed from the Shaker "classic," some changes were made to the design.

DOWELS. For one thing, Shaker rockers included legs that were tapered and often given a slight bend. But you don't need a lathe or a steam box to build this chair. The legs and the rails that connect them are made from straight dowels that are $1^1/_2$", 1", and $^3/_4$" in diameter.

SQUARE STOCK. But where do you find $1^1/_2$"-dia. dowels — especially ones over 42" long? The solution is simple. You can make the dowels yourself. If you don't have a lathe, you can make the dowels with a router table and a few roundover bits. The technique is straightforward. (There's a separate article on making dowels on page 37.)

There was even an unexpected benefit to this. The chair requires two sets of holes along each leg. And because the seat is tapered front to back, these holes aren't 90° to each other. Working with store-bought dowels would have required a special holding jig. But with our method, the holes could be drilled in the square maple blanks before they were "turned" into dowels.

WEAVING. The woven seat is another common feature on Shaker rockers. And here I pretty much stuck to tradition — except for the stuffing between the two layers of webbing. I used a 1"-foam pad instead of what the Shakers used — horse hair. Other than that, the technique is the same. It's all explained beginning on page 40. Plus there are some alternate patterns you can weave into the chair back. These are shown in the Designer's Notebook on page 42.

FOOTSTOOL. We've also designed a footstool to go with the rocker. It uses many of the same techniques. That project begins on page 43.

EXPLODED VIEW

OVERALL DIMENSIONS:
$25\frac{3}{8}$W x $32\frac{1}{2}$D x $43\frac{1}{2}$H

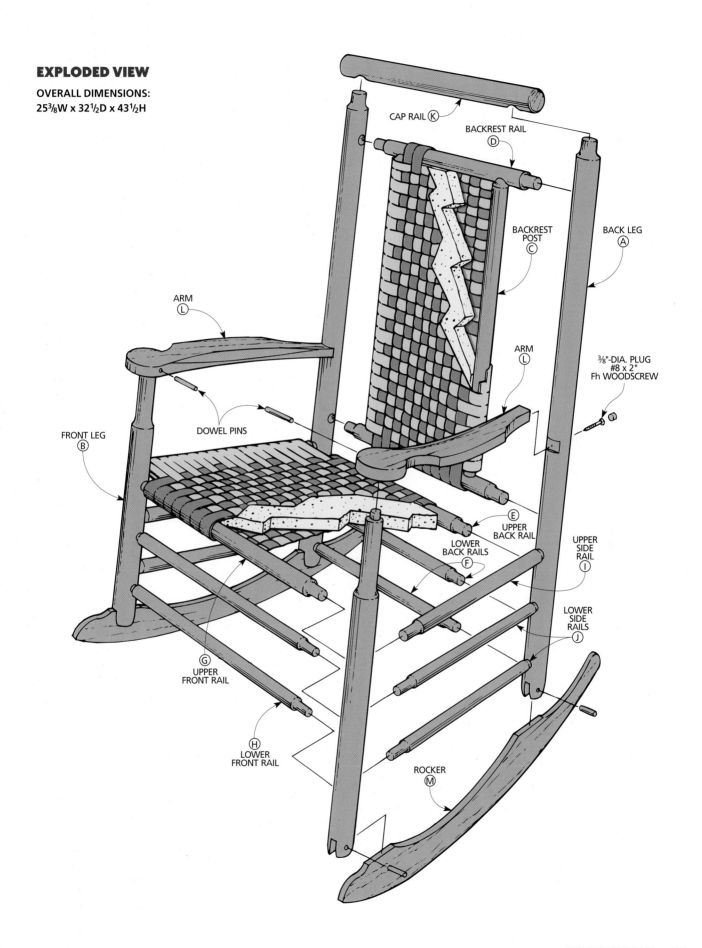

CAP RAIL (K)

BACKREST RAIL (D)

BACKREST POST (C)

BACK LEG (A)

ARM (L)

ARM (L)

$\frac{3}{8}$"-DIA. PLUG
#8 x 2"
Fh WOODSCREW

FRONT LEG (B)

DOWEL PINS

(E) UPPER BACK RAIL

LOWER BACK RAILS (F)

UPPER SIDE RAIL (I)

LOWER SIDE RAILS (J)

(G) UPPER FRONT RAIL

(H) LOWER FRONT RAIL

ROCKER (M)

1

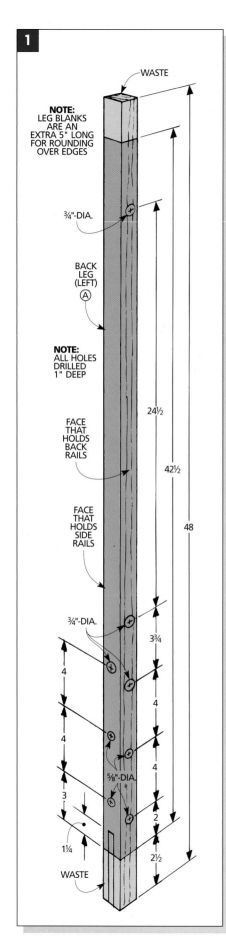

WASTE

NOTE:
LEG BLANKS ARE AN EXTRA 5" LONG FOR ROUNDING OVER EDGES

¾"-DIA.

BACK LEG (LEFT)
Ⓐ

NOTE:
ALL HOLES DRILLED 1" DEEP

FACE THAT HOLDS BACK RAILS

FACE THAT HOLDS SIDE RAILS

¾"-DIA.

⅝"-DIA.

WASTE

24½

42½

48

3¾

4

4

4

2

2½

4

4

4

3

1¼

CUTTING DIAGRAM

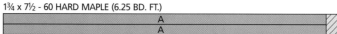

1¾ x 7½ - 60 HARD MAPLE (6.25 BD. FT.)

A
A
B
B
K

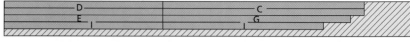

1 x 5 - 60 HARD MAPLE (2.6 BD. FT.)

D
E
I
C
G

¾ x 4 - 60 HARD MAPLE (1.7 BD. FT.)

J
J
F
H

¾ x 5 - 48 HARD MAPLE (1.7 BD. FT.)

L
L

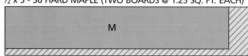

½ x 5 - 36 HARD MAPLE (TWO BOARDS @ 1.25 SQ. FT. EACH)

M

2

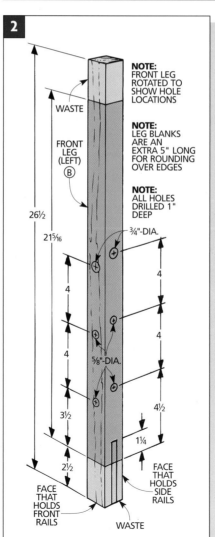

WASTE

FRONT LEG (LEFT)
Ⓑ

26½

21⁵⁄₁₆

¾"-DIA.

⅝"-DIA.

3½

2½

FACE THAT HOLDS FRONT RAILS

WASTE

NOTE:
FRONT LEG ROTATED TO SHOW HOLE LOCATIONS

NOTE:
LEG BLANKS ARE AN EXTRA 5" LONG FOR ROUNDING OVER EDGES

NOTE:
ALL HOLES DRILLED 1" DEEP

4

4

4

4½

1¼

FACE THAT HOLDS SIDE RAILS

MATERIALS LIST

WOOD

A	Back Legs (2)	1½ x 48 rgh.
B	Front Legs (2)	1½ x 26½ rgh.
C	Backrest Posts (2)	1 x 29½ rgh.
D	Backrest Rails (2)	1 x 23½ rgh.
E	Upper Back Rail (1)	1 x 23½ rgh.
F	Lower Back Rails (2)	¾ x 23½ rgh.
G	Upper Front Rail (1)	1 x 27½ rgh.
H	Lower Front Rails (2)	¾ x 27½ rgh.
I	Upper Side Rails (2)	1 x 23½ rgh.
J	Lower Side Rails (4)	¾ x 23½ rgh
K	Cap Rail (1)	1½ x 21½
L	Arms (2)	¾ x 5 - 20
M	Rockers (2)	½ x 5 - 33

HARDWARE SUPPLIES

(2) No. 8 x 2" Fh woodscrews
(2) ¾"-dia. flathead wood plugs
(1) ³⁄₁₆"-dia. dowel 6" long
(1) ⅜-dia. dowel 6" long
(80 yds.) Cotton Shaker tape
(8) ½"-long upholstery tacks
(1) 1"-thick foam pad 18 x 20
(1) 1"-thick foam pad 12 x 23

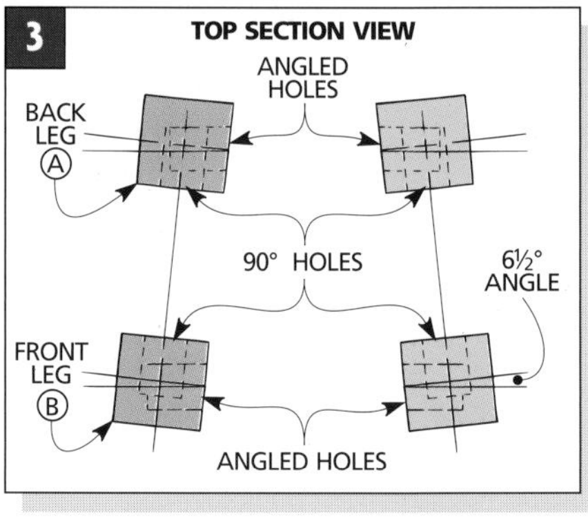

3 TOP SECTION VIEW

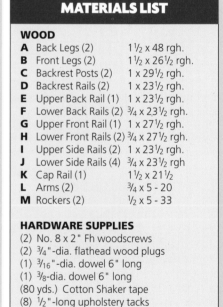

ANGLED HOLES

BACK LEG Ⓐ

90° HOLES

6½° ANGLE

FRONT LEG Ⓑ

ANGLED HOLES

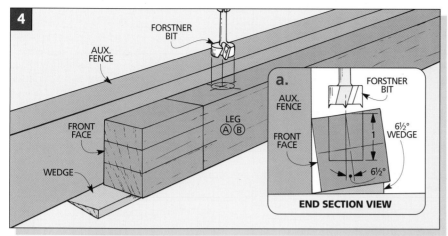

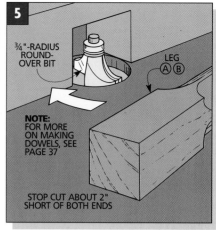

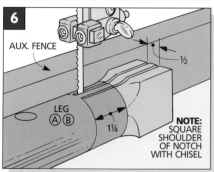

LEGS

To build the rocker, I began with the four square leg blanks. It may seem a bit odd to start off with square blanks when the legs are going to end up as dowels — but that's exactly how this project begins.

CUT TO SIZE. First cut four leg blanks $1^{1}/2$" thick and $1^{1}/2$" wide. Then the back legs (A) and front legs (B) can be cut to rough length — I sized mine an extra 5" longer than the finished length of the legs. (This may seem plenty long, but the extra length is needed when you round over the blanks to make dowels.)

LAY OUT BLANKS. The next step is to carefully lay out the finished length and the holes on the blanks *(Figs. 1 and 2)*. First, I measured up $2^{1}/2$" from the end of each blank to mark what will be the bottom edge. Then measuring from this mark, I laid out the top end of each leg.

Next, mark the position of the holes for the rails. There are a couple things to keep in mind when doing this.

For one thing, you don't lay out the front (or back) legs exactly the same — they're mirror images of each other *(Fig. 3)*. I found it helped prevent confusion if I labeled the end of each leg with its position on the chair (front left, front right, back left, back right).

Also, note that the positions for the side rail holes on the front and back legs are not the same. The holes in the back legs are $1^{1}/2$" closer to the bottom end. Later, when the chair is assembled with the rockers, this offset helps the chair tip back at a comfortable angle.

The last things to lay out are the notches for the rockers *(Figs. 1 and 2)*. I drew them on both faces of the legs to help me keep things oriented.

DRILL HOLES. With the legs laid out, the next step is to drill the holes. First I drilled all the 90° holes for the side rails. Just keep in mind that there are two hole sizes. The holes for the upper side rails are $3/4$" in diameter *(Figs. 1 and 2)*. The lower rails require $5/8$"-dia. holes.

The holes for the front and back rails are a little different. They're drilled at a $6^{1}/2$° angle *(Fig. 3)*. To do this, I just cut a wedge from some scrap to set the blank on *(Fig. 4)*.

To avoid drilling these angled holes in the wrong direction, I marked the front face of each leg. Then make sure this face sets against the fence as you drill.

Note: Each back leg needs two additional $3/4$"-dia. angled holes for the backrest rails *(Fig. 1)*.

ROUND OVER EDGES. With the holes drilled, the next step is to use a $3/4$" roundover bit in the router table to turn the square blanks into dowels *(Fig. 5)*. For more information on how to do this, see the Technique box on page 37.

CUT NOTCHES. Now before cutting the dowels to final length, I cut the $1/2$"-wide notches for the rockers on the bottom of each leg *(Fig. 6)*. I used a band saw for this, cleaning up the top shoulder with a sharp chisel.

CUT TO LENGTH. Finally, the legs are ready to be cut to final length *(Figs. 1 and 2)*. Cut carefully to the layout lines (though you may need to lay them out again since you've routed the edges).

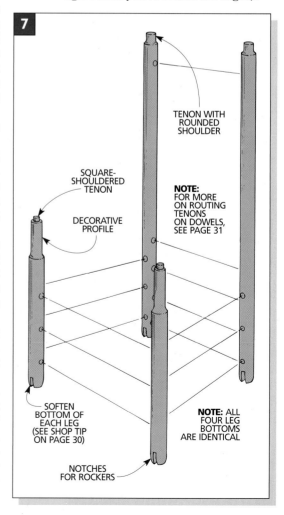

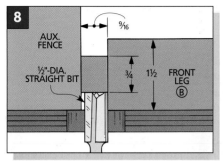

8

AUX. FENCE

9/16

1/2"-DIA. STRAIGHT BIT

3/4

1 1/2

FRONT LEG Ⓑ

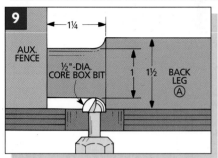

9

1 1/4

AUX. FENCE

1/2"-DIA. CORE BOX BIT

1

1 1/2

BACK LEG Ⓐ

10

TOP VIEW

5 1/16"

4 1/2"

CLAMP BOTH SUPPORT BLOCKS TO TABLE

AUX. FENCE

1/2" CORE BOX BIT

FRONT LEG Ⓑ

SAFETY NOTE: ADD SECOND SUPPORT BLOCK FOR LONG PROFILE ROUTING

a.

9/16"

SIDE VIEW

4 1/2"

NOTE: SUPPORT BLOCKS REMOVED FOR CLARITY

AUX. FENCE

1/2" CORE BOX BIT

1/8"

FRONT LEG Ⓑ

CREATE TENONS. The only thing left on the legs is to shape the ends (refer to *Fig. 7* on the previous page). The top of each leg gets a round tenon. But they're not the same size or shape.

On the top of the front legs (B), a square-shouldered tenon provides solid support for the arms later. To do this, I used a straight bit to rout a 3/4"-dia. tenon 9/16" long *(Fig. 8)*. (For more on routing tenons on dowels, see the Technique box on the opposite page.)

The back legs (A) also have a tenon on the top that's created with the same routing technique. But this time, the 1"-diameter, 1 1/4"-long tenon has a round shoulder that's created with a 1/2"-dia. core box bit *(Fig. 9)*.

ROUT PROFILE. I also decided to "lighten" the top of the front leg (B) with a decorative profile. This 4 1/2"-long profile is created just like the tenon on

each back leg *(Fig. 10)*. But this time, the cut is shallower (only 1/8").

Safety Note: Since this profile is so long, I added a second support board to the table. This kept my fingers a safe distance from the bit *(Fig. 10)*.

TAPER LEGS. To complete the legs, all that's left is to soften the bottom end of each. This is easy to do with a file and a little sandpaper. (For more on this, see the Shop Tip below.)

SHOP TIP . . . . *Shaping Leg Bottoms*

To keep the legs of the rocking chair from looking too square and bulky, I shaped the bottom of each leg, see photo. The shape of the legs is really a cross between a taper and a roundover. It's more like a "contoured taper."

In addition to improving

the way the legs look, the tapers serve another purpose — they help to prevent the bottoms of the legs from splintering.

Although the tapers are shaped by hand, I found it helpful to draw some layout lines on each leg. To start with, I laid out the narrow end of the taper on the bottom of each leg. To do this, I simply traced around a twenty-five cent piece.

Each taper starts about an inch from the bottom of the

leg (see detail "a" in drawing). To mark this point, I used a pencil and a combination square to draw a line around each leg 1" from the end.

To shape the ends of the legs, first clamp the leg in a vise to hold it securely. Then use a file to rough

out the material between the two layout lines.

Note: The layout lines are a guide only — you'll still have to use your "eye" to refine the leg's shape.

After you've got the leg roughly shaped with the file, sand the profile smooth and round.

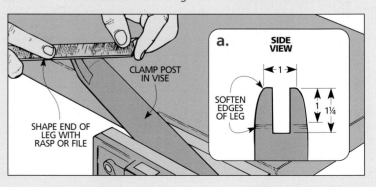

CLAMP POST IN VISE

SHAPE END OF LEG WITH RASP OR FILE

a. SIDE VIEW

1

SOFTEN EDGES OF LEG

1

1 1/4

Cutting tenons on dowels is easy on a router table. And by using different bits, you can cut two kinds of tenons. Using a straight bit, you can cut square-shouldered tenons (left photo), and by using a core box bit, you can cut round-shouldered tenons (right photo).

On the rocking chair, almost all of the tenons have round shoulders. The only place you need square-shouldered tenons is on the tops of the front legs to help support the arms *(Fig. 1)*.

The difference between these two types is more than skin deep. A square-shouldered tenon is like a traditional tenon in that its *shoulder-to-end* dimension is important. On the other hand, the round-shouldered tenon is more decorative. The tenon actually bottoms out in the mortise, so what's important is its *overall* length. This also means the tenon must be longer than the depth of the mortise. (On the rocker, for example, I cut 1¼"-long tenons for the 1"-deep mortises.)

PROCEDURE

The tenons are cut by pushing the end of the dowel into the bit.

SETUP. The dowel is guided by a support block clamped to the table *(Fig. 2)*. When positioning the support block, make sure the dowel is centered over the bit *(Fig. 2b)*.

Note: You'll have to reposition the support block when routing dowels of different diameters.

An auxiliary fence covering the router fence opening serves as a stop block to set the tenon's length *(Fig. 2a)*.

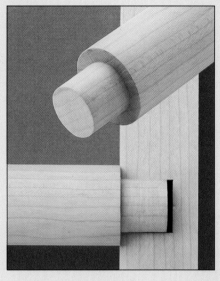

You'll need to sneak up on the final bit height, testing the fit of the tenon in the mortise. I like to leave the tenon just slightly oversize. Then it can be sanded for an exact fit *(Fig. 3a)*.

TECHNIQUE. To rout a tenon, first hold the dowel against the support block, then push it into the bit until it butts into the auxiliary fence *(Fig. 2)*. Now form the shoulder of the tenon by rotating the dowel clockwise. Then back the dowel out.

Next, remove the waste around the tenon in small bites *(Fig. 3)*. Simply push the dowel into the bit and pull it straight out. Then rotate the dowel slightly and repeat this procedure until the tenon is formed.

This same procedure (with a second support block added) is used to cut the profile on the tops of the front legs (refer to *Fig. 9* on previous page).

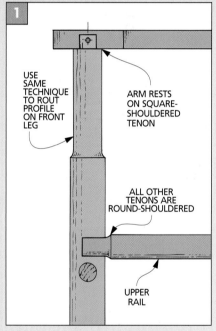

1

USE SAME TECHNIQUE TO ROUT PROFILE ON FRONT LEG

ARM RESTS ON SQUARE-SHOULDERED TENON

ALL OTHER TENONS ARE ROUND-SHOULDERED

UPPER RAIL

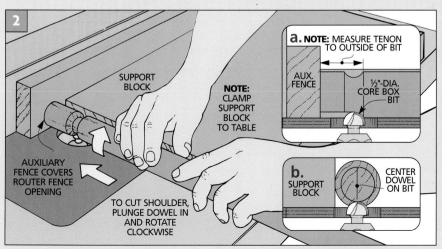

2

SUPPORT BLOCK

NOTE: CLAMP SUPPORT BLOCK TO TABLE

AUXILIARY FENCE COVERS ROUTER FENCE OPENING

TO CUT SHOULDER, PLUNGE DOWEL IN AND ROTATE CLOCKWISE

a. NOTE: MEASURE TENON TO OUTSIDE OF BIT

AUX. FENCE

½"-DIA. CORE BOX BIT

b. SUPPORT BLOCK

CENTER DOWEL ON BIT

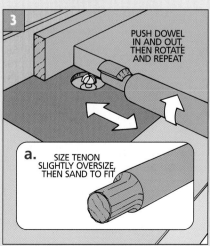

3

PUSH DOWEL IN AND OUT, THEN ROTATE AND REPEAT

a. SIZE TENON SLIGHTLY OVERSIZE, THEN SAND TO FIT

Now that the legs are complete, it's time to connect them with the chair rails and the backrest. The backrest will be sandwiched between the back legs. And below that, on each of the four sides of the chair, there's a 1"-dia. upper rail that the cotton webbing wraps around and two ¾"-dia. lower rails.

Though there are a lot of pieces here, the most efficient method is to make them all at the same time. That's because they all share many of the same techniques and setups.

CUT TO SIZE. Like the legs, I made all the backrest posts (C) and rails (D) and the back rails (E, F), front rails (G, H), and side rails (I, J) out of square blanks. The diameters and final lengths of all these pieces are given in *Fig. 11*.

DRILL BACKREST HOLES. Of the sixteen square blanks you just cut, only the two backrest rails (D) require holes. These have a ¾"-dia. hole drilled ½"-deep and 3³⁄₁₆" from each finished end (*Fig. 13*). (Lay out the ends of the pieces first and then locate the holes.)

ROUND OVER EDGES. With these holes drilled in the backrest rails, you can round over the edges of all the pieces. This is the same process used on the leg blanks earlier. The only difference is the size of the roundover bits. For the ¾"-dia. dowels, you'll need a ⅜"-radius bit, while the 1" dowels require a ½"-radius bit.

CUT TO LENGTH. After all the pieces have been routed, they can be cut to finished length. You'll want to pay special attention to the backrest rails. They should be cut so the holes you just drilled in them are equally spaced from the ends (*Fig. 12*).

The others can simply be cut to finished length. However, because the tenons on these pieces will bottom out in the mortises, it's important that the rails on each side of the chair are exactly the same length. To do this, I used a stop block clamped to an auxiliary miter gauge fence.

CUT TENONS. After the pieces have been cut and sanded smooth, the next thing to do is rout the round-shouldered tenons on the ends (*Figs. 11 and 14*). The only trick is cutting the correct-size tenons on each piece.

I started with the ¾"-long tenons on the backrest posts (C). Set the core box bit to rout a ¾"-dia. tenon. (Mine was ⅛" high.) But again for a good fit, sneak up on the height of the router bit.

Next, I cut the ¾"-dia. tenons on the other 1" dowels (backrest rails D and upper rails E, G, and I). The height of the bit should be the same (but test it to make sure). However, you will need to adjust the fence so the tenons end up 1¼"-long (*Fig. 14a*).

Finally, the tenons on the ¾"-dia. pieces (the lower rails F, H, and J) can be routed. You'll need to lower the bit so it leaves a ⅝"-dia. tenon. (My bit was ¹⁄₁₆" high.)

Note: With the bit lower, you may need to reposition the fence slightly to end up with 1¼"-long tenons.

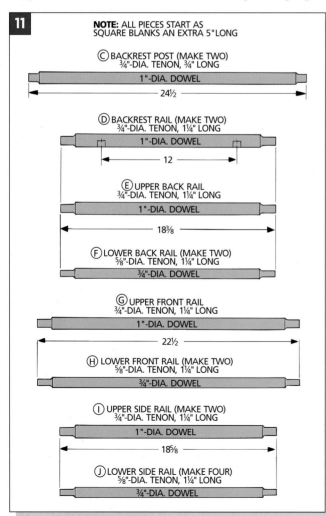

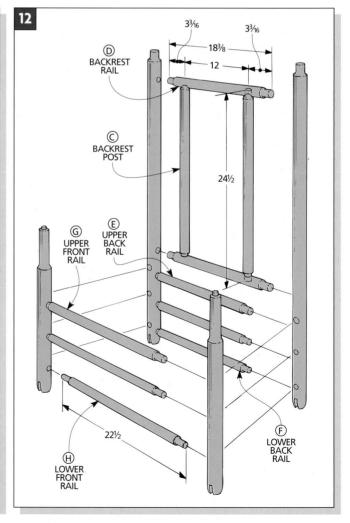

With all the tenons routed, the chair frame is ready to be assembled.

SUB-ASSEMBLIES. The first thing I did was to assemble the front and back sub-assemblies *(Fig. 12)*. As with any assembly, your goal is to get them flat and square. But because you're working with dowels here, you can't approach them in the usual way.

I used clamps to pull each sub-assembly together *(Fig. 16)*. Then I measured the width at the top and bottom of the legs. This will tell you if the legs are parallel or not. Then I removed the clamps and set the assemblies on a flat surface. If they were twisted, I flattened them out.

SIDE RAILS. When the glue is dry on both sub-assemblies, they can be joined with the side rails *(Fig. 15)*. The key here is to make sure the notches for the rockers line up. So I created two temporary alignment pieces that were $1/2$"-thick and had a $1\frac{1}{2}$" offset. Then I placed them in the notches at the bottom of the legs while the chair was being assembled.

CAP RAIL. The last dowel to add is the cap rail (K) that fits over the top of the back legs *(Fig. 15)*. I saved this rail until now because it's a different diameter than the other rails ($1\frac{1}{2}$"). Also, I wanted to drill the holes to fit the tenons on the tops of the legs *(Fig. 15a)*.

After the cap rail was rounded and cut to final length ($21\frac{1}{2}$"), I routed a $1/8$" chamfer on both ends of the piece. This is the same technique used to create the tenons on the other rails, except you use a chamfer bit and the piece stops against the bearing on the bit. After the chamfers are routed, the cap rail can be glued onto the back legs.

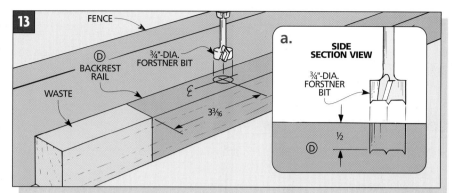

13 FENCE · BACKREST RAIL · $3/4$"-DIA. FORSTNER BIT · WASTE · 3 · $3\frac{3}{16}$

a. SIDE SECTION VIEW · $3/4$"-DIA. FORSTNER BIT · $1/2$ · D

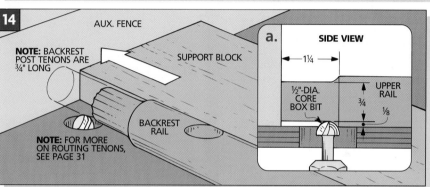

14 AUX. FENCE · SUPPORT BLOCK · NOTE: BACKREST POST TENONS ARE $3/4$" LONG · BACKREST RAIL · NOTE: FOR MORE ON ROUTING TENONS, SEE PAGE 31

a. SIDE VIEW · $1\frac{1}{4}$ · $1/2$"-DIA. CORE BOX BIT · UPPER RAIL · $3/4$ · $1/8$

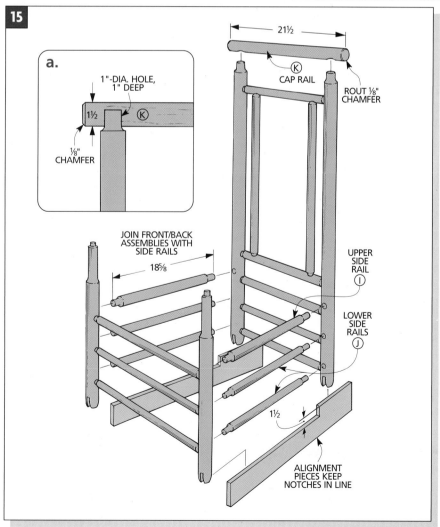

15

a. 1"-DIA. HOLE, 1" DEEP · $1\frac{1}{2}$ · K · $1/8$" CHAMFER

$21\frac{1}{2}$ · K · CAP RAIL · ROUT $1/8$" CHAMFER

JOIN FRONT/BACK ASSEMBLIES WITH SIDE RAILS · $18\frac{5}{8}$ · UPPER SIDE RAIL (I) · LOWER SIDE RAILS (J) · $1\frac{1}{2}$ · ALIGNMENT PIECES KEEP NOTCHES IN LINE

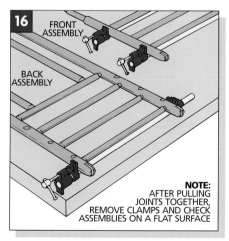

16 FRONT ASSEMBLY · BACK ASSEMBLY

NOTE: AFTER PULLING JOINTS TOGETHER, REMOVE CLAMPS AND CHECK ASSEMBLIES ON A FLAT SURFACE

At this point, all that's left to be added are the arms and rockers. I saved the rockers for last so the chair wouldn't rock while I was trying to add the arms.

CUT TO SHAPE. The arms (L) start out as a pair of $3/4$"-thick blanks (5" x 20"). The first thing I did was to draw the shape of the arm on the blanks, see pattern below. (**Note:** Full-size patterns are available. See Sources on page 126.)

Before cutting the arms to shape, I drilled a $3/4$"-dia. hole $9/16$"-deep on the bottom face for the tenon on each front leg (*Fig. 17a*). Make sure you don't drill through the top face of the arm.

Next I used a band saw to rough out the arm. Then for most of the arm, I sanded up to the line with a drum sander and finished by hand sanding.

CREATE BEVEL. Before attaching the arm to the chair, I removed the sharp inside edge by creating a tapered chamfer that's $1/2$" x $1/2$" at its deepest point (*Fig. 18*). To do this, I drew the chamfer on the top face of the arm (refer to pattern). And I scribed a line $1/2$" down from the top face. Then to do the chamfering, I used a spokeshave (though you could use a rasp for this).

ATTACH ARM. Now the arm is ready to be mounted to the chair. This is a little trickier than it looks. To give the arm plenty of support, I cut a notch in each back leg for the arm to rest on. (For more on this, see the Technique box on the opposite page.) Then I set the arm on the tenon on the front leg and sanded it in back until it fit snugly in the notch (*Fig. 19*).

After the arm fits in the notch, its outside edge can be sanded flush with the leg (*Fig. 19a*). Then it's pinned at the front inside edge with a $3/16$"-dia. dowel (*Fig. 17b*). And in the back, the arm is secured with a No. 8 x 2" Fh woodscrew (*Fig. 19a*). (The screw is counterbored and plugged so it won't be visible.)

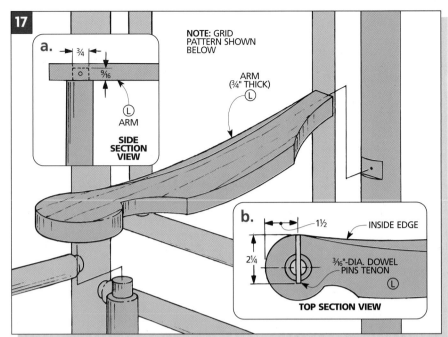

17

a. ¾ 9/16
L ARM
SIDE SECTION VIEW

NOTE: GRID PATTERN SHOWN BELOW

ARM ($3/4$" THICK) L

b. 1½ — INSIDE EDGE
2¼ $3/16$"-DIA. DOWEL PINS TENON L
TOP SECTION VIEW

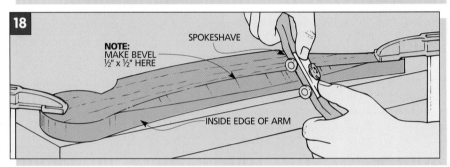

18

NOTE: MAKE BEVEL $1/2$" x $1/2$" HERE
SPOKESHAVE
INSIDE EDGE OF ARM

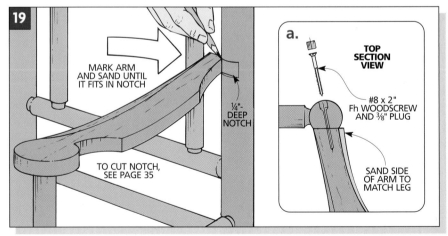

19

MARK ARM AND SAND UNTIL IT FITS IN NOTCH
$1/4$"- DEEP NOTCH
TO CUT NOTCH, SEE PAGE 35

a. **TOP SECTION VIEW**
#8 x 2" Fh WOODSCREW AND $3/8$" PLUG
SAND SIDE OF ARM TO MATCH LEG

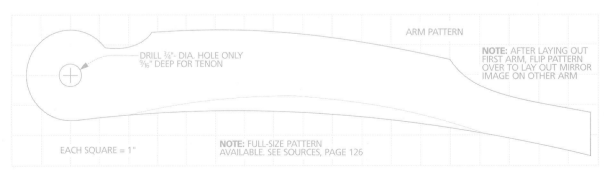

ARM PATTERN
DRILL $3/4$"- DIA. HOLE ONLY $9/16$" DEEP FOR TENON
NOTE: AFTER LAYING OUT FIRST ARM, FLIP PATTERN OVER TO LAY OUT MIRROR IMAGE ON OTHER ARM
EACH SQUARE = 1"
NOTE: FULL-SIZE PATTERN AVAILABLE. SEE SOURCES, PAGE 126

TECHNIQUE... *Notching Round Stock*

I didn't want the arms of the rocker to work loose, so I cut a notch in each back leg and let in the ends of the arms. But trying to lay out a square notch on a round dowel can be tricky.

TEMPLATE. To help lay out the notch accurately, I made a template with a shallow arc on one side. The arc matches the curve of the back leg so that you can trace the outline of the notch.

To make the template, I marked centerlines on a square block of wood and then drilled a $1\frac{1}{2}$"-dia. hole through the center *(Fig. 1)*. (This block should be the same thickness as the arms of the chair.) Then I cut the block in two pieces so I had a $\frac{1}{4}$"-deep arc in one piece *(Fig. 1a)*.

SPACER BLOCK. To keep the arms of the chair flat, the notch needs to be positioned at the same height as the tenon on the front leg. To do this, first I cut a spacer block the

same length as the distance from the upper side rail to the shoulder of the tenon on the front leg *(Fig. 2)*.

Then I just set the template against the back leg on top of this spacer block and traced along the top and bottom edges to establish the top and bottom of the notch *(Figs. 2 and 2a)*.

LAYOUT. The next step is to lay out the ends of the notch. To do this, place a framing square across both back legs and measure in half the diameter of the leg ($\frac{3}{4}$" in my case) *(Figs. 3 and 3a)*. This will be the center of the notch. Make a mark at this point.

Now place the template against the leg again, lining up the centerpoint on the leg with the centerpoint on the template. Mark the ends of the template arc onto the leg to designate the ends of the notch *(Fig. 4)*.

To cut the notches, carefully saw along the top and bottom layout lines with a hand saw *(Fig. 5)*. Then chisel out the waste down to the end lines of the notch *(Fig. 6)*.

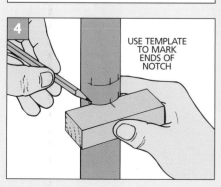

1

NOTE: BLOCK SHOULD MATCH THICKNESS OF ARM

3
$1\frac{1}{2}$
$\frac{1}{2}$
$\frac{3}{4}$
3
CUT BLOCK HERE

a.

TOP VIEW
$\frac{1}{4}$
MARK CENTERLINE ON TEMPLATE

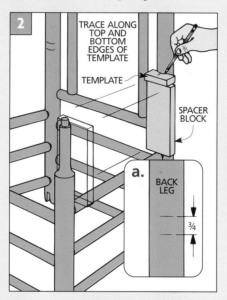

2

TRACE ALONG TOP AND BOTTOM EDGES OF TEMPLATE

TEMPLATE

SPACER BLOCK

a.

BACK LEG
$\frac{3}{4}$

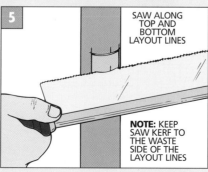

3

DRAW CENTERLINE FOR ALIGNING TEMPLATE

a.

FRAMING SQUARE

$\frac{3}{4}$

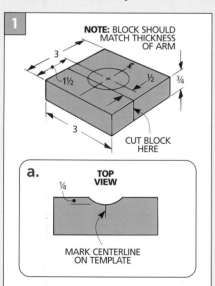

4

USE TEMPLATE TO MARK ENDS OF NOTCH

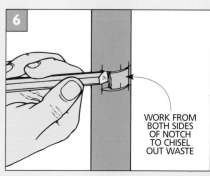

5

SAW ALONG TOP AND BOTTOM LAYOUT LINES

NOTE: KEEP SAW KERF TO THE WASTE SIDE OF THE LAYOUT LINES

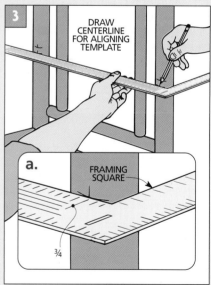

6

WORK FROM BOTH SIDES OF NOTCH TO CHISEL OUT WASTE

ROCKERS

The rockers are curved like the arms, but they're much less work. They're simply cut to shape from 1/2"-thick stock and pegged to the legs.

CUT TO SHAPE. First, I cut two blanks to rough size (5" x 33") and taped them together with carpet tape. This way, you only need to draw the pattern on one blank (see pattern below). Then the rockers (M) can be cut out at the same time on the band saw and sanded smooth with a drum sander.

PEG TO LEGS. Now the rockers can be attached to the chair. To do this, I flipped the chair upside-down and set the rockers in the notches, making sure the legs were centered on the flat spots on the rocker pieces.

Next, I drilled a 3/8"-dia. hole 1 1/4" deep through the outside face of each leg and through the rockers *(Fig. 20a)*. This hole stops short of the inside face of the leg. (Use a brad point bit to get a clean hole.) And finally, I pinned the rocker with a 3/8"-dia. dowel.

FINISH & SEAT WEAVING

With the rocker built, there are still two things left to do: apply the finish and weave the seat. The round surfaces make it difficult to brush on even coats of finish, so I used a wipe-on oil finish.

After the finish had dried, I noticed a few runs and rough spots left by dust. These were easily removed with a light buffing with 0000 steel wool.

When you are satisfied with the finish, you can begin to weave the seat. Refer to the Technique article that begins on page 38. ■

ROCKER PATTERN

EACH SQUARE = 1"

NOTE: FULL-SIZE PATTERN AVAILABLE. SEE SOURCES, PAGE 126

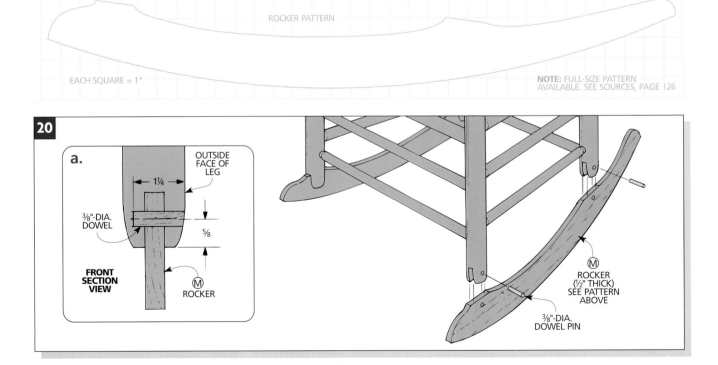

20

a.

OUTSIDE FACE OF LEG

1 1/4

3/8"-DIA. DOWEL

5/8

FRONT SECTION VIEW

Ⓜ ROCKER

Ⓜ ROCKER (1/2" THICK) SEE PATTERN ABOVE

3/8"-DIA. DOWEL PIN

Make your own dowels — why go through all the work? Well, there are quite a few reasons. For the rocker and footstool in this book, I had a hard time finding 1½"-dia. dowels, so making them was about my only option. Plus, I could build these projects out of any wood I wanted. I wasn't limited to what was "in stock."

Then while building the rocker, I ran into a couple other benefits. The real trick would have been steadying dowels while drilling the two sets of holes in each leg. But by starting with square stock, laying out and drilling the holes was a simple procedure.

Safety Note: The technique shown here will work for ½"-dia. and larger dowels. If you try to make smaller dowels this way, the stock will vibrate too much as it passes over the bit.

PREPARING STOCK

The first step is getting your stock to the proper width and thickness.

MAKE SQUARE BLANKS. Before you can make a dowel, make sure the stock is square. Both the width and the thickness of the blank should match the finished diameter of the dowel. So for a 1½"-dia. dowel, for example, you'll need a 1½" x 1½" blank *(Fig. 1)*.

The other thing about these blanks is that I don't rout to the ends *(Fig. 2)*. Otherwise, the blank would tend to roll as the last edge was being routed. So to get the correct dowel length and still keep the ends square, I cut the blanks 5" longer than the final dowel length.

ROUNDING OVER

Once your stock is prepared, the next step is to set up the router table.

SET UP ROUTER TABLE. First, choose a roundover bit that's half the diameter of the completed dowel. (For a 1½"-dia. dowel, you'll need a ¾"-radius bit.)

When setting up the bit, the key is to get its cutting edge flush with both the top of the router table and the face of the fence, *(Fig. 1a)*. If the fence isn't aligned or the bit is too high or low, you'll end up with small shoulders or large flat spots on the dowel — and this translates into quite a bit of sanding (something I like to avoid).

Note: One way to set the height of the bit is to place a rule across the opening in the fence and the table. With the router unplugged, turn the bit by hand — the cutting edge at the ends should just "tick" the ruler.

ROUND OVER EDGES. To round the edges, set the right end of the blank against the fence and pivot the other end into the bit about 2" from the left end *(Fig. 2)*. Then push the stock to the left, stopping 2" from the opposite end.

Now rotate the stock and rout the other three sides *(Fig. 2a)*. Then cut the dowel to finished length.

Finally, no matter how carefully you set up the bit, you'll still need to sand some small, flat edges.

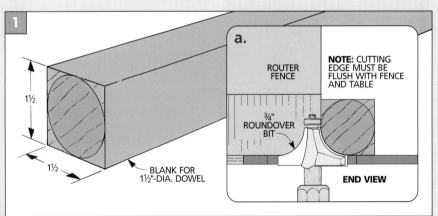

1
1½
1½
BLANK FOR 1½"-DIA. DOWEL

a.
ROUTER FENCE
NOTE: CUTTING EDGE MUST BE FLUSH WITH FENCE AND TABLE
¾" ROUNDOVER BIT
END VIEW

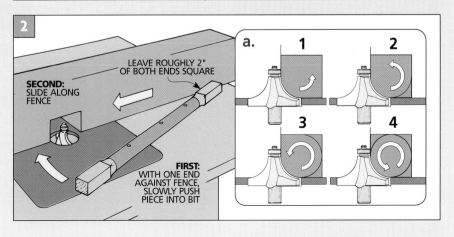

2
SECOND: SLIDE ALONG FENCE
LEAVE ROUGHLY 2" OF BOTH ENDS SQUARE
FIRST: WITH ONE END AGAINST FENCE, SLOWLY PUSH PIECE INTO BIT

a.
1
2
3
4

Weaving a seat isn't a typical woodworking technique. And frankly, I was a little bit nervous about getting it right. But after weaving the rocking chair and the footstool, I realized that there's not much to it. In fact, I'd have to say that Shaker-style weaving is downright easy. It doesn't require a lot of tools, materials, or a lot of time. So once your rocking chair or footstool has a few coats of finish and is dry, you can jump right in.

Of course, the best part is how great the project looks when you're done. Interesting color combinations can make a simple project striking. Or for a look that's more subdued, you can weave a project all in one color.

NEW TERMS

When weaving for the first time, there are a few new terms you'll have to get used to. For starters, the cotton webbing is called "tape," but it's not sticky. Plus, the tape has a different name depending on which direction you're working. I better explain.

WARP AND WEFT. The first piece of tape you work with is called the "warp" *(Fig. 1)*. This isn't anything to avoid, as in woodworking. Instead, the "warp" is the long piece of tape that's wrapped around the front and back rails of a project (like on the seat of the rocker), or the top and bottom rails (as on the rocker's backrest).

The other piece of tape is called the "weft" (or sometimes, the "woof"). This long piece is woven through the warp from left to right *(Fig. 1)*.

GETTING STARTED

Now that you're familiar with the terms I'll be using, it's time to get started. The first thing to do is to get all the materials together. There are really only three things you need: cotton tape, a piece of 1"-thick foam pad, and a handful of upholstery tacks.

Note: There are several sources for the cotton tape and foam pad. Refer to page 126 for a list.

ESTIMATING THE TAPE LENGTH. To figure out how much tape is needed, you have to keep two things in mind. First, each seat or backrest will have two layers — the tape is woven around both the top and bottom (or front and

back) of the chair. (The 1" foam pad ends up between these two layers.) The second thing to keep in mind is that it's better to end up with too much tape rather than too little. Although tape can be spliced to make it longer, you don't want to risk having that splice show up in the middle of your pattern. (When ordering the tape, you can ask for help. All you'll need are the dimensions of your chair.)

To estimate the amount of tape you'll need, first measure one complete row by wrapping a string completely around the rails *(Fig. 2)*. Then multiply this measurement by the number of rows you'll end up with (I also add a few extra rows for waste — just to be safe). The number of rows will depend on the width of the tape. Most tape is 1" wide, which makes the math easy. But $5/8$"-wide tape is available too.

The measurement you just arrived at is just for the warp piece of tape. Now you can follow the same procedure to estimate the weft piece.

WRAPPING THE WARP

When you have the weaving supplies in hand and the project has had several coats of finish applied to it, you can begin weaving the chair back.

As I mentioned, the first piece of tape is called the "warp." It's one long piece that's wrapped around the top and bottom backrest rails of the chair.

(For the chair seat and the footstool,

MATERIALS LIST

WEAVING SUPPLIES
Cotton Shaker tape (1" wide)
$1/2$"-long upholstery tacks
1" thick foam pad
Tack hammer
Spring clamp
Needle nose pliers
Scissors
Needle and thread or 5-minute epoxy

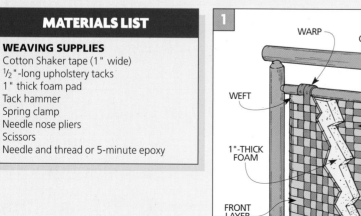

1 WARP — BACK LAYER OF TAPE
WEFT
1"-THICK FOAM
FRONT LAYER OF TAPE

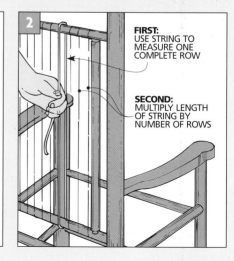

2 FIRST: USE STRING TO MEASURE ONE COMPLETE ROW

SECOND: MULTIPLY LENGTH OF STRING BY NUMBER OF ROWS

the warp also covers the front and back rails. See page 41.)

Note: If you're using two colors for your chair it's best to use the darker color for the warp. On the seat, the front edge gets much more wear than the sides, so the darker color will help "hide" the dirt better.

SECURING THE TAPE. To begin wrapping the warp, the first thing to do is anchor it to the frame. I did this with a couple of $\frac{1}{2}$"-long upholstery tacks.

The end of the tape should end up hidden as much as possible. So I tacked it to the inside edge of the backrest post on the side (not the rail on top or bottom) *(Step 1)*. Though it isn't critical where you tack the tape, I like to tack it near the end of the rail. This way when hammering the tack in place, the rail has a little more support than if you were to tack it in the middle.

Now you can begin wrapping the tape around the rails, starting from the back *(Step 2)*. Starting this way allows the tape to run straight up and down in front, which is what you want. This means the rows in back will angle just

slightly, but that's okay — you want to put your best face forward.

After weaving about halfway across the rails, I stopped and cut the foam pad to size *(Step 3)*. Then I inserted the foam between the front and back layers of the warp *(Step 4)*. When someone sits in the chair, this pad helps distribute some of the weight to the back layer of tape.

Once the last row of the warp is done

in front, wrap the tape around to the back and then up to the top of the side rail *(Step 5)*. To keep the tape taut, clamp the tape to the cap rail (or wrap it around the rail a few times). Then tack the tape in place and trim off the excess.

While wrapping the warp, the one thing to avoid is pulling the tape too tight. It shouldn't sag, but if the tape is tight now, you'll have a harder time weaving the next layer — the weft.

1 Working from the back side of the chair, use an upholstery tack to secure the end of the tape along the bottom inside edge of the side rail.

2 Now wrap the tape around the top and bottom rails, positioning the tape edge-to-edge. Make sure the tape in front is perfectly vertical.

3 With half the tape wrapped, clamp it to a rail (refer to Step 4). Cut a foam pad to fit between the rails with a $\frac{1}{2}$" gap around each edge.

4 With the tape still clamped, feed the foam between the two layers of tape. Continue to wrap the warp until you reach the opposite side rail.

5 After the last row is completed in front, wrap the tape around to the back and up to the top of the side rail. Tack it in place and trim the excess.

SPLICING THE TAPE

Depending on the roll of tape, you may need to splice two of the ends together. This is easy enough to do. Just make sure the splice weaves into the back (or bottom) layer so it's hidden.

The traditional way to splice tape is with a needle and thread (see left photo). But for the rocker, I used a five-minute epoxy (see right photo).

At this point, it's time to begin weaving the weft piece of tape through the warp. This is what creates the "checkerboard" look. (There are also a couple of additional weaving patterns you might want to try. See the Designer's Notebook on page 42.)

By the way, you don't have to use contrasting colors for the warp and the weft, as I did. With just one color of tape on the chair, the pattern will draw less attention to itself, but still add an extra bit of interest.

GETTING STARTED

Whatever pattern you choose to weave into your chair, weaving the weft begins the same way.

TACKING THE WEFT. Like the warp, the first thing to do is anchor the weft to the chair frame. But there's an important difference here. Instead of being tacked on the backrest post near the bottom, I secured the weft piece on the underside of the top rail *(Step 6)*. (For the chair seat or the footstool, the weft

is tacked on the inside edge of the back rail near one of the legs.)

To do this, first move to the back of the chair (or flip it over if you're working on the seat) and weave the weft tape under and over the warp pieces from one end to the other *(Step 6)*. Then push some of the warp pieces aside so you can tack the end of the weft piece to the backrest rail. (As you can see in *Step 6*, the small head on a tack hammer is especially useful for reaching into this tight space.)

WEAVING. Now it's time to weave the

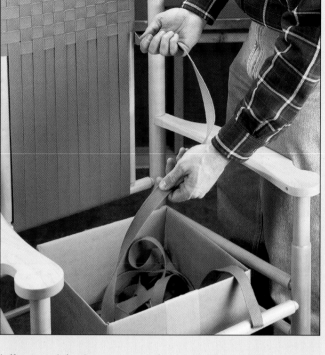

rest of the weft. This piece is woven through the warp at both the front and back sides of the chair.

Unlike the warp, the weft can't be left in a roll. You have to pull all the tape through the warp (see the photo above). And because there ends up being a big pile of tape, I found it helped to feed the weft into a cardboard box. And after weaving a couple of rows, I also discovered another trick. Let the end of the tape hang over the edge of the box so you can find it easily.

You'll also find the tape gets pretty twisted in the process. The simple way to straighten it out is to force all the twists through the warp before the tape gets pulled to the very end.

While weaving the backrest, you'll be moving from the front side of the chair to the back as you weave the two layers. Pull each row tight as you complete it, though don't pull so hard that you bend the backrest posts.

As you start each row, check that you're weaving a pattern that is opposite the row above it. You don't want to discover a mistake several rows later and have to undo your work.

Also, while weaving the weft, you want to push each row up against the one before it *(Step 9)*. When you do this, make sure the rows on the front (or on top) are straight and square to the warp rows.

6 Weave the tape across the back of the chair. Then push aside the warp pieces and tack the end in place.

7 Moving to the front, weave the tape over and under the warp pieces. Then repeat this on the back side.

8 At the start of each weft row, make sure you are weaving opposite the pattern of the row that's above it.

9 Stop occasionally to push the rows together, making sure those in front of the chair are straight.

FINISHING UP

For most of the chair, weaving the weft over and under doesn't change. But when you get close to the end, there are some things to be aware of.

COMPLETING THE WEFT. As you weave the last few rows, you'll notice the weaving gets harder because the tape gets tighter. (Needle nose pliers come in handy here.) The weft should end on the back side of the backrest. Simply weave it as far as you can. Then pull a couple warp pieces aside and tack the tape to the backrest rail *(Step 11)*. Now just cut off the excess and push the warp pieces back in place.

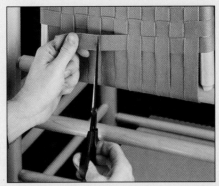

10 *If you find yourself running short of tape and need to make a splice, try to position the cut so the splice will be hidden beneath a warp piece on the back or underside of the weave.*

11 *Complete the weft on the back side, weaving it as far as possible. Then to anchor the weft, move a couple of the warp pieces and tack the weft to the backrest rail. Move the warp pieces back.*

WEAVING A TAPERED CHAIR SEAT

There's one big difference when it comes to weaving the rocker seat — unlike the parallel sides of the chair back, the seat tapers from front to rear.

WARP PIECES. Like the backrest, the first thing to do on the seat is wrap the warp around the front and back rails *(Fig. 1)*. But since the front is wider than the back, you can't cover the entire front rail. There's a little bit on each end that's exposed.

To cover these sections, add a couple short strips of tape to each side *(Fig. 1 and Step 1)*. With the chair upside down, tack one end of the tape to the back inside edge of the side rail. Then wrap it around the front rail and tack it again to the inside edge of the side rail. That's all there is to it. But there are a couple other tips I can pass along.

When positioning the filler strips, it's important that they are as parallel as possible to the other warp pieces. I positioned the first strip near the back leg, but the second looked better when tacked near the middle *(Fig. 1)*. Also, when trimming the tape, I tapered the top edge so it wouldn't cause the weft pieces to bulge.

WEFT PIECES. With the filler strips in place, you can weave the weft pieces. I put a strip of double-sided tape on the sides of the rails *(Step 2)*. This does two things: It helps hold the tape as you're weaving. And later, it prevents the tape from slipping to the back.

While weaving, you can "ignore" the filler strips at first. Then after a few rows, they can be worked into the weaving pattern *(Step 3)*.

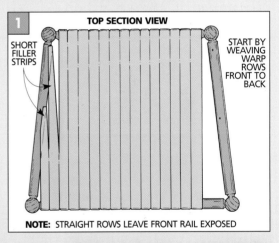

1 TOP SECTION VIEW

SHORT FILLER STRIPS

START BY WEAVING WARP ROWS FRONT TO BACK

NOTE: STRAIGHT ROWS LEAVE FRONT RAIL EXPOSED

1 *To cover the front rail at each end, tack short filler strips to the inside of the side rails. Position the strips so they're parallel with the warp pieces.*

2 *Before weaving the weft, place a strip of double-sided tape on the outside of each side rail. Remove the tape backing as you weave each row.*

3 *Weave over the filler strips on the sides for several rows. Then when it looks "natural," begin incorporating them into the weaving pattern.*

DESIGNER'S NOTEBOOK

Changing the pattern in the weave can give your chair a distinctive look. We offer a couple of different designs here, but you can easily design many more with just a sheet of graph paper.

WEAVING PATTERNS

■ To weave the diamond pattern (top), there has to be an odd number of rows in the warp. **Note:** If you plan to weave the diamond on the chair seat or on the footstool, first resize the pattern by drawing it out on graph paper rather than experimenting on the project.

■ The herringbone pattern (bottom), is similar to the checkerboard. But instead of going over one row and under the next, weave over two rows, then under two rows. Pay special attention to the start of each row. Some begin with one over, then two under or vice versa. This pattern works well with an even or odd number of rows.

DIAMOND PATTERN

DIAMOND PATTERN

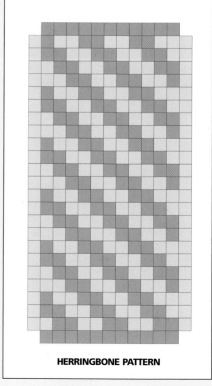

HERRINGBONE PATTERN

Shaker-Style Footstool

It doesn't take long to build this footstool to match the rocker. From making your own dowels to weaving the seat, these two projects share many of the same techniques.

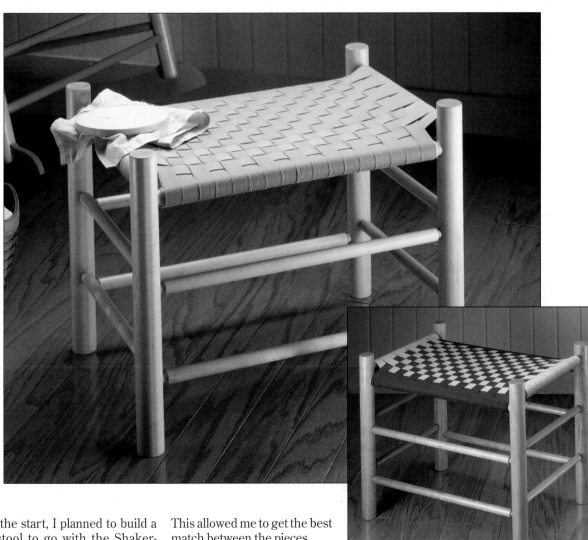

From the start, I planned to build a footstool to go with the Shaker-style rocker on page 26. Besides being a nice place to rest your feet, the stool features many of the same techniques used to build the rocker. So if you'd like to practice some of these before you "work up" to the rocker, this is the perfect project.

MATERIALS. Since the idea was to match the footstool to the rocker, I used hard maple. In fact, since I knew I was going to build both projects, I bought the wood for them at the same time.

This allowed me to get the best match between the pieces.

CHERRY. Building the maple version only took a weekend, so I decided to make a second stool to give as a gift. This time I decided to use cherry (see inset photo).

I chose cherry for a couple of reasons. First, the Shakers frequently used this wood to build furniture. That's because it was readily available in the northeastern United States (where the Shakers settled).

Second, I really like the deep-red color cherry takes on as it ages. Although the Shakers frowned on unnecessary "frills" decorating their furniture, they did appreciate the natural beauty of the wood.

FINISH. And with that Shaker notion in mind, I used four coats of a wipe-on oil finish on both the maple and the cherry versions.

EXPLODED VIEW

OVERALL DIMENSIONS:
$20\frac{1}{2}$W x $14\frac{1}{2}$D x $16\frac{1}{2}$H

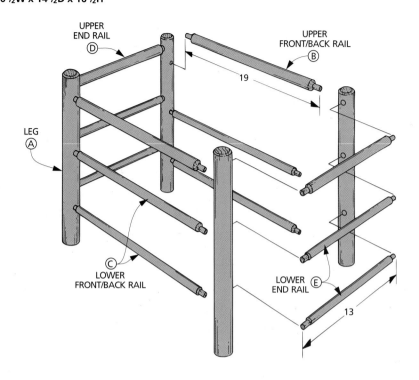

UPPER
END RAIL
D

UPPER
FRONT/BACK RAIL
B

19

LEG
A

LOWER
FRONT/BACK RAIL
C

LOWER
END RAIL
E

13

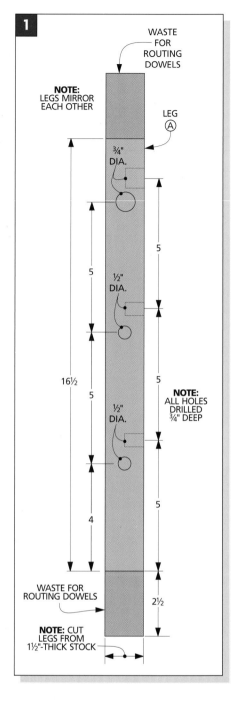

1

WASTE
FOR
ROUTING
DOWELS

NOTE:
LEGS MIRROR
EACH OTHER

LEG
A

$\frac{3}{4}$"
DIA.

5

$\frac{1}{2}$"
DIA.

5

NOTE:
ALL HOLES
DRILLED
$\frac{3}{4}$" DEEP

5

$\frac{1}{2}$"
DIA.

$16\frac{1}{2}$

5

5

4

WASTE FOR
ROUTING DOWELS

$2\frac{1}{2}$

NOTE: CUT
LEGS FROM
$1\frac{1}{2}$"-THICK STOCK

MATERIALS LIST

WOOD

A	Legs (4)	$1\frac{1}{2}$ x $21\frac{1}{2}$ rgh.
B	Upper Fr./Bk. Rails (2)	1 x 24 rgh.
C	Lower Fr./Bk. Rails (4)	$\frac{3}{4}$ x 24 rgh.
D	Upper End Rails (2)	1 x 18 rgh.
E	Lower End Rails (4)	$\frac{3}{4}$ x 18 rgh.

HARDWARE SUPPLIES

(30 yds.) 1"-wide cotton Shaker tape
(8) $\frac{1}{2}$"-long upholstery tacks
(1) 1"-thick foam pad, 12" x 17"

CUTTING DIAGRAM

$1\frac{3}{4}$ x 4 - 24 (Two Boards @ 1.3 Bd. Ft. Each)

A
A

1 x 5 - 24 (1 Bd. Ft.)

B
D

$\frac{3}{4}$ x 4 - 24 (.7 Bd. Ft.)

C
C

$\frac{3}{4}$ x 4 - 24 (.7 Bd. Ft.)

E
E

LEGS

The legs start out as overlong square blanks. After holes are drilled, they are rounded over and then cut to length.

SQUARE BLANKS. To begin, I cut four legs (A) $1\frac{1}{2}$" square *(Fig. 1)*. The final length of these pieces will be $16\frac{1}{2}$", but I cut mine 5" longer. (This extra length comes in handy when it comes time to rout the square blanks into round dowels.)

LAYOUT. The next step is to lay out the locations of the finished top and bottom ends (the finished length of the legs), and the holes that will be drilled to hold the rails later. Just keep in mind that these legs aren't identical. They create two pairs that mirror each other. So after laying them out, stand the four legs up on end to make sure each set of holes aligns.

The first thing to do is to measure up from the bottom of each blank $2\frac{1}{2}$" *(Fig. 1)*. This will be the bottom end of the finished leg. To make sure you rout

far enough when rounding over the leg, make a mark around the blank at this point. Then lay out the top end of the leg, $16\frac{1}{2}$" above this line, and make a second mark around the leg. And finally, mark on adjacent faces the locations of the six holes.

DRILL HOLES. Once the hole locations are marked, you can drill them. They are all flat-bottomed holes $\frac{3}{4}$" deep. But they're not all the same diameter. The *top* hole on each face is $\frac{3}{4}$" in diameter to match the tenon on the upper rail

(Fig. 1). The *bottom* two holes are $1/2$" in diameter to fit the tenons on the lower rails. (I drilled these using Forstner bits in the drill press.)

ROUND OVER EDGES. At this point, the square leg blanks are ready to be "turned" into dowels. And to do this, I routed them on a router table using a $3/4$"-radius roundover bit *(Fig. 2)*. Each leg requires four "stopped" passes over the bit. See the Technique box on page 37 for more about this.

Once the square blanks have been turned into round legs, they can be cut to finished length ($16^{1}/_{2}$"). This has to be done accurately, so the holes are aligned exactly from one leg to another.

Note: Routing the roundovers on the legs removed your original layout lines, so you'll have to measure again. Make sure you measure from the bottom end of each piece.

Then to complete the legs, I sanded them smooth and routed a $1/8$" chamfer on each end *(Fig. 3)*. This helps keep the ends of the legs from splintering.

RAILS

The front/back rails (B, C) and end rails (D, E) that connect the legs start out as square blanks that are 5" longer than finished length, just like the legs.

There are no holes to drill in these pieces, so the first thing to do is round over their edges. I used a $1/2$"-radius roundover bit for the 1"-dia. upper rails (B, D) and a $3/8$"-radius bit for the $3/4$"-dia. lower rails (C, E).

Once the rails are rounded over, they can be cut to final length (19" for the front and back rails and 13" for the ends). Then I cut tenons on both ends of each piece using a $1/2$"-dia. core box bit *(Figs. 4, 5,* and the Technique box on page 31). Even though there are two different diameters for the tenons, the height of the bit should be the same for both of them ($1/8$"). But the important thing is that the tenons fit the holes in the legs. So it's a good idea to start with the bit slightly lower than $1/8$" and sneak up on the final size.

ASSEMBLY

With the tenons cut, the frame of the footstool can be assembled. I glued up the end assemblies first *(Fig. 6)*. With round mortises and tenons, it's easy for an assembly to get racked out of square.

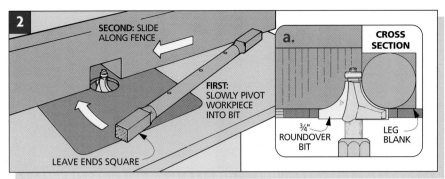

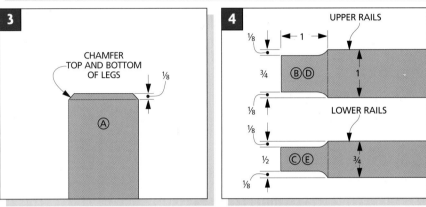

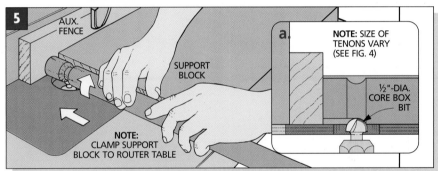

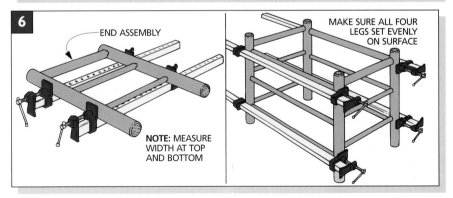

So to make sure they weren't twisted, I set them on a flat surface. And I also measured the widths at the top and bottom of the assembly to make sure they were the same.

When the glue is dry on the end assemblies, they can be connected with the front and back rails *(Fig. 6)*. To make sure the stool didn't rock, I made sure all four legs were resting on a flat surface. (If the stool does rock, put a little bit of weight on it.)

At this point, the "woodworking" is done, so you can apply a finish to the footstool. (I wiped on four coats of an oil finish to match the rocker.)

To complete the footstool, you can weave the seat with cotton tape. Refer to the Technique box starting on page 38 for more on how to do this. ■

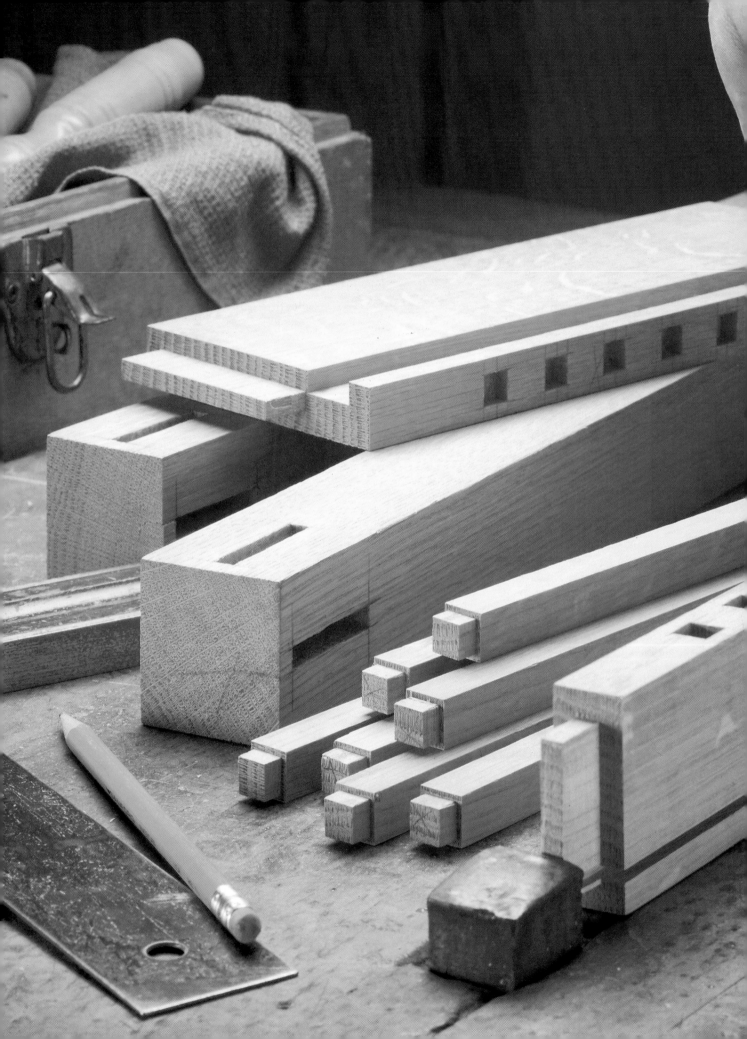

MISSION PROJECTS

Mission-style furniture should be simple and functional. Oak and cherry are the materials of choice, as they were in the early 1900s. These projects utilize a variety of hand and power tools to highlight contrasts in grain and the distinctive joinery.

A space-saving clothes tree, made of red oak, features distinctive and functional "Lincoln Log" cross pieces.

The sofa table is built entirely from quartersawn oak with traditional mortised spindles at either end.

Complementing the sofa table is a coffee table with a similar design. But this table has a beveled glass top and offers a simplified technique for making a series of mortises.

Finally, the cherry bookcase has characteristic through mortise and tenon joinery, ball-tipped hinges, and shop-built door pulls. It's a project that truly shows off your craftsmanship.

Hall Clothes Tree   48

Shop Tip: Special Sanding Block 50

Oak Sofa Table   54

Shop Jig: Chisel Guide 57
Shop Jig: Bevel Jig 61

Glass-Top Coffee Table   62

Shop Tip: Drawing an Arc 65
Technique: Simple Mortises 70
Designer's Notebook: Solid Wood Top 71

Mission Bookcase   72

Shop Tip: Frame Assembly 75
Shop Tip: Scraping and Sanding Corners 78
Shop Tip: Adding Decorative Pegs 79
Shop Tip: Shop-Built Door Pulls 83
Joinery: Through Mortise and Tenon 84
Designer's Notebook: Open Bookcase 87

Hall Clothes Tree

A special interlocking design brings this red oak hall tree together with a distinctive, Mission-style look. It also makes it strong and stable, without the need for a massive single "trunk."

There's not much to this hall tree: posts, hooks, feet and cross pieces. But as simple as it is, working out the final design took quite a few revisions.

POST. For one thing, a hall tree requires a center post. A solid post would have been hard to find — and pretty heavy. Plus, it would've had a tendency to warp, particularly with seasonal changes in humidity.

I considered laminating the post from two or three pieces of thinner stock. But then there would have been visible joint lines running the length of the post.

INTERLOCKED JOINTS. So instead of a single, solid post, I decided on four narrower posts (each 1" thick). These posts are connected by the hooks, feet and some special cross pieces in an interlocking style (refer to the Exploded View on the opposite page).

This "Lincoln Log" approach lightened the weight of the tree, and also made it quite a bit more interesting to look at (and build). The exposed joints and contrasting grain give it a distinct Craftsman/Mission look.

HOOKS & FEET. With the post designed, next I worked on the hooks and feet. Of course, these pieces have to look right. But changing their size (and shape) also affected the stability and utility of the tree.

So I played with the shape and lengths of the pieces, trying to get a balanced look that worked well when coats, hats, and umbrellas were hung on it (see photo at left).

This required building several prototypes. But that wasn't a big deal; you don't have to cut any tenons on the inside edges of the hooks or feet. Instead, the pieces are simply sandwiched between the posts.

MATERIALS. The hall tree shown here was made from red oak. Oak was a popular material to use for Craftsman-style or Mission furniture, particularly in northern regions where it was abundantly available.

Oak is very hard and durable, and it planes well. And when finished with oil (as this project was) red oak can develop a rich, natural color — almost an orange hue.

Of course, you could also use nearly any other hardwood to build this project. And no hardware is needed, as the interlocking design makes it sturdy just with glue.

PATTERNS. Scaled-down grid patterns are shown for the top hooks, bottom hooks, and feet of the hall tree (see opposite page).

But if you prefer not to try to transfer these patterns to your workpieces, you can purchase full-size patterns. For more information, see page 126.

CUTTING DIAGRAM

NOTE: ALL PIECES CUT FROM ⁵⁄₄ STOCK (PLANED 1" THICK)

1 x 5 - 60 RED OAK (2.6 Bd. Ft.)

| E | E | E | E | |

1 x 4 - 84 RED OAK (2.9 Bd. Ft.)

| C | C | C | C | D | D | D | D | |

1 x 5 - 84 RED OAK (3.6 Bd. Ft.)

| A | | | B | B | |

EXPLODED VIEW

OVERALL DIMENSIONS:
$22^{3}/_{8}$W x $22^{3}/_{8}$D x $69^{3}/_{4}$H

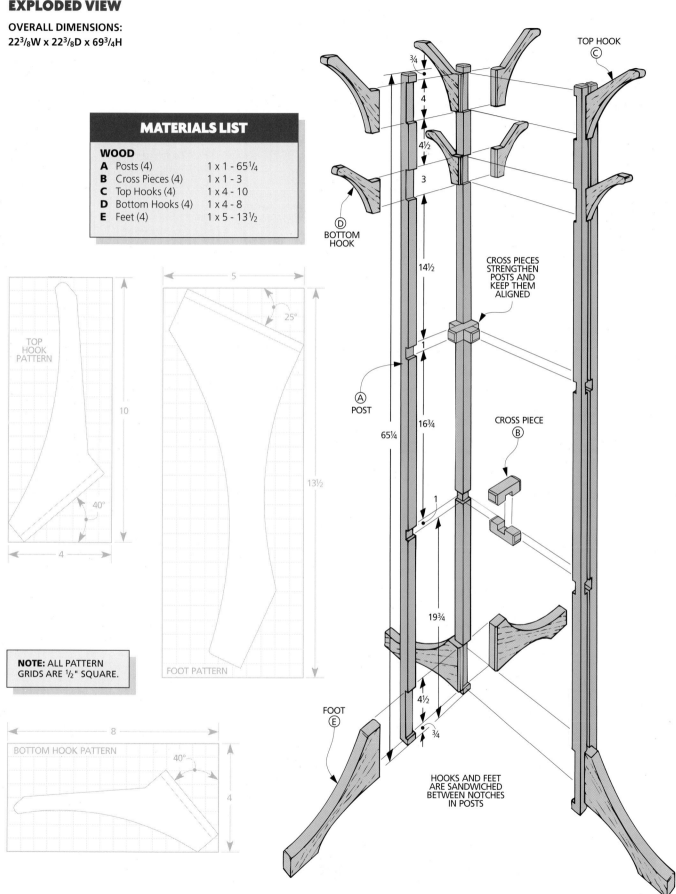

TOP
HOOK
PATTERN

10

40°

4

5

25°

$13^{1}/_{2}$

FOOT PATTERN

NOTE: ALL PATTERN
GRIDS ARE $^{1}/_{2}$" SQUARE.

8

BOTTOM HOOK PATTERN

40°

4

TOP HOOK
C

$^{3}/_{4}$

4

$4^{1}/_{2}$

3

BOTTOM
HOOK
D

CROSS PIECES
STRENGTHEN
POSTS AND
KEEP THEM
ALIGNED

$14^{1}/_{2}$

1

A
POST

$65^{1}/_{4}$

$16^{3}/_{4}$

CROSS PIECE
B

1

$19^{3}/_{4}$

FOOT
E

$4^{1}/_{2}$

$^{3}/_{4}$

HOOKS AND FEET
ARE SANDWICHED
BETWEEN NOTCHES
IN POSTS

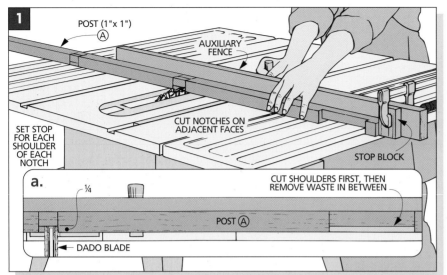

1 POST (1" x 1") Ⓐ
AUXILIARY FENCE
CUT NOTCHES ON ADJACENT FACES
SET STOP FOR EACH SHOULDER OF EACH NOTCH
STOP BLOCK

a. ¼
CUT SHOULDERS FIRST, THEN REMOVE WASTE IN BETWEEN
POST Ⓐ
DADO BLADE

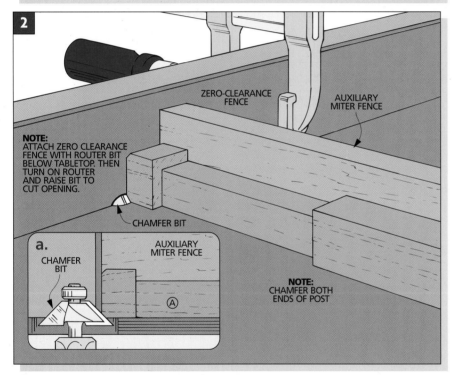

2 ZERO-CLEARANCE FENCE
AUXILIARY MITER FENCE

NOTE: ATTACH ZERO CLEARANCE FENCE WITH ROUTER BIT BELOW TABLETOP. THEN TURN ON ROUTER AND RAISE BIT TO CUT OPENING.

CHAMFER BIT

a. CHAMFER BIT
AUXILIARY MITER FENCE
Ⓐ

NOTE: CHAMFER BOTH ENDS OF POST

POSTS

To build this hall tree, I started with the "trunk." This trunk is made up of four long posts (refer to the Exploded View on page 49). Each post has a series of notches cut on two adjacent faces. These notches hold the hooks, cross pieces, and feet.

To make the posts, I started with a 5"-wide blank of 5/4 stock planed 1" thick. Keep in mind when you're choosing and milling this blank that the straighter these pieces are now, the easier it will be to cut the notches and assemble the tree later.

CUT TO LENGTH. With the blank ready, I cut it to final length ($65^1/_4$") and ripped it into four 1"-wide posts (A) (see Cutting Diagram on page 48). This way, all the pieces will end up *exactly* the same length, which is important when it comes time to cut the notches.

CUT NOTCHES. With the posts cut to size, I began work on the notches. These are cut on the inside faces of each post *(Fig. 1)*. And since they trap the hooks and feet, it's important that they line up across the four posts.

To do this, first I laid out the notches on a single post (see Exploded View). (Note that the top and bottom notches are the same distance from the ends of the post, but they're *not* the same length. The bottom notch is longer.)

With the notches laid out on one post, I set the dado blade to make a $^1/_4$"-deep cut. And I added a long auxiliary fence to the miter gauge to support the piece *(Fig. 1)*.

The trick to making sure that the notches are identical is to use a stop block *(Fig. 1)*. After setting it to cut the

SHOP TIP . . . . *Special Sanding Block*

If the notches on the posts for the hall tree aren't smooth, you'll notice it when the hooks and feet are glued between them later.

So I created a simple sanding block out of plywood and ¼" hardboard (see drawing).

The "handle" of the block spans the notches so their depth stays consistent and their edges aren't rounded over.

POST Ⓐ
SANDING BLOCK

a. ¾" PLYWOOD
ADHESIVE-BACKED SANDPAPER
¼" HARDBOARD
1

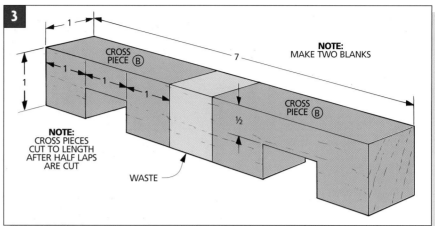

first shoulder, I made two passes on each piece, rolling the post between passes so the notches ended up on adjacent faces.

When the first shoulder had been cut on all the posts, I moved the stop block to cut the second shoulder of the notch. After making this cut, any waste between the two shoulders can be removed with overlapping passes. Then I worked on the next notch, following the same procedure (Fig. 1a).

Note: Because of the length of the posts, you'll need to flip them around halfway through this process.

When the notches were cut, I noticed they had some shallow kerf marks left by my dado blade. I was concerned that these marks would be visible after assembly. So to remove them, I made a simple sanding jig (see the Shop Tip box on the opposite page).

CHAMFER ENDS. With the saw marks removed, all that's left is to chamfer the ends on the router table (Fig. 2). These pieces are so long that I was concerned about routing this chamfer, but I found that holding them flat on the table wasn't difficult, especially when using the miter gauge and an auxiliary fence to support the piece. But to keep the pieces from catching in the fence opening, I added a zero-clearance fence made of 1/8" hardboard with an opening sized to cut the chamfer (Fig. 2).

CROSS PIECES

With the posts completed, I started on the cross pieces. Each cross piece assembly consists of two individual pieces stacked together. They connect the posts in the middle so the spacing stays even (see photo above).

OVERSIZE BLANKS. The cross pieces (B) fit in the notches in the center of the post. (Mine were 1" x 1".) Their final length will be 3". However, since this is

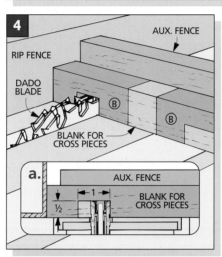

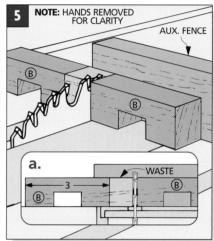

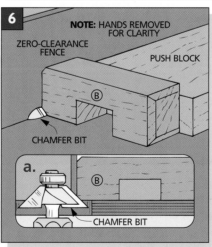

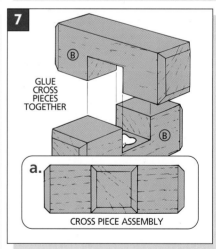

a bit short to work with on the table saw safely, I started out with two 7"-long blanks (Fig. 3).

With the two blanks in hand, I cut a half lap near both ends of each so the cross pieces would overlap (Fig. 4). To support these blanks, I attached an auxiliary fence to the miter gauge and used the rip fence as a stop.

CUT TO SIZE. Now the blanks can be cut into four cross pieces (Fig. 5). (This

time, you can't use the rip fence as a stop, because the piece will kick back.)

Then all that's left is to chamfer the ends of the cross pieces (Fig. 6). Here again, I used the zero-clearance insert. But this time, I supported the pieces with a push block.

Now the cross pieces can be glued together and set aside until after the hooks and feet are made and the tree is ready to be assembled (Fig. 7).

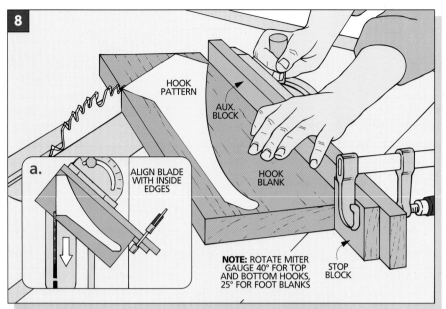

8

a. ALIGN BLADE WITH INSIDE EDGES

HOOK PATTERN

AUX. BLOCK

HOOK BLANK

NOTE: ROTATE MITER GAUGE 40° FOR TOP AND BOTTOM HOOKS, 25° FOR FOOT BLANKS

STOP BLOCK

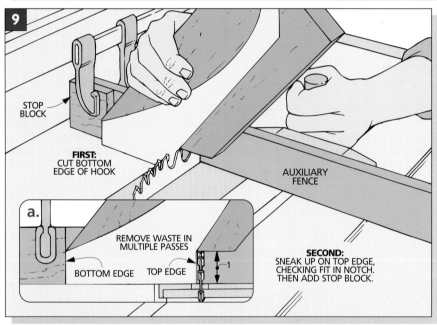

9

STOP BLOCK

FIRST: CUT BOTTOM EDGE OF HOOK

AUXILIARY FENCE

a. REMOVE WASTE IN MULTIPLE PASSES

BOTTOM EDGE   TOP EDGE   1

SECOND: SNEAK UP ON TOP EDGE, CHECKING FIT IN NOTCH. THEN ADD STOP BLOCK.

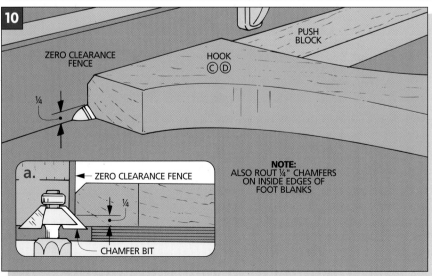

10

ZERO CLEARANCE FENCE

PUSH BLOCK

HOOK Ⓒ Ⓓ

¼

a. ZERO CLEARANCE FENCE

¼

CHAMFER BIT

NOTE: ALSO ROUT ¼" CHAMFERS ON INSIDE EDGES OF FOOT BLANKS

The last pieces to make are the hooks and feet. There are twelve different pieces to make, but the procedure is identical (the only difference is the shape). The initial (straight) cuts are made on a table saw for accuracy, while the curved cuts are made on a band saw.

I started by cutting the blanks for the top (C) and bottom hooks (D) from 1"-thick stock. (Top hook blanks are 4" x 10"; bottom blanks are 4" x 8".)

PATTERN. With the blanks cut to size, I created patterns for the top and bottom hooks (see page 49). Then I mounted them to two of the blanks.

INSIDE EDGE. The next step is to shape the inside edge of each blank (the one that fits into the notches on the posts). This is a two-step process. First I angled the miter gauge and cut the inside edge of each piece *(Fig. 8)*.

Note: Both hook blanks are cut with the miter gauge angled to 40°.

With the inside edge cut, next I cut the top and bottom edges so the hooks fit in the notches in the post. I cut the bottom edge first with the blank standing on the inside edge. (I cut the blank with the pattern first and then traced this cut on the other blanks.)

Next, I cut the top edge of the hook *(Figs. 9 and 9a)*. Here, instead of following the pattern, you'll want to sneak up on the final height (width) of the piece so it fits snug in the notches in the posts. When it does, you can clamp a stop block to the auxiliary fence so all the other blanks will be identical.

Note: You'll need to reset the stop block for the other set of hook blanks.

CUT TO SHAPE. Now the rest of the pattern can be cut out. I cut oversize on the band saw and sanded up to the line. When this piece was complete, I traced it on the other blanks so they could be cut and sanded to match.

FEET. Next you can work on the feet (E). The procedure here is the same. The only differences are that the blank is larger (5" x 13½") (see page 49) and to cut the inside edge, the miter gauge is rotated 25°.

CHAMFER INSIDE EDGE. When the feet are cut out and sanded, there's still one more step for both the hooks and feet. I routed chamfers on the inside edges of each piece *(Figs. 10 and 10a)*. These ¼" chamfers allow all four pieces to come together in the center.

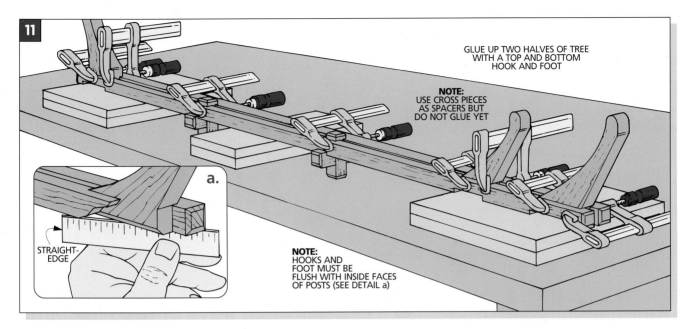

11

GLUE UP TWO HALVES OF TREE
WITH A TOP AND BOTTOM
HOOK AND FOOT

NOTE:
USE CROSS PIECES
AS SPACERS BUT
DO NOT GLUE YET

a.

STRAIGHT-
EDGE

NOTE:
HOOKS AND
FOOT MUST BE
FLUSH WITH INSIDE FACES
OF POSTS (SEE DETAIL a)

ASSEMBLY

Now that the hooks and feet are complete, the hall tree can be assembled. Here it begins to look like a large "Lincoln Log" project. But fortunately, there's not much to the assembly, if you take it in steps.

GLUE UP HALVES. The first thing I did was glue up one set of hooks (top and bottom) and a foot between two posts *(Fig. 11)*. I used the cross piece assemblies to help keep the posts aligned. But

the important thing is that the inside edges of all the posts, hooks, and feet are flush *(Fig. 11a)*.

When one half is glued together, I did the same with the other. Then I connected the two halves by gluing the cross piece assemblies between them *(Fig. 12)*.

Now the remaining pairs of hooks and feet can be glued into the notches *(Fig. 12)*. I added one at a time, inserting it into the notch and clamping it tight.

Note: To prevent squeeze-out, apply glue only to the notches on the post.

After all the hooks and feet were in place, I checked to see if there was a shoulder at the bottom of the hooks. If there was, I sanded the hooks so they made a smooth transition into the posts. Then I softened all the "hard" edges on the hooks and feet.

FINISH. The last thing to do is apply the finish. Because of the tight spaces between the posts, a spray gun would work best. But if you don't have a spray gun, you can do what I did. Wipe on about three coats of an oil finish. ■

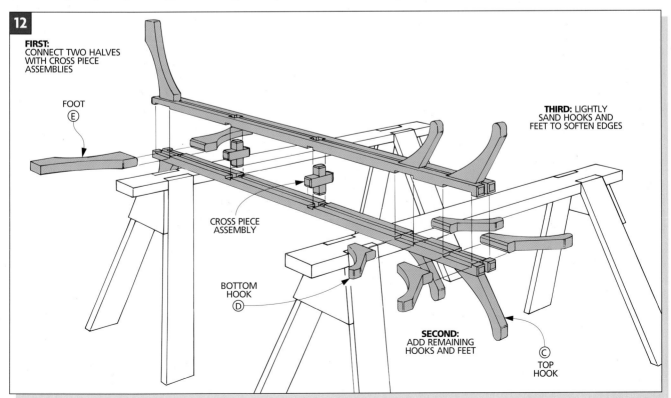

12

FIRST:
CONNECT TWO HALVES
WITH CROSS PIECE
ASSEMBLIES

FOOT
E

THIRD: LIGHTLY
SAND HOOKS AND
FEET TO SOFTEN EDGES

CROSS PIECE
ASSEMBLY

BOTTOM
HOOK
D

SECOND:
ADD REMAINING
HOOKS AND FEET

TOP
HOOK
C

Oak Sofa Table

Everything you'd expect of a Mission-style sofa table is featured in this project, including quartersawn oak, square spindles, and authentic mortise and tenon joinery.

Plywood or solid wood? That's the choice you have to make when a project includes wide panels, such as the top and shelf on this sofa table. Often, I choose plywood since it won't expand and contract with changes in humidity as much as solid wood.

But I chose solid wood on this table, for two reasons. I wanted to use quartersawn oak, typical of Mission (or Craftsman style) furniture, and quartersawn oak is hard to find in plywood. Also, beveling a plywood edge wouldn't work without hardwood edging.

WOOD MOVEMENT. Since solid wood was the best option, I needed a way to allow the panels to expand and contract.

This wasn't a problem with the top, or the front and back of the shelf. I used some simple Z-shaped fasteners. But the *ends* of the shelf were a concern.

The problem is that the shelf fits between the legs, so when the panel expands, it will tend to push the legs apart, and when it contracts, there will be a gap. So I made a pocket for the shelf by extending the groove on the rails into the legs (see inset photo).

FINISH. I used a light cherry stain and topped it with two coats of an oil and urethane combination. Then I rubbed on paste wax and buffed it to a satin sheen.

EXPLODED VIEW

OVERALL DIMENSIONS:
50L x 17D x 28H

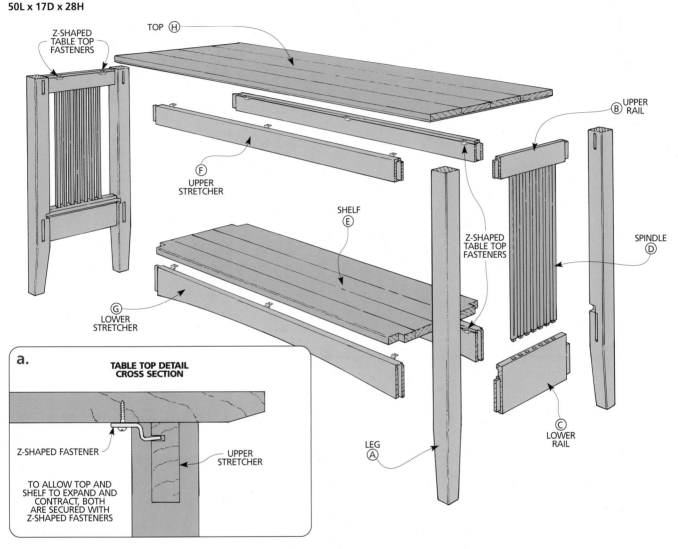

Z-SHAPED
TABLE TOP
FASTENERS

TOP (H)

(B) UPPER
RAIL

UPPER
STRETCHER (F)

SHELF
(E)

Z-SHAPED
TABLE TOP
FASTENERS

SPINDLE
(D)

LOWER
STRETCHER (G)

LEG
(A)

(C) LOWER
RAIL

a.

**TABLE TOP DETAIL
CROSS SECTION**

Z-SHAPED FASTENER

UPPER
STRETCHER

TO ALLOW TOP AND
SHELF TO EXPAND AND
CONTRACT, BOTH
ARE SECURED WITH
Z-SHAPED FASTENERS

MATERIALS LIST

WOOD

A	Legs (4)	$1\frac{3}{4}$ x $1\frac{3}{4}$ - $27\frac{1}{4}$
B	Upper Rails (2)	$\frac{3}{4}$ x 2 - $11\frac{1}{4}$
C	Lower Rails (2)	$\frac{3}{4}$ x $4\frac{1}{8}$ - $11\frac{1}{4}$
D	Spindles (14)	$\frac{1}{2}$ x $\frac{1}{2}$ - $15\frac{1}{8}$
E	Shelf (1)	$\frac{3}{4}$ x $12\frac{3}{4}$ - 40
F	Upr. Stretchers (2)	$\frac{3}{4}$ x 2 - $39\frac{3}{4}$
G	Lwr. Stretchers (2)	$\frac{3}{4}$ x 3 - $39\frac{3}{4}$
H	Top (1)	$\frac{3}{4}$ x 17 - 50

HARDWARE SUPPLIES

(16) No. 8 x $\frac{5}{8}$" Rh woodscrews
(16) Z-shaped table top fasteners

CUTTING DIAGRAM

$1\frac{3}{4}$ x 4 - 60 QUARTERSAWN WHITE OAK (3.3 Bd. Ft.)

A	A

$\frac{3}{4}$ x 4 - 84 QUARTERSAWN WHITE OAK (2 Boards @ 2.3 Bd. Ft. Each)

E	E

$\frac{3}{4}$ x 5 - 96 QUARTERSAWN WHITE OAK (2 Boards @ 3.3 Bd. Ft. Each)

H	G

D

$\frac{3}{4}$ x 5 - 96 QUARTERSAWN WHITE OAK (3.3 Bd. Ft.)

H	F

$\frac{3}{4}$ x 5 - 96 QUARTERSAWN WHITE OAK (3.3 Bd. Ft.)

H	C	C	B

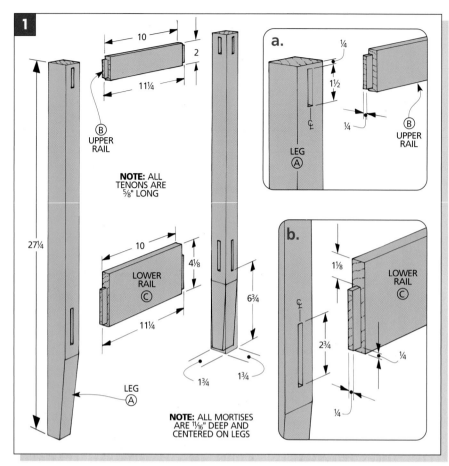

1

10

2

11¼

B
UPPER
RAIL

NOTE: ALL
TENONS ARE
⅝" LONG

27¼

10

4⅛

LOWER
RAIL
C

11¼

LEG
A

a.

¼

1½

¢

¼

LEG
A

B
UPPER
RAIL

b.

1⅛

LOWER
RAIL
C

2¾

¼

¼

6¾

1¾   1¾

NOTE: ALL MORTISES
ARE ¹¹⁄₁₆" DEEP AND
CENTERED ON LEGS

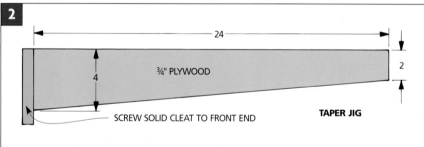

2

24

4

¾" PLYWOOD

2

SCREW SOLID CLEAT TO FRONT END

TAPER JIG

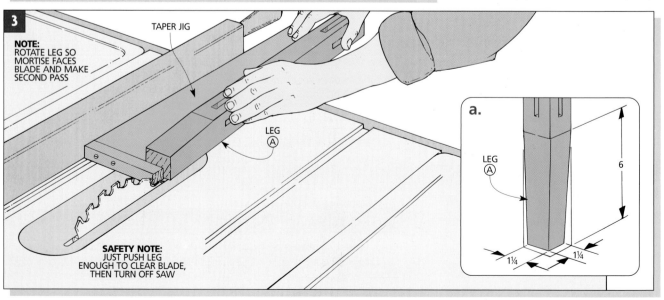

3

TAPER JIG

NOTE:
ROTATE LEG SO
MORTISE FACES
BLADE AND MAKE
SECOND PASS

LEG
A

SAFETY NOTE:
JUST PUSH LEG
ENOUGH TO CLEAR BLADE,
THEN TURN OFF SAW

a.

LEG
A

6

1¼   1¼

LEGS

To build the sofa table, I started by working on the legs.

With some projects, keeping all of the legs oriented correctly in relation to each other requires some mental gymnastics. But it's easy on this table since the four legs (A) are identical.

The legs are cut from 8/4 stock to a length of 27¼" and 1¾" square (Fig. 1).

MORTISES. Next, I made centered mortises for the rails and stretchers (Figs. 1a and 1b). To do this, drill overlapping ¼"-dia. holes ¹¹⁄₁₆" deep on adjacent faces of the legs. Then square up the sides and ends with a chisel.

TAPERS. Finally, I tapered the inside faces of each leg (the same faces that the mortises are on). Start the tapers 6" up from the bottom end (Fig. 3a).

To do this, I made a jig for the table saw (Fig. 2). It's just a scrap piece with a tapered edge and a small cleat at one end. The jig acts as an angled spacer between the rip fence and the leg. You push the leg through the blade, and the cleat causes the jig to ride along (Fig. 3).

When one taper is cut, rotate the leg so the other mortised face is toward the blade and make a second pass.

RAILS

Now the legs can be set aside and work can begin on the rails that will join the legs at the ends of the table.

The upper and lower rails (B, C) are cut from ¾"-thick stock and are the same length (11¼"). But the upper rail isn't as wide (2") as the lower one (4⅛")

(Fig. 1). The extra width on the lower rail allows room for a groove to accept the shelf that's added later.

TENONS. After cutting the rails to final size, tenons can be cut on the ends of the rails. Since the tenons are centered, I cut them on the table saw with a dado blade, flipping the rails between passes to sneak up on the thickness.

Then I cut the shoulders on the tenons, which are all 1/4" except the upper shoulder on the lower rail (C). Here, it's 1 1/8" because of the shelf groove that's added later *(Fig. 1b)*.

SPINDLE MORTISES. With the tenons cut, it's time to lay out the spindle mortises. There are seven mortises in each rail. For a good fit, these mortises should align between the top and bottom rails. To ensure this, I clamped the four rails together and marked the centers of all the mortises *(Figs. 4 and 4a)*.

Next, unclamp the rails and set up the drill press to bore a 3/8"-dia. hole 5/16" deep that's centered on the thickness of the rail *(Fig. 5)*. Then drill a single hole for each mortise.

Finally, I squared up the mortises with a chisel. To keep them identical, I made a chisel guide (see the Shop Jig below).

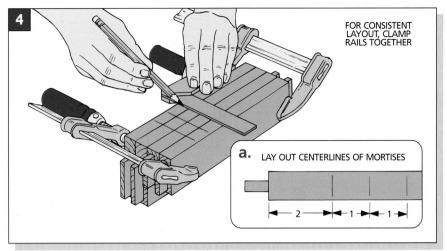

4 FOR CONSISTENT LAYOUT, CLAMP RAILS TOGETHER

a. LAY OUT CENTERLINES OF MORTISES

2 — 1 — 1

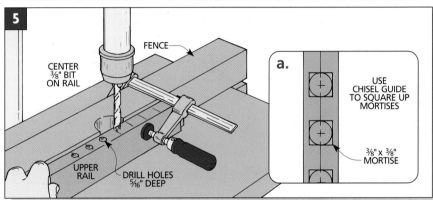

5 CENTER 3/8" BIT ON RAIL · FENCE · UPPER RAIL · DRILL HOLES 5/16" DEEP

a. USE CHISEL GUIDE TO SQUARE UP MORTISES · 3/8" x 3/8" MORTISE

SHOP JIG . . . . *Chisel Guide*

Getting all the spindle holes on the sofa table rails squared up can be difficult. To speed up the process, I made a simple jig to guide my chisel.

This jig is just a piece of aluminum angle with a square hole filed in the middle. The key to this jig is cutting the square hole so it's centered perfectly over the drilled holes in the rails.

This is easy to do. Once the holes for the mortises are drilled *(Fig. 1)*, clamp

the aluminum angle to the front of your workpiece *(Fig. 2)*. Don't move the fence on your drill press, but change to a twist bit to drill the aluminum.

Now drill the hole and square it up with a small file until it's the size needed for the mortise (3/8" x 3/8") *(Fig. 3)*.

To use the jig, position it over the holes and clamp it in place (see photo). The jig guides your chisel to cut mortises that match the spindle tenons.

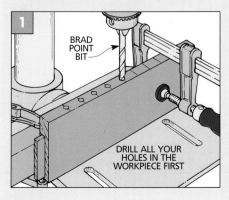

1 BRAD POINT BIT · DRILL ALL YOUR HOLES IN THE WORKPIECE FIRST

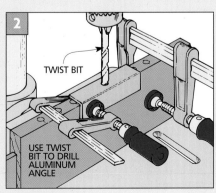

2 TWIST BIT · USE TWIST BIT TO DRILL ALUMINUM ANGLE

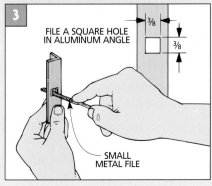

3 FILE A SQUARE HOLE IN ALUMINUM ANGLE · 3/8 · 3/8 · SMALL METAL FILE

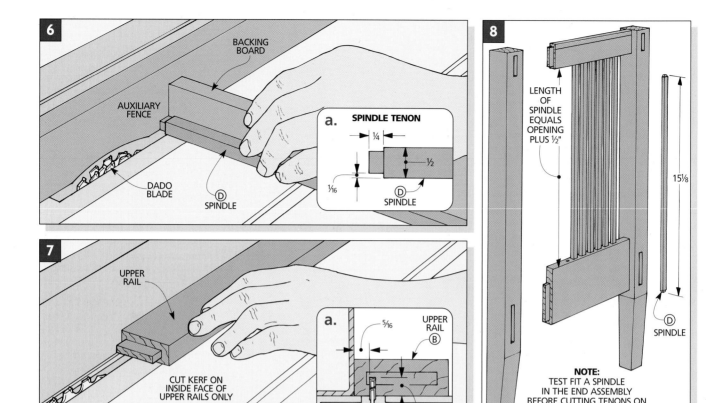

6

BACKING BOARD

AUXILIARY FENCE

DADO BLADE

Ⓓ SPINDLE

a. SPINDLE TENON

1/4

1/16

1/2

Ⓓ SPINDLE

7

UPPER RAIL

CUT KERF ON INSIDE FACE OF UPPER RAILS ONLY

a.

5/16

UPPER RAIL Ⓑ

3/8

8

LENGTH OF SPINDLE EQUALS OPENING PLUS 1/2"

15⅛

Ⓓ SPINDLE

NOTE:
TEST FIT A SPINDLE IN THE END ASSEMBLY BEFORE CUTTING TENONS ON ALL THE SPINDLES

SPINDLES

Once all the mortises in the rails are drilled and squared up, they are ready for the square spindles.

CUT TO SIZE. To find the length of the spindles, first dry-assemble the rails and legs into an end unit. Then measure the distance between the rails (refer to *Fig. 8*). This will give you the *shoulder-to-shoulder* distance of the spindles.

Now add 1/2" to this measurement to allow for the 1/4"-long tenons on each end. (My spindles were 15⅛" long.)

Next, to cut the spindles (D) to size, I began with 1/2"-thick stock cut to finished length. Then I ripped 1/2"-square spindles from the blank.

Note: It's probably a good idea to make a few extra spindles. This will help you set up the cut for the tenons.

TENONS. Once the spindles are cut to width, square tenons can be cut on their ends to fit the mortises in the rails. I like to do this on the table saw with a dado blade buried in an auxiliary fence. To do this, leave 1/4" of the blade exposed and raise it 1/16" above the table *(Fig. 6)*.

But before cutting tenons on all the pieces, start with a test piece and check the fit. This means more than just trying the tenon in the mortise. It also means making sure the spindles fit between the upper and lower rails.

KERF IN RAIL. Now, to complete the upper rails (B), I cut a 1/8" kerf in each rail's top inside edge *(Figs. 7 and 8)*. This is for the hardware used to attach the top panel later.

SHELF JOINERY

There's just a couple more steps before the end units of the table can be assembled. First, there has to be some way to hold the shelf in place between the ends. It's done a little differently than with the table top.

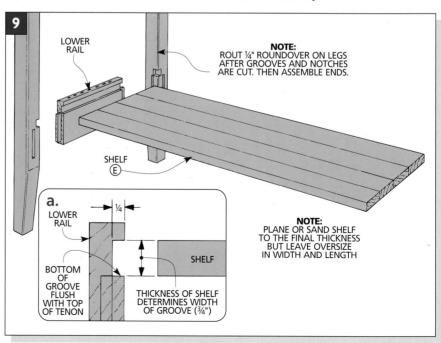

9

LOWER RAIL

NOTE:
ROUT 1/4" ROUNDOVER ON LEGS AFTER GROOVES AND NOTCHES ARE CUT. THEN ASSEMBLE ENDS.

SHELF Ⓔ

a.

1/4

LOWER RAIL

BOTTOM OF GROOVE FLUSH WITH TOP OF TENON

THICKNESS OF SHELF DETERMINES WIDTH OF GROOVE (¾")

SHELF

NOTE:
PLANE OR SAND SHELF TO THE FINAL THICKNESS BUT LEAVE OVERSIZE IN WIDTH AND LENGTH

To support the shelf and prevent it from cupping, I cut a groove in the lower rails. Easy enough. But since the shelf will be notched to fit between the legs, I had to come up with a way to allow the panel to easily expand and contract. If it were just glued in the groove, the shelf would likely split or leave gaps with changes in humidity.

The solution is to extend the groove into the legs so there's a notch for the shelf to expand into (*Figs. 9 and 10* and the inset photo on page 54).

SHELF. Creating the groove for the shelf isn't difficult. But since the final thickness of the shelf (E) determines the width of the grooves, I glued the shelf up now and planed and sanded it down to final thickness (*Fig. 9a*). (You can leave it at rough width and length for now.)

GROOVE. After determining the thickness of the panel, the first step is to lay out the location of the groove in the rail. Mark the bottom edge of this groove so it will be flush with the top edge of the tenon on the rail (*Fig. 9a*). Then cut the groove $1/4$" deep.

NOTCH. Now dry-assemble the legs and rails into an end unit again, and transfer the depth and height of the groove to the leg (*Fig. 10*). Then lay out the notch on the leg. Once the layout is complete, you can notch the leg. To remove most of the waste, I used my drill press to drill $3/8$"-deep overlapping holes. Then I pared up to the layout lines with a sharp chisel (*Fig. 11*).

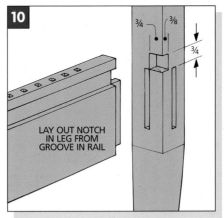

10 LAY OUT NOTCH IN LEG FROM GROOVE IN RAIL

$3/4$ $3/8$ $3/4$

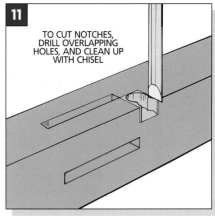

11 TO CUT NOTCHES, DRILL OVERLAPPING HOLES, AND CLEAN UP WITH CHISEL

After all the notches are cut, you can test the fit of the shelf in the grooves and notches.

ROUND OVER LEGS. Once the shelf fits in the grooves and notches, there's one more step before the ends can be assembled. Use the router table and a fence to rout a $1/4$" roundover on all four edges of the legs.

ASSEMBLE ENDS. At this point, the ends of the table can be assembled. I positioned the spindles in their mortises between the rails. Then I glued the legs to the rails.

STRETCHERS

Next, the stretchers (F, G) can be made (*Fig. 12*). They're cut to identical lengths ($39^3/4$"), but the upper stretchers are 2" wide, while the lower ones are 3" (*Fig. 12a*).

TENONS. Next, cut $5/8$"-long tenons centered on the stretchers to fit the mortises in the legs. Note that the tenons on the lower stretchers don't have shoulders along their top edges. That's because the shelf sits directly on top and will hide any gaps.

KERFS AND ARCS. There are two more steps to complete the stretchers. First, the hardware that holds the shelf and top in place (refer to *Fig. 14a*) requires a kerf cut along the inside faces of the stretchers (*Fig. 12a*).

The second step is to lay out and cut an arc on the bottom of each of the lower stretchers (*Fig. 12*). This arc should be 2" down from the top edge of the stretcher at its highest point.

To lay out this arc, you can use a flexible straightedge, a couple of pointed scraps, and a pencil (refer to the Shop Tip box on page 65).

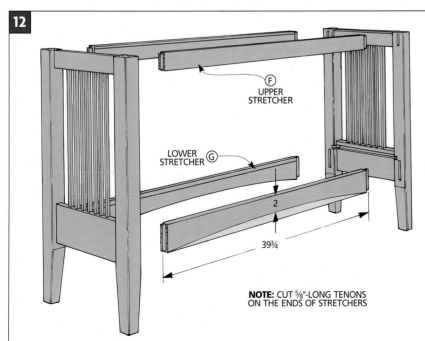

12

F UPPER STRETCHER

LOWER STRETCHER G

2

$39^3/4$

NOTE: CUT $5/8$"-LONG TENONS ON THE ENDS OF STRETCHERS

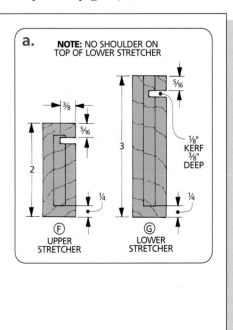

a. **NOTE:** NO SHOULDER ON TOP OF LOWER STRETCHER

$3/8$ $5/16$ $5/16$ 3 $1/8$" KERF $3/8$" DEEP

2   $1/4$ $1/4$

F UPPER STRETCHER

G LOWER STRETCHER

Before connecting the end assemblies with the stretchers, you need to cut the shelf panel to final size. To do this, you'll have to dry-assemble the table again *(Fig. 13)*.

The overall length of the shelf equals the distance between the bottoms of the grooves in the rails. (Mine was 40" long.) The overall width equals the distance across the stretchers plus $1/8$" overhang on each side *(Fig. 13a)*. (Mine ended up $12^3/4$" wide.)

NOTCHES. After the shelf is cut to size, the corners need to be notched to fit around the legs (and into the notches in the legs) *(Fig. 13b)*. To find the depth of the shelf notch, measure from the bottom of the groove in the rail to the inside edge of the leg. (Mine was $3/4$".)

The width of the notch is a little trickier. First measure from the outside edge of the stretcher to the edge of the notch in the leg ($7/8$") *(Fig. 13b)*. Add $1/8$" for the overhang on the outside of the stretcher. Then add another $1/8$" for a gap inside the notch that allows the shelf to expand and contract. (My notch was $1^1/8$" wide.)

Note: It's a good idea to double-check your measurements before cutting the notches on the shelf. The length between the legs should equal the length between these notches. Then once the notches are cut, dry-assemble the table one last time to

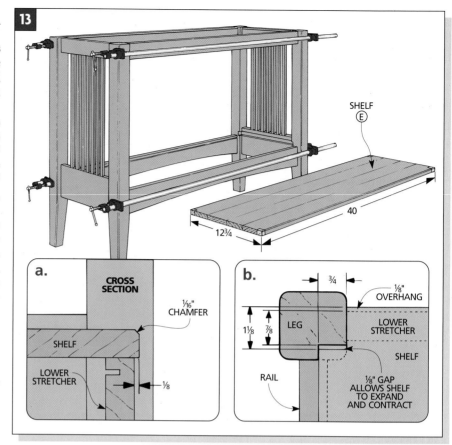

make sure everything fits.

ASSEMBLY. When everything fits, rout a $1/16$" chamfer on the top edge of the shelf *(Fig. 13a)*. Then glue up the table. (Don't glue in the shelf panel.)

TOP. Now all that's left is to add the top (H). Glue up a $3/4$"-thick panel and

cut it to finished size *(Fig. 14)*. Then rout a bevel around the bottom edge (see the Shop Jig on the opposite page).

Finally, to attach the top (and the front and back of the shelf), I used table top fasteners *(Fig. 14a)*. These fit into the kerfs in the stretchers and rails. ■

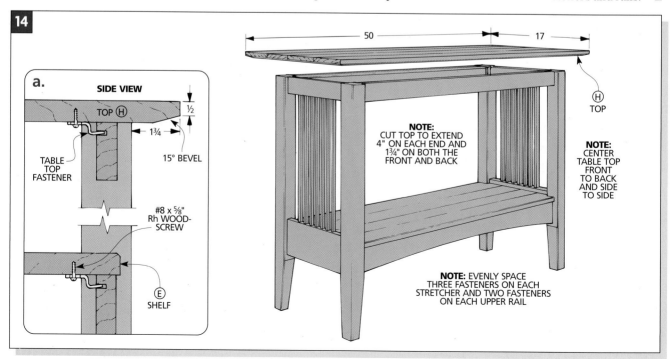

SHOP JIG .... *Bevel Jig*

Typically, I like to use a table saw to cut a bevel on a workpiece. But trying to bevel the bottom side of the sofa table top created a problem. It just wasn't safe to stand this large panel on end and use the table saw.

The solution was a shop-made jig that holds a router at an angle *(Fig. 2)*. With a straight bit in the router, it's easy to rout the bevel.

Note: The flute length on the bit has to be long enough to cut the full width of the bevel. Mine was $1^1/4"$ long.

JIG CONSTRUCTION. The jig consists of four pieces: a fence, a bit guard, a router base plate, and a handle *(Fig. 1)*. To build the jig, start with the fence and

bit guard. First, cut a notch at the center of the fence to provide clearance for the bit. Then you can glue the bit guard and fence together.

To make this jig work, simply cut an angle on one end of the fence and bit

guard that matches the bevel you need on your workpiece (15° for the sofa table). Then when you add the base plate, it tips your router to match the bevel. The $1/4"$ hardboard base plate is simply screwed into the fence. Finally, screw a handle to the fence.

SETTING DEPTH. Since this jig is designed to cut the bevel in several passes, you adjust the depth of cut by pivoting the auxiliary base *(Fig. 3)*. An arched slot allows the router to swing up or down to the required depth before locking it in position with a screw.

USING THE JIG. Start with the depth set shallow. Then increase the depth gradually until your bevel is complete.

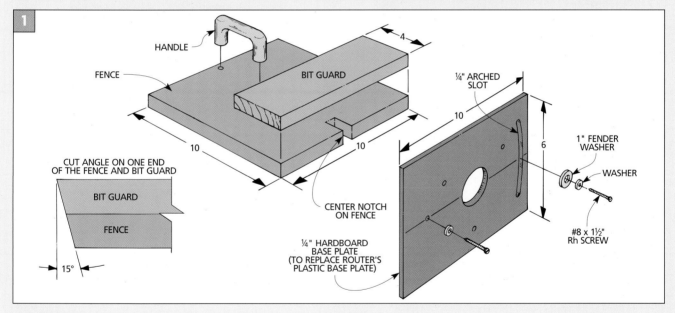

1

HANDLE

FENCE

BIT GUARD

4

$1/4"$ ARCHED SLOT

10

10

10

6

1" FENDER WASHER

WASHER

#8 x $1^1/2$" Rh SCREW

CUT ANGLE ON ONE END OF THE FENCE AND BIT GUARD

BIT GUARD

FENCE

15°

CENTER NOTCH ON FENCE

$1/4$" HARDBOARD BASE PLATE (TO REPLACE ROUTER'S PLASTIC BASE PLATE)

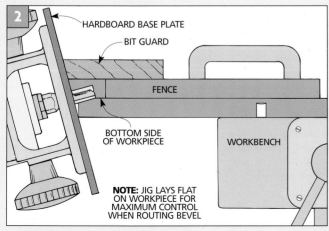

2

HARDBOARD BASE PLATE

BIT GUARD

FENCE

BOTTOM SIDE OF WORKPIECE

WORKBENCH

NOTE: JIG LAYS FLAT ON WORKPIECE FOR MAXIMUM CONTROL WHEN ROUTING BEVEL

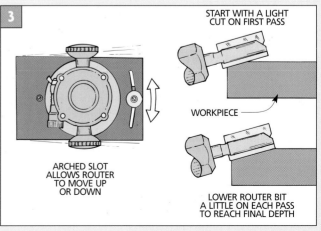

3

START WITH A LIGHT CUT ON FIRST PASS

WORKPIECE

ARCHED SLOT ALLOWS ROUTER TO MOVE UP OR DOWN

LOWER ROUTER BIT A LITTLE ON EACH PASS TO REACH FINAL DEPTH

Glass-Top Coffee Table

Made of quartersawn oak, this traditional Mission-style coffee table is enhanced with a beveled glass top and a series of narrow spindles. There's also an option for a solid wood top.

D rilling a round hole to create a mortise for a square tenon has always struck me as a bit odd. But aside from investing in an expensive machine for making mortises, the only solutions I could come up with in the past were to round the tenon or to square up the mortise with a chisel.

Now, if you're only talking about a few mortises, that's not a big deal. In fact, it's kind of relaxing. That's what I did for the spindles on the Sofa Table shown on page 54.

But on this coffee table there are 26 spindles, which means a total of 52 mor-

tises to drill and square up. You could spend the better part of a day on this part of the project alone.

So I decided to try something different this time around. The new procedure I came up with is both quick and accurate. (I'll give you a hint — it doesn't involve using a drill press or a chisel. See the Technique on page 70.)

GLASS TOP. But the mortises aren't the only feature of this table worth mentioning. The beveled glass top is also a little out of the ordinary.

Now at first, I was worried that the beveled glass top would look too

"modern" for this style of table. But actually, it complements the style by giving you a clear view of the spindles from just about any angle.

However, if you prefer the look of a solid wood top (that matches the one on the Sofa Table), we've included that as an option. See the Designer's Notebook on page 71.

MATERIALS. All the wooden parts for the table shown here are quartersawn white oak, a typical material for Mission-style projects.

No hardware is required for this table other than ordinary woodscrews.

EXPLODED VIEW

OVERALL DIMENSIONS:
38W x 30D x 17H

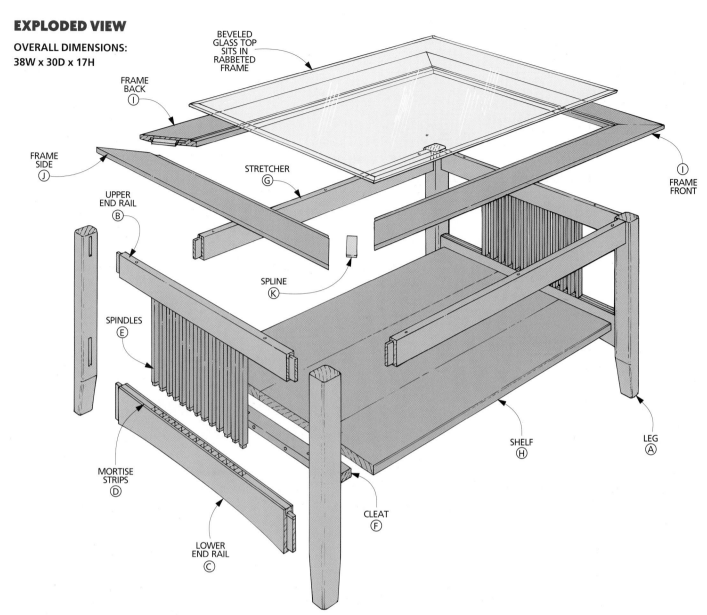

BEVELED GLASS TOP SITS IN RABBETED FRAME

FRAME BACK ⓘ

FRAME SIDE ⓙ

FRAME FRONT ⓘ

STRETCHER ⓖ

UPPER END RAIL ⓑ

SPLINE ⓚ

SPINDLES ⓔ

SHELF ⓗ

LEG ⓐ

MORTISE STRIPS ⓓ

CLEAT ⓕ

LOWER END RAIL ⓒ

MATERIALS LIST

WOOD

A	Legs (4)	$1\frac{3}{4} \times 1\frac{3}{4} - 16\frac{1}{4}$
B	Upper End Rails (2)	$\frac{3}{4} \times 2 - 24\frac{1}{2}$
C	Lower End Rails (2)	$\frac{3}{4} \times 3 - 24\frac{1}{2}$
D	Mortise Strips (4)	$\frac{1}{2} \times \frac{3}{8} - 24\frac{1}{2}$
E	Spindles (26)	$\frac{1}{2} \times \frac{1}{2} - 8\frac{1}{4}$
F	Cleats (2)	$\frac{3}{4} \times 1\frac{1}{2} - 17$
G	Stretchers (2)	$\frac{3}{4} \times 2 - 32\frac{1}{2}$
H	Shelf (1)	$\frac{3}{4} \times 22 - 32$
I	Frame Fr./Bk. (2)	$\frac{3}{4} \times 3\frac{1}{2} - 38$
J	Frame Sides (2)	$\frac{3}{4} \times 3\frac{1}{2} - 30$
K	Splines (4)	$\frac{1}{4} \times 1 - 1\frac{3}{4}$

HARDWARE SUPPLIES

(1) $\frac{1}{4}$" beveled glass, 24" x 32"
(6) #8 x 1$\frac{1}{4}$" Fh woodscrews
(18) #8 x 2" Fh woodscrews

CUTTING DIAGRAM

$1\frac{3}{4}$ x 4 - 48 QUARTERSAWN WHITE OAK (2.7 Bd. Ft.)

$\frac{3}{4}$ x 5$\frac{1}{2}$ - 84 QUARTERSAWN WHITE OAK (3.2 Bd. Ft.)

$\frac{1}{2}$ x 3$\frac{1}{2}$ - 72 QUARTERSAWN WHITE OAK (1.8 Sq. Ft.)

$\frac{3}{4}$ x 5 - 60 QUARTERSAWN WHITE OAK (2.1 Bd. Ft.)

$\frac{3}{4}$ x 5 - 72 QUARTERSAWN WHITE OAK (Two Boards @ 2.5 Bd. Ft. Each)

$\frac{3}{4}$ x 4 - 84 QUARTERSAWN WHITE OAK (2.3 Bd. Ft.)

$\frac{3}{4}$ x 4 - 72 QUARTERSAWN WHITE OAK (2 Bd. Ft.)

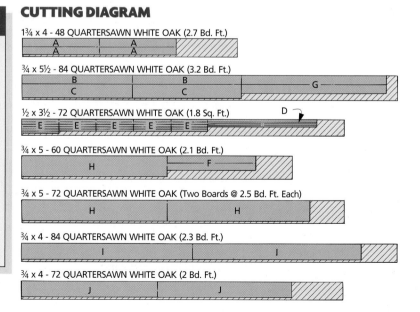

The coffee table is just two end frames joined by a top and shelf. And each end frame has a pair of legs, a pair of rails, and a row of spindles. I started building these frames by making the legs.

LEGS. The legs (A) begin as four squared-up blanks cut from 1³/₄"-thick stock *(Fig. 1)*. After cutting the blanks to length, I laid out the mortises for the rails on each leg *(Figs. 1 and 1a)*.

You can't go wrong laying out the two mortises at the top of each leg — they're on adjacent faces. But when laying out the lower mortise on each leg, pay attention to the orientation of the legs. The right and left legs are mirror images of one another *(Figs. 1 and 1a)*.

To make the mortises, I removed most of the waste by drilling a row of overlapping holes on a drill press. Then I used a chisel to clean up the sides.

Once the mortises are complete, the legs can be tapered and shaped. A table saw and a simple taper jig make quick work of the tapers on the inside faces of each leg *(Fig. 3)*. The jig I used is just a piece of plywood with a hardwood cleat attached to one end *(Fig. 2)*.

After cutting the tapers, I routed a chamfer on the inside corner of each leg on a router table *(Fig. 4)*. But don't try to chamfer the tapered edge. Just push the leg straight through the router table — the chamfer will narrow to a point at the bottom of the leg *(Fig. 1a)*.

For the three outside corners of the leg, I wanted a softer look. So I routed ¹/₄" roundovers on the edges, again using the router table *(Fig. 1)*.

Finally, to prevent the legs from splintering if the table is dragged across a floor, I rounded over the bottom edges of each leg slightly with sandpaper.

At this point, I put the legs aside and began work on the other parts of the end frames.

END RAILS. I cut the upper and lower end rails (B, C) to size from ³/₄"-thick stock first. All the rails are 24¹/₂" long,

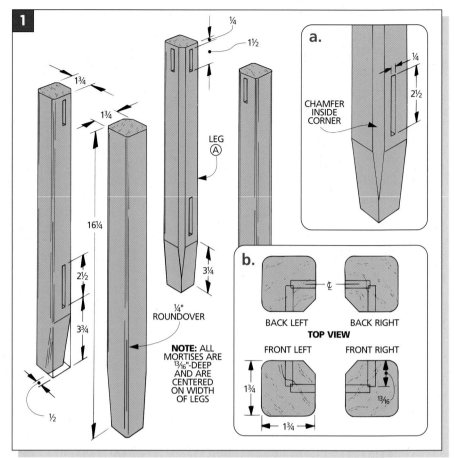

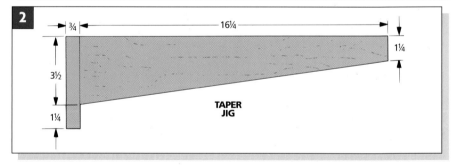

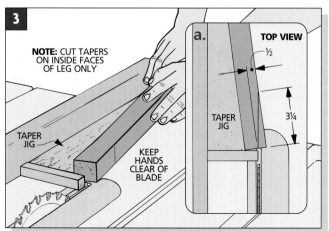

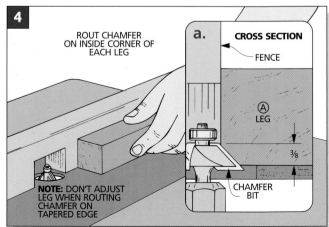

but the lower rails are an inch wider than the upper rails (*Fig. 5*).

The next step is to make the mortises for the spindles. But instead of drilling holes and squaring them up with a chisel, I used a different approach.

MORTISE STRIPS. First, I cut a groove on one edge of each rail (*Fig. 6*). Then I glued in a strip of wood with a row of notches (*Figs. 6 and 6a*). Once these mortise strips (D) are glued into the grooves, the notches become mortises. For more on this technique, see page 70.

TENONS. After gluing the strips into the rails and sanding them flush, tenons are cut on the ends of the rails to fit the mortises in the legs (*Figs. 7 and 7a*).

Note: The ends of the mortise strips become part of these tenons (*Fig. 7a*). This is why the tenons are cut *after* the mortise strips are glued in place.

ARCS. On the lower rails, I cut a gentle arc along the bottom edge (*Fig. 8*). To lay out this arc, I used a pencil, a flexible straightedge, and a couple of blocks of wood (see the Shop Tip box below).

I cut these arcs with a band saw and sanded them smooth with a drum sander. But you could use a jig saw and a rounded sanding block.

To complete the upper rails, I drilled counterbored shank holes in each rail (*Fig. 8*). These are for screws that fasten the top later. The shank holes are slightly oversize ($3/16$"-dia.) to allow room for wood movement (especially if you build the solid wood top).

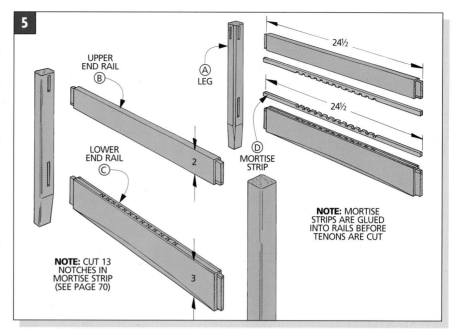

5

UPPER END RAIL — Ⓑ

LEG — Ⓐ

24½

24½

LOWER END RAIL — Ⓒ

MORTISE STRIP — Ⓓ

2

3

NOTE: CUT 13 NOTCHES IN MORTISE STRIP (SEE PAGE 70)

NOTE: MORTISE STRIPS ARE GLUED INTO RAILS BEFORE TENONS ARE CUT

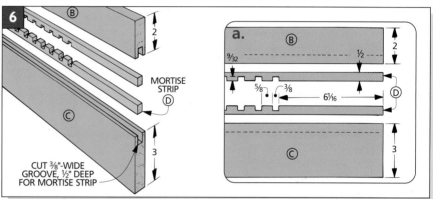

6

Ⓑ — 2

MORTISE STRIP — Ⓓ

Ⓒ — 3

CUT ⅜"-WIDE GROOVE, ½" DEEP FOR MORTISE STRIP

a. Ⓑ — 2

9/32 — ½

⅝ — ⅜

6 1/16 — Ⓓ

Ⓒ — 3

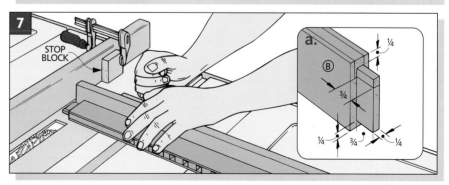

7

STOP BLOCK

a. Ⓑ

¼ ¼

¾ ¾

¼ ¾ ¼

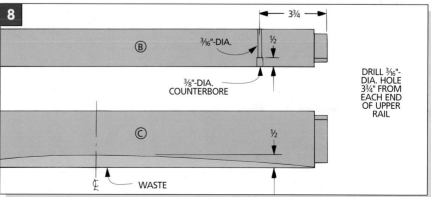

8

Ⓑ

3¾

3/16"-DIA.

½

⅜"-DIA. COUNTERBORE

Ⓒ

½

WASTE

DRILL 3/16"-DIA. HOLE 3¾" FROM EACH END OF UPPER RAIL

SHOP TIP

Drawing an Arc

To flex the straightedge and lay out the arcs, clamp a couple of pointed scraps to the ends of the rails.

SPINDLES. The rails and legs are the main components of the end frames. But the spindles are what catch your eye.

Making the twenty-six spindles (E) isn't difficult, just a little repetitive. The spindles are first cut to size from $1/2$"-thick stock *(Fig. 9a)*.

Then the tenons on the ends of each spindle are cut with a table saw and dado blade, rotating each piece a quarter turn between passes *(Fig. 9b)*. To keep the shoulders even and the shoulder-to-shoulder distance the same on each spindle, I used a stop block clamped to my miter gauge fence.

Normally you would glue up the end frames next. But because the spindles are so narrow and spaced so closely, I decided to stain them before assembly. I also stained the end rails. This way, I didn't have to worry about trying to work the stain in around the spindles after the table was assembled.

ASSEMBLY. Don't worry about trying to assemble all the spindles between the end rails before the glue sets up. The spindles aren't glued in place — they're captured between the rails.

I used a two-step procedure to assemble the end frames. First, I fit the spindles between the rails and held them in place with band clamps. Then I glued and clamped the legs to the rails *(Fig. 10)*. Not having to worry about the spindles makes the gluing up process a lot easier.

CLEATS. After assembling the end frames, there's still one more piece to add to each frame — a cleat.

The cleat (F) is attached to the lower end rail of each frame to support a shelf *(Figs. 9 and 11)*. These cleats are just narrow strips of $3/4$"-thick stock.

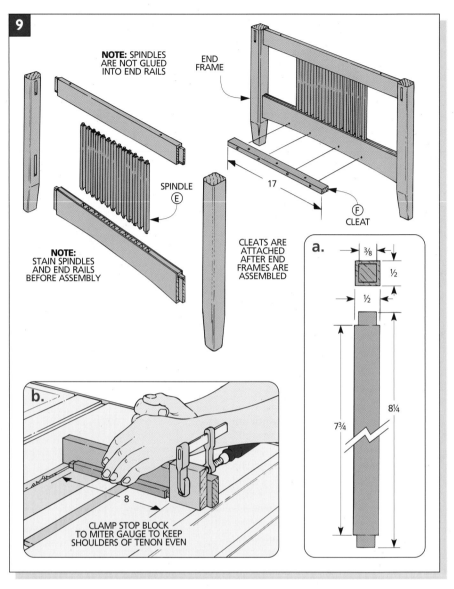

Before attaching the cleats to the end frames, I drilled three $3/16$"-dia. countersunk shank holes in each cleat for the screws that will be used to attach the shelf *(Figs. 11 and 11a)*.

Then I simply glued and screwed the cleats to the inside of the lower rails *(Figs. 11 and 11b)*.

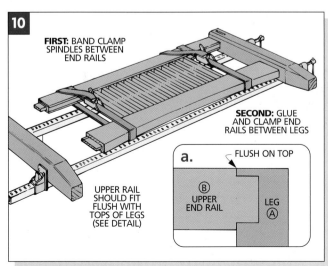

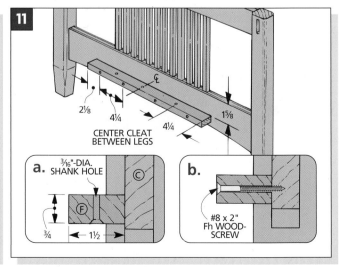

With the end frames completed, you're more than halfway home. All that remains is to join the two end frames with stretchers and a shelf, and add a top. I made the stretchers first so I could assemble the base and take measurements for the shelf *(Fig. 12).*

STRETCHERS. Each stretcher (G) is cut from a piece of ³/₄"-thick stock. A tenon is cut on each end to match the mortises in the legs *(Fig. 12a).*

Like the upper end rails, each stretcher is drilled and counterbored for three screws that will be used to attach the top *(Fig. 12a).*

SHELF. Aside from holding books or magazines, the shelf (H) serves another purpose. It acts as a lower stretcher, tying the base of the table together. I made the shelf from an oversized, glued-up panel of ³/₄"-thick stock.

Note: If you plan to build a solid wood top (see the Designer's Notebook on page 71) you may also want to glue up a panel for the top at this time.

After gluing up the shelf, I ripped it to finished width (22") *(Fig. 14).* In order to determine the exact length, I measured the distance between the upper end rails (32" in my case). Then I trimmed the ends of the shelf to match this measurement.

Before attaching the shelf, I took the time to break the sharp edges by routing a small (¹/₁₆") chamfer along the front and back edges (both top and bottom) *(Fig. 14a).* (The ends of the shelf are not chamfered.)

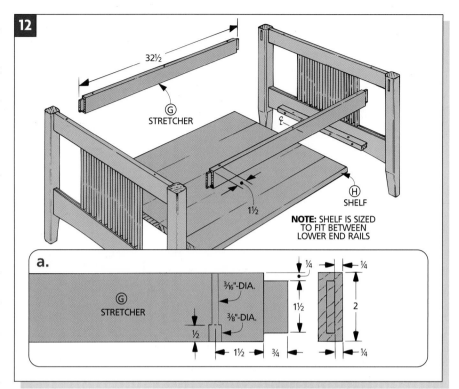
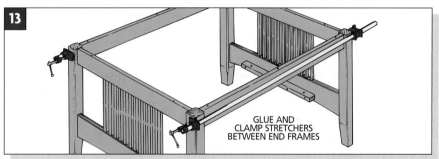

To attach the shelf, I placed it on the cleats and centered it front-to-back. Then, using clamps to pull the end frames tight against the shelf, I drove screws up through the cleats into the bottom of the shelf *(Figs. 15 and 15a).*

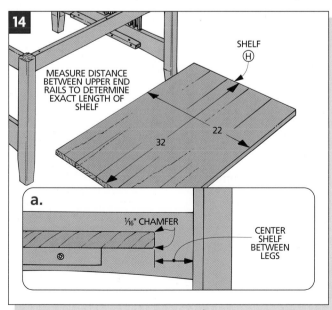

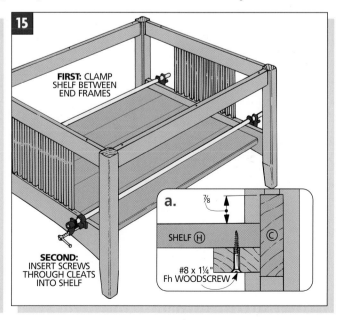

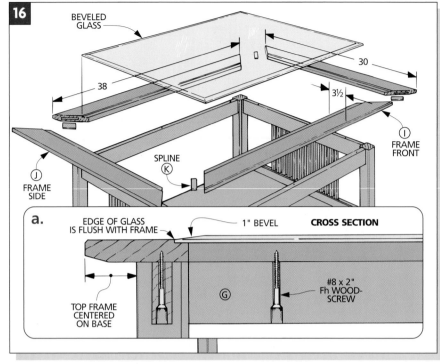

16

BEVELED GLASS

30

38

3½

FRAME FRONT

SPLINE K

FRAME SIDE J

I

a. CROSS SECTION

EDGE OF GLASS IS FLUSH WITH FRAME

1" BEVEL

TOP FRAME CENTERED ON BASE

#8 x 2" Fh WOOD-SCREW

G

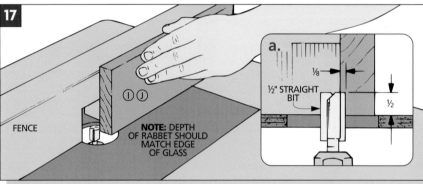

17

FENCE

I J

NOTE: DEPTH OF RABBET SHOULD MATCH EDGE OF GLASS

a.

½" STRAIGHT BIT

⅛

½

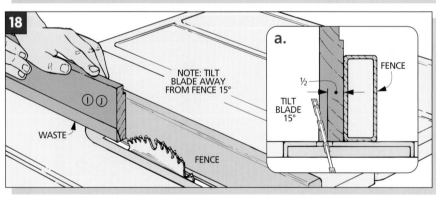

18

I J

WASTE

NOTE: TILT BLADE AWAY FROM FENCE 15°

FENCE

a.

FENCE

½

TILT BLADE 15°

FENCE

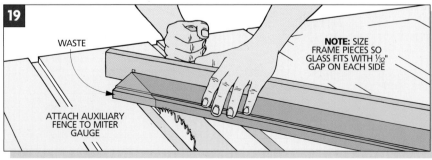

19

WASTE

NOTE: SIZE FRAME PIECES SO GLASS FITS WITH 1/32" GAP ON EACH SIDE

ATTACH AUXILIARY FENCE TO MITER GAUGE

The top of the coffee table is something like a picture in a frame — a really big frame. But the "picture" in this case is a piece of beveled glass.

BEVELED GLASS. If you've never worked with beveled glass before, there are a couple of things you should know. First off, the piece of glass I used is fairly large (1/4" thick and 24" x 32"). So don't expect to simply run down to your local hardware store and find it in stock.

I had to order the beveled glass specially from a local glass shop, and it took a week to fill the order. Try looking in the yellow pages to find a glass shop in your area.

Another important thing to know about ordering glass is that the final measurements aren't always exactly what you request. Because of the cutting and polishing process, the glass can vary as much as 1/8" from what you specify when you order it. But this isn't a problem as long as you obtain the glass *before* you cut the top frame pieces to length.

The frame front/back (I) and frame sides (J) are cut from 3/4"-thick stock. They can be ripped to finished width (3½"), but don't cut them to length just yet. They will be mitered to length a little later.

Before mitering the frame pieces, I cut a rabbet on one edge of each piece *(Figs. 17 and 17a)*. This rabbet creates a ledge for the glass top to rest on.

Note: The rabbet should be deep enough so the beveled edge of the glass will sit flush with the top surface of the frame (1/8" in my case) *(Fig. 16a)*.

Then to keep the outside edges of the top from looking too thick and heavy, I beveled the underside of each frame piece *(Figs. 18 and 18a)*. I did this by running the pieces through the table saw on edge and then sanding off the saw marks.

After rabbeting and beveling the frame pieces, they can be mitered to length to fit the beveled glass *(Fig. 19)*.

Note: To avoid making the opening for the glass too tight, allow a little extra (1/16") when figuring the length of the frame pieces.

SPLINES. To strengthen the miter joints, I added splines. But the splines serve another purpose as well. They help keep all the pieces even when gluing and clamping them together.

To cut the slots for the splines, I used a hand-held router and a slot-cutting bit *(Figs. 20 and 20b).* Just be sure to stop the slot short of the edges of the workpiece *(Fig. 20a).*

After routing these slots, I cut the $\frac{1}{4}$"-thick splines (K) to fit. The thing to remember here is that in order to get a strong joint, the grain of the spline needs to run *across* the joint line of the miters *(Fig. 20a).*

ASSEMBLING THE TOP. Before gluing up the top, I dry-assembled the pieces and clamped them together with band clamps to check the fit of the beveled glass *(Fig. 21).*

But because I didn't want to take a chance on breaking the glass, I made a template out of hardboard the same size as the glass and used that to check the fit instead.

Once I was satisfied with the fit of the miters and the size of the glass opening, I glued up the top frame pieces and clamped them back together. Then I used the hardboard template to check the glass opening one more time with the clamps in place.

CHAMFER. As a final detail, I relieved the sharp edges by routing very small ($\frac{1}{16}$") chamfers all around the edges of the top *(Figs. 22 and 22a).*

To attach the top, I simply centered it front-to-back and side-to-side. Then I drove screws up through the counterbored holes in the stretchers and upper end rails and into the top *(Fig. 23).*

FINISH. I stained the table with a light cherry stain and topped it with a tung oil and urethane combination finish. After drying, it was rubbed and buffed to a satin sheen with paste wax.

After the entire table was finished, I added the glass top. ◾

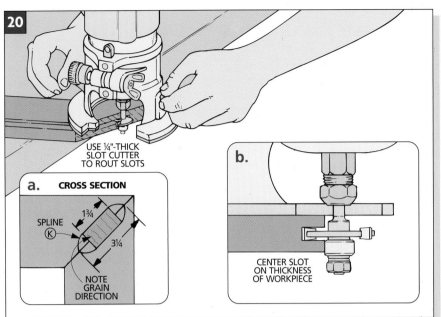

20 USE ¼"-THICK SLOT CUTTER TO ROUT SLOTS

a. CROSS SECTION
SPLINE (K)
1¾
3¼
NOTE GRAIN DIRECTION

b. CENTER SLOT ON THICKNESS OF WORKPIECE

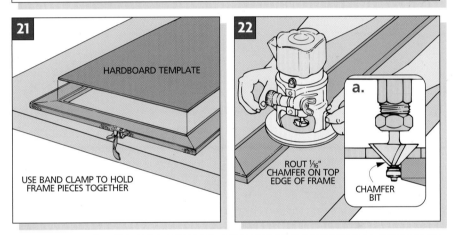

21 HARDBOARD TEMPLATE
USE BAND CLAMP TO HOLD FRAME PIECES TOGETHER

22 ROUT ¹⁄₁₆" CHAMFER ON TOP EDGE OF FRAME
a. CHAMFER BIT

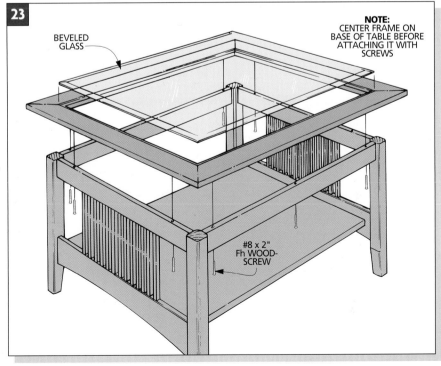

23
BEVELED GLASS
NOTE: CENTER FRAME ON BASE OF TABLE BEFORE ATTACHING IT WITH SCREWS
#8 x 2" Fh WOOD-SCREW

TECHNIQUE .... Simple Mortises

Instead of making individual mortises for the spindles in the coffee table, I used a different approach. First I cut a groove on one edge of each end rail. Then I glued in a "mortise strip."

GROOVES. There's not much to making the grooves. I cut them in two passes, flipping each rail end for end between passes to ensure that the grooves will be centered on the thickness of the workpiece (*Figs. 1 and 1a*).

MORTISE STRIPS. The mortise strips are just narrow strips with notches cut in them. When glued into the grooves, they create mortises for the spindles.

But instead of trying to cut the notches in narrow strips, I started with a wide blank cut to the same length as the rails (24¹⁄₂"). After the notches are cut, the blank will be ripped into strips. (I made the thickness of the blank equal the depth of the grooves in the rails.) If you want the strips to be nearly undetectable, you can make them from the same piece of wood as the rails.

NOTCHES. To cut the notches, I used a dado blade and a table saw. The trick is to keep the notches evenly spaced. To do this, I used a simple indexing jig.

To make the jig, clamp an auxiliary fence to the front of the miter gauge. Then cut a dado through the center of the blank and the auxiliary fence (*Fig. 2*).

To keep the notches evenly spaced, I glued an index key into the notch in the auxiliary fence (*Fig. 2a*). Then I readjusted the fence so the key was ⁵⁄₈" from the edge of the blade (*Figs. 3 and 3a*).

Next, I cut six more notches on one side of the center notch (*Fig. 4*). To do this, I simply placed each newly cut notch over the key to cut the next one.

After cutting the notches on one side, I turned the piece around and cut six notches on the other side of the center notch, following the same procedure.

Note: You should end up with a total of 13 notches.

RIPPING. Before ripping the strips, I drew a reference line on one end of the blank (*Fig. 5*). Later when the rails are glued between the legs, this line will help orient the end rails so the mortises align (*Fig. 6*).

Note: When gluing the strips into the rails, use a sparing amount of glue to avoid getting any in the mortises.

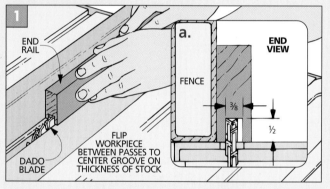

1

END RAIL

FLIP WORKPIECE BETWEEN PASSES TO CENTER GROOVE ON THICKNESS OF STOCK

DADO BLADE

a. FENCE

END VIEW

³⁄₈

¹⁄₂

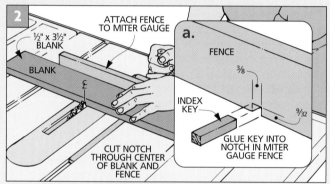

2

ATTACH FENCE TO MITER GAUGE

¹⁄₂" x 3¹⁄₂" BLANK

BLANK

CUT NOTCH THROUGH CENTER OF BLANK AND FENCE

a. FENCE

³⁄₈

INDEX KEY

⁹⁄₃₂

GLUE KEY INTO NOTCH IN MITER GAUGE FENCE

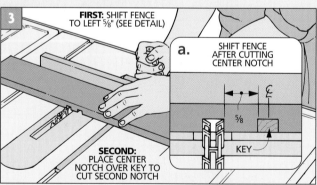

3

FIRST: SHIFT FENCE TO LEFT ⁵⁄₈" (SEE DETAIL)

a. SHIFT FENCE AFTER CUTTING CENTER NOTCH

⁵⁄₈

KEY

SECOND: PLACE CENTER NOTCH OVER KEY TO CUT SECOND NOTCH

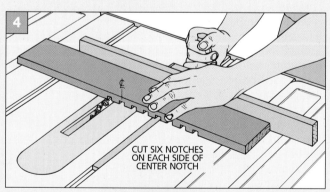

4

CUT SIX NOTCHES ON EACH SIDE OF CENTER NOTCH

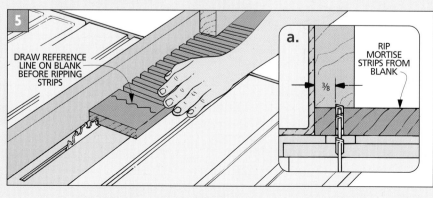

5

DRAW REFERENCE LINE ON BLANK BEFORE RIPPING STRIPS

a. RIP MORTISE STRIPS FROM BLANK

³⁄₈

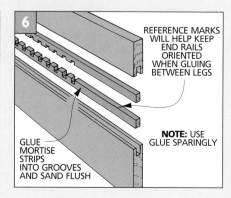

6

REFERENCE MARKS WILL HELP KEEP END RAILS ORIENTED WHEN GLUING BETWEEN LEGS

NOTE: USE GLUE SPARINGLY

GLUE MORTISE STRIPS INTO GROOVES AND SAND FLUSH

DESIGNER'S NOTEBOOK

Replacing the frame and beveled glass top with a panel built from solid wood gives the coffee table a more traditional look. And it's a simple addition to build.

CONSTRUCTION NOTES:

■ If you prefer a more traditional look for your coffee table, you can build a solid wood top instead of the frame and glass one shown on page 62.

Note: This version also matches the Sofa Table on page 54, if you'd like to build both as a set.

■ To make the solid wood top, start by gluing up an oversized panel from 3/4"-thick stock (just like you did for the shelf earlier).

■ When the glue is dry, you can trim the panel to its finished dimensions of 30" x 38".

■ After the panel is cut to size, the bottom edges need to be beveled like the frame pieces for the glass top. But trying to stand a panel this large on edge and running it through the table saw could create numerous problems, even with a tall auxiliary fence.

So I used a bevel jig with a hand-held router to produce the same look. This jig is the same one used for the top of the Sofa Table. The basic construction and procedure for this jig are shown on page 61.

■ Since you're using a solid wood top instead of a frame, you'll need to allow room for the wood to expand and contract. To do this, you could use Z-shaped fasteners like on the Sofa Table

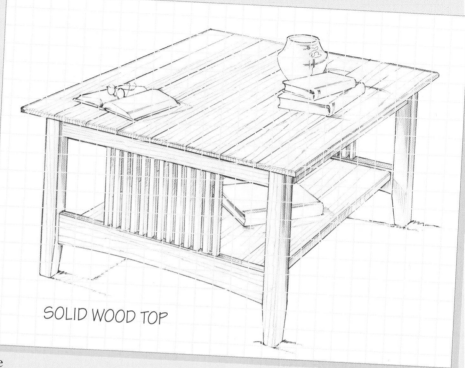

SOLID WOOD TOP

(see page 60). But this would require cutting kerfs in the upper end rails and stretchers, which could be visible if you ever wanted to switch to the glass top.

Instead, I made the counterbored holes in the rails and stretchers a little larger (almost like a slot) to allow the wood to move (see detail 'a' in drawing

below). Then you can center the top on the frame and screw it down.

Note: While the glass top provides a convenient surface for glasses and other items (since it won't mark or stain), the solid top may require some extra protection. So you may want to finish it with polyurethane.

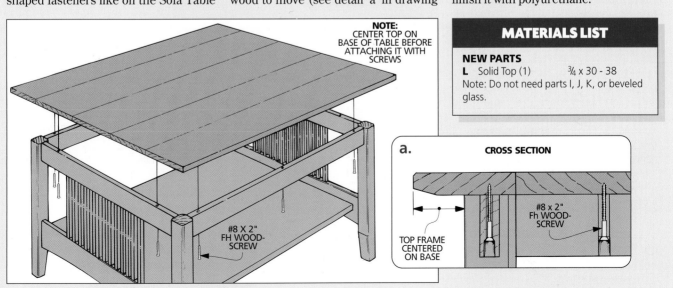

NOTE:
CENTER TOP ON
BASE OF TABLE BEFORE
ATTACHING IT WITH
SCREWS

#8 X 2"
FH WOOD-
SCREW

MATERIALS LIST

NEW PARTS
L   Solid Top (1)   3/4 x 30 - 38
Note: Do not need parts I, J, K, or beveled glass.

a.   **CROSS SECTION**

TOP FRAME
CENTERED
ON BASE

#8 x 2"
Fh WOOD-
SCREW

Mission Bookcase

Built with machinery and handwork, this cherry bookcase features through mortise and tenon joints for an impressive look. There's also an option for a shorter bookcase without the glass doors.

This bookcase is a good example of straightforward Mission-style furniture, with sturdy mortise and through tenon construction, square pegs, and shop-made door pulls.

When Gustav Stickley started designing furniture like this in the early 1900s, he had the "common man" in mind. Out with the ornate — furniture should be simple and functional. The result was the Mission style (sometimes called "Craftsman" style furniture).

MACHINE AND HAND TOOLS. But Stickley was not just concerned with design. Furniture also had to be built in the tradition of the master craftsman. His furniture was built with a combination of machinery and handwork.

That's what I like most about this bookcase. It's built in the same tradition. Heavy and repetitive tasks (cutting, planing, and drilling) can be done by machine, while the finer details (the through tenons, square pegs, and door dividers) require careful handwork. The whole process reflects Stickley's concern for quality and craftsmanship.

WOOD. You might be surprised to see that I used cherry to build the bookcase. Much of the Mission-style furniture was originally built out of quartersawn oak. But after doing a little research, I discovered that cherry was used by Stickley as well.

I thought the brass ball-tipped hinges I wanted to use would look good with the cherry, once the wood darkened to a deep brownish-red.

FINISH. To protect the bookcase, I brushed on four coats of a tung oil and urethane combination finish. While this isn't an authentic Mission finish, I did follow Stickley's technique in a way. I waxed the bookcase after the finish had set a few days (to give it time to cure).

I applied several coats of a high quality paste wax. The one I found was a mixture of carnauba and beeswax.

To apply the wax, wipe on a thin layer with a cotton cloth and let it dry for a few minutes. (Several thin coats are easier to apply than one thick one.) Then buff it to a shine with a clean cloth.

SHORT OPEN BOOKCASE. For a different look (and a simpler project), see the shorter bookcase without doors in the Designer's Notebook on page 87.

EXPLODED VIEW

OVERALL DIMENSIONS:
48W x 14D x 59H

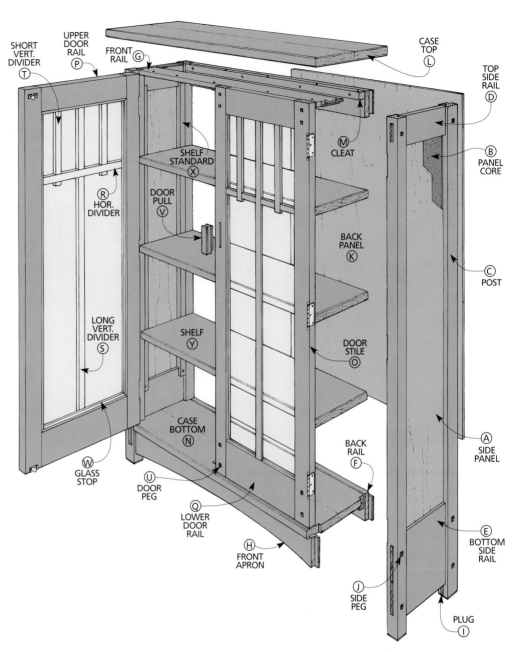

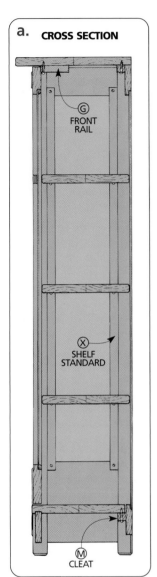

a. **CROSS SECTION**

MATERIALS LIST

CASE
A	Side Panels (4)	1/4 ply - 9³/₁₆ x 44³/₁₆
B	Panel Cores (2)	1/8 hdbd. - 9³/₁₆ x 44³/₁₆
C	Posts (4)	1³/₄ x 1³/₄ - 58
D	Top Side Rails (2)	1 x 3¹/₂ - 11⁵/₈
E	Btm. Side Rails (2)	1 x 9¹/₂ - 11⁵/₈
F	Back Rails (2)	³/₄ x 3¹/₂ - 41¹/₂
G	Front Rail (1)	³/₄ x 3¹/₂ - 42¹/₄
H	Front Apron (1)	³/₄ x 3³/₄ - 41¹/₂
I	Plugs (4)	³/₈ x ¹/₂ - 2⁵/₁₆
J	Side Pegs (12)	³/₈ x ³/₈ - 1⁹/₁₆
K	Back Panel (1)	1/4 ply - 41¹/₂ x 49¹/₂
L	Case Top (1)	1 x 14 - 48
M	Cleats (2)	1 x 1 - 40¹/₂
N	Case Bottom (1)	1 x 11¹/₄ - 41¹/₄

DOORS
O	Door Stiles (4)	1 x 2¹⁷/₃₂ - 51⁷/₈
P	Upr. Door Rails (2)	1 x 3¹/₂ - 19¹/₈
Q	Lwr. Door Rails (2)	1 x 5 - 19¹/₈
R	Horiz. Divid. (2)	¹/₂ x 1 - 15⁷/₈
S	Long Ver. Divid. (2)	¹/₂ x 1 - 44¹/₈
T	Short Ver. Divid. (4)	¹/₂ x 1 - 11⁵/₁₆
U	Door Pegs (16)	³/₈ x ³/₈ - ¹³/₁₆
V	Door Pulls (2)	³/₄ x 1¹/₈ - 4
W	Glass Stops (1)	³/₈ x ³/₈ - 20 ft. rgh.

STANDARDS & SHELVES
X	Shelf Standards (4)	⁵/₈ x 1 - 45¹/₂
Y	Shelves (3)	1 x 10⁵/₈ - 40⁷/₁₆

HARDWARE SUPPLIES
(8) No. 6 x ⁵/₈" Fh woodscrews
(12) No. 6 x 1" Fh woodscrews
(23) No. 8 x 1¹/₂" Rh woodscrews
(3 pr.) 2¹/₂" x 2" ball-tipped hinges w/ screws
(4) Double-ball door catches w/ screws
(12) Shelf pins
(100) ⁵/₈" wire brads
(2) 15³/₄" x 44" glass panes*
* Use 1/8"-thick tempered glass. Have the glass cut to fit the opening on the back of each door, minus 1/8" in both length and width, so it will fit easily.

CUTTING DIAGRAM

$1\frac{3}{4} \times 7\frac{1}{2} - 60$ (6.25 Bd. Ft.)

C
C
C
C

$1 \times 8 - 96$ (Two Boards @ 6.7 Bd. Ft. Each)

L   N
S   M

$1 \times 5\frac{1}{2} - 96$ (Three Boards @ 4.6 Bd. Ft. Each)

Y   Y   E

$1 \times 7 - 96$ (5.8 Bd. Ft.)

O
O
Q   Q
X   X

$1 \times 7 - 72$ (4.4 Bd. Ft.)

O
O
E
W

$1 \times 5 - 72$ (3.1 Bd. Ft.)

P   P   D   D   T   J & U
I
R

$\frac{3}{4} \times 7\frac{1}{2} - 96$ (5 Bd. Ft.)

F   G   V
F   H

NOTE: ALSO NEED ONE 4' x 8' SHEET ¼" PLYWOOD, ONE 2' x 4' SHEET ⅛" HARDBOARD

PANELS

To build this Mission bookcase, I started by making the framed side units. Each unit consists of two posts, two rails and a panel assembly (refer to *Fig. 2* on opposite page). I built up the panel assemblies first.

When making a framed panel, I generally use plywood for the panel. Unlike solid wood, plywood isn't drastically affected by changes in humidity.

I designed each side unit to have ½"-thick plywood panels with two good sides. (Both the inside and the outside of each panel will be seen when the project is completed.) Unfortunately, finding ½" cherry plywood with two good faces isn't easy. And it would also be quite expensive.

A simple solution to this problem was to cut two separate pieces of ¼" cherry plywood to make each panel *(Fig. 1)*. Then these side panels (A) can be set back-to-back so there are two good sides visible.

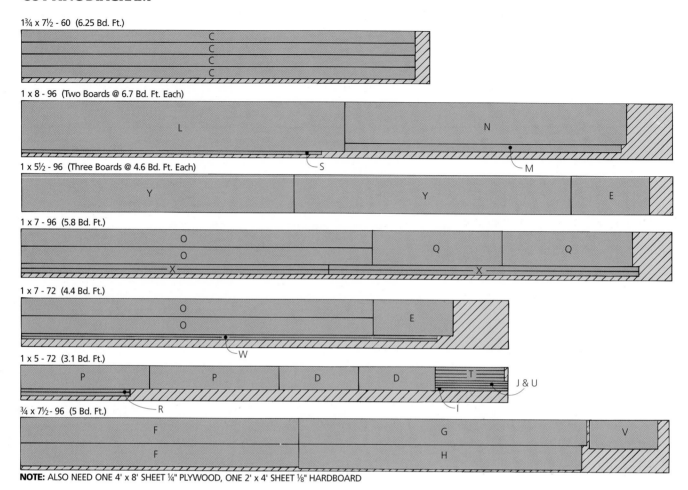

1

SIDE PANEL CORE
(⅛" HARDBOARD)
Ⓑ

Ⓐ

SIDE PANELS
(¼" PLYWOOD)

$44\frac{3}{16}$

$9\frac{3}{16}$

NOTE:
MAKE TWO SIDE
PANEL ASSEMBLIES

Note: All the plywood pieces for this project can be cut from one 4x8 sheet of ¼" plywood.

But there's still a problem. Most ¼" hardwood plywood is quite a bit less than ¼" thick. The plywood I used was actually only a hair over 3/16" thick.

So, to get the panels closer to a thickness of ½" (they don't need to be exact

since you'll cut grooves to fit them later), I sandwiched a ⅛"-thick piece of hardboard between the panels to serve as a panel core (B) *(Fig. 1)*.

Note: The three layers for each side panel could be glued together. But this is not necessary. The frames built around the panels will hold them together just fine.

SIDE UNITS

When the side panels are complete, a grooved frame can be built to fit around each side panel.

First, I cut all the pieces for both side frames *(Fig. 2)*. The posts (C) are cut from $1^3/_4$"-thick stock, and the top (D) and bottom side rails (E) from 1" stock.

GROOVES. The grooves in the posts and rails must match the thickness of the panel. And the grooves should be centered on each piece.

Since the posts and rails are different thicknesses, each requires its own setup to cut the grooves. Here, you have two options. You can reset the fence, or keep the fence in the same position but clamp a shim to it (refer to *Fig. 5*).

To find the thickness of this shim, figure the difference between the thickness of the posts and rails ($^3/_4$" in my case). Then, divide this number by two. My shim ended up $^3/_8$" thick *(Fig. 5)*.

SETUP. To cut the grooves, I first mounted a $^3/_8$" dado blade in the table saw and raised it $^3/_8$" *(Fig. 3)*. Then I set the fence so the blade was slightly off-center on the piece.

I cut each groove in two passes, flipping the board between each pass *(Figs. 3 and 4)*. (Flipping the piece centers the groove.)

Note: Test the setup first with a scrap piece.

Once the groove is cut, check if the panel fits. If you need to, adjust the fence and make another test cut.

CUT GROOVES. When the test piece fits, cut the grooves on the four posts.

Next, to cut the grooves in the top and bottom rails, either reset the fence or add the shim *(Fig. 5)*.

SHOP TIP...... Frame Assembly

When making framed panels, grooves are usually cut in the frame to fit the panel. But that doesn't mean it will go together easily.

If either piece is twisted or bowed, getting them together can be difficult.

To make it easier to assemble and avoid tearout on the edges of the grooves, I first round over the edges of the panel with a sanding block.

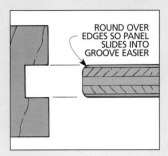

ROUND OVER EDGES SO PANEL SLIDES INTO GROOVE EASIER

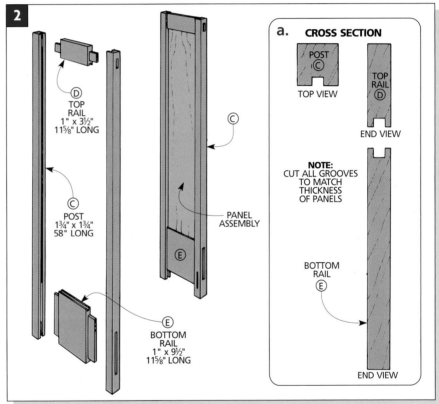

2

TOP RAIL
1" x $3^1/_2$"
$11^5/_8$" LONG

POST
$1^3/_4$" x $1^3/_4$"
58" LONG

C

PANEL ASSEMBLY

E

BOTTOM RAIL
1" x $9^1/_2$"
$11^5/_8$" LONG

a. CROSS SECTION

POST
C
TOP VIEW

TOP RAIL
D
END VIEW

NOTE:
CUT ALL GROOVES TO MATCH THICKNESS OF PANELS

BOTTOM RAIL
E

END VIEW

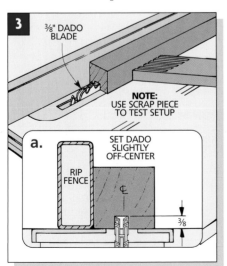

3

$^3/_8$" DADO BLADE

NOTE:
USE SCRAP PIECE TO TEST SETUP

a.

RIP FENCE

$^3/_8$

SET DADO SLIGHTLY OFF-CENTER

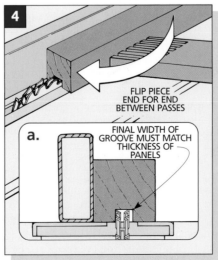

4

FLIP PIECE END FOR END BETWEEN PASSES

a.

FINAL WIDTH OF GROOVE MUST MATCH THICKNESS OF PANELS

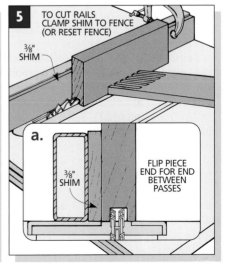

5

TO CUT RAILS CLAMP SHIM TO FENCE (OR RESET FENCE)

$^3/_8$" SHIM

a.

$^3/_8$" SHIM

FLIP PIECE END FOR END BETWEEN PASSES

TENONS

The mortises and through tenons on the bookcase demand careful handwork, but you actually get to *see* the joint. (For more on this joint, see page 84.)

I usually start with the mortises, but this time I worked backwards. The tenons are cut first to fit the grooves cut in the posts. Like a mortise, the grooves act as a gauge for sizing the tenons.

TWO TENONS. There are two different length tenons on each rail *(Fig. 6)*. On the front is a long tenon that fits through a front post. The tenon in back stops short in a typical (blind) mortise.

TWO STEPS. The setup for both rails is the same *(Figs. 7 and 8)*. First, cut the cheek of the tenon *(Step 1)*. (Test the fit with a scrap piece before cutting on the rails.) Next, set the piece on edge and cut the tenon to width *(Step 2)*.

MORTISES

When all the tenons are cut, it's time to cut mortises in the posts. Again, there are two types of mortises: through and blind.

All the mortises are the same width as the grooves for the panels. This makes the setup easy. Just position the post so a $1/2$"-dia. drill bit is centered in the groove. Then clamp a fence to the drill press table so it's against the post.

BLIND MORTISES. After laying out each mortise, I drilled the blind ones in the back posts first *(Fig. 9)*. (Drill them $1^5/16$" deep to allow $1/16$" for excess glue.)

THROUGH MORTISES. When the mortises in the back posts are complete, drill mortises through the front posts.

Note: Drill these mortises halfway through from both sides to avoid chipout.

MORTISES FOR APRON. There's one more set of mortises to cut in the front posts. An apron that joins the front posts at the bottom requires $1/4$"-wide by $9/16$"-deep mortises *(Fig. 9)*.

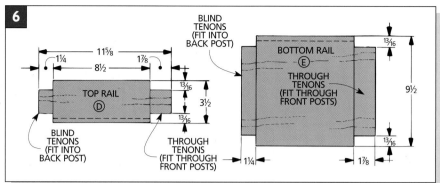

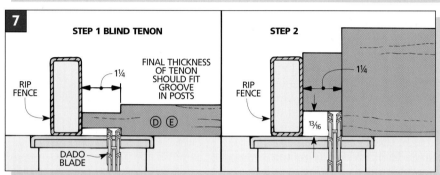

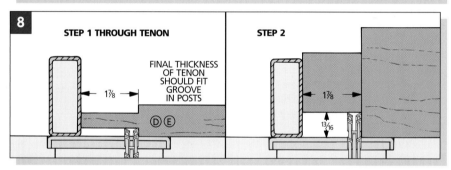

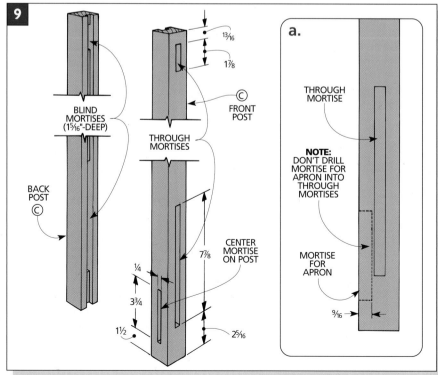

RAILS & APRON

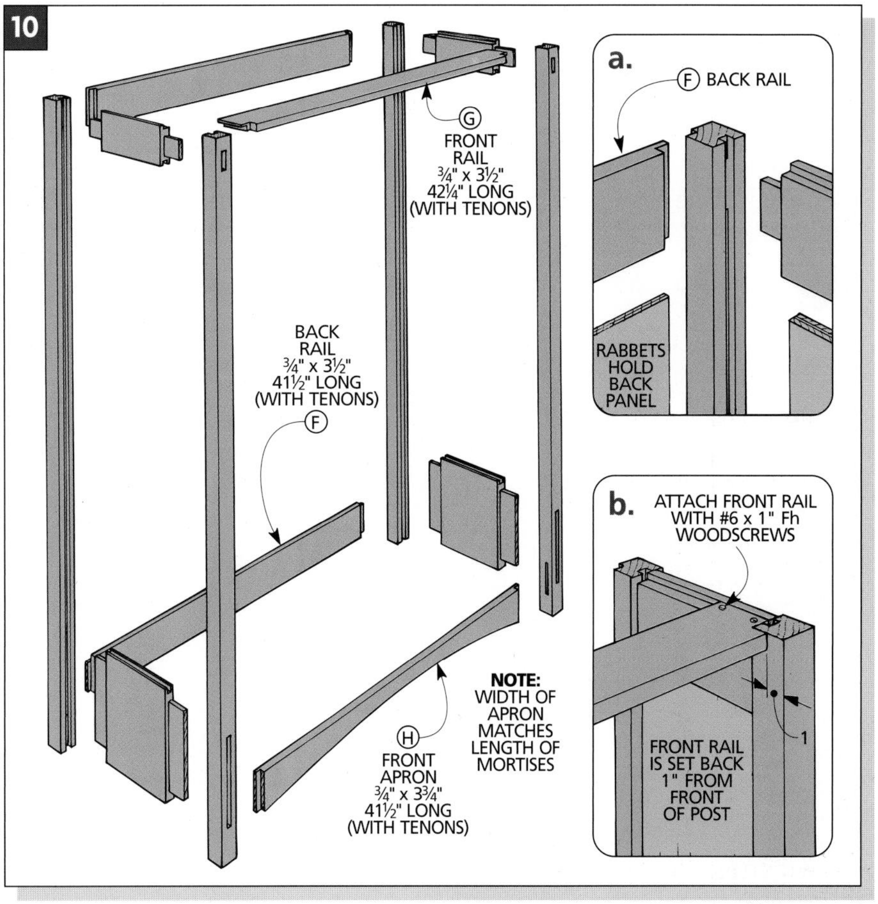

10
FRONT RAIL ¾" x 3½" 42¼" LONG (WITH TENONS)
Ⓖ
BACK RAIL ¾" x 3½" 41½" LONG (WITH TENONS)
Ⓕ
NOTE: WIDTH OF APRON MATCHES LENGTH OF MORTISES
Ⓗ FRONT APRON ¾" x 3¾" 41½" LONG (WITH TENONS)
a.
Ⓕ BACK RAIL
RABBETS HOLD BACK PANEL
b.
ATTACH FRONT RAIL WITH #6 x 1" Fh WOODSCREWS
FRONT RAIL IS SET BACK 1" FROM FRONT OF POST
1

Before the side units can be put together, there must be some way to connect them. So next I cut out the pieces that connect the units.

CUT TO SIZE. Begin by cutting two back rails (F) and a front rail (G) to size *(Fig. 10)*. Then cut out a front apron (H).

Note: The width of this apron should match the mortises in the posts — the apron doesn't have a top or bottom shoulder (refer to *Fig. 15a*).

RABBETS. To hold these pieces, I rabbeted some of the side unit pieces. First, each top side rail (D) is rabbeted on the top inside edge to hold the front rail *(Figs. 10b and 11)*.

Then the two back posts (C) are rabbeted on the back inside edges to hold the back rail and the back panel (added later) *(Figs. 10a and 12)*.

The back rails (F) also hold the back panel in place. So, I rabbeted the back edges of these rails too *(Fig. 13)*.

Note: All these pieces don't end up identical — they're actually *mirrored*. So to keep them straight, mark the pieces before you cut the rabbets.

TONGUES. The next step is to cut tongues on the pieces that will connect the side units *(Fig. 10)*. Rabbet the ends of the back rails (F) and the front rail (G) *(Figs. 13 and 14)*. The tongues should fit the rabbets in the side pieces.

After these rabbets are cut, the front rail needs to be notched at the front corners so it will fit around the front posts *(Figs. 10b and 14)*. When in place, the rail should set back 1" from the front. This allows the rail to act as a door stop.

RABBET APRON. The last piece to rabbet is the front apron (H) *(Fig. 15)*. Again, you're creating tongues on the ends. But this time, they fit the mortises in the posts.

The apron also has a gentle arc on the bottom that can be laid out and cut at this time *(Fig. 15a)*.

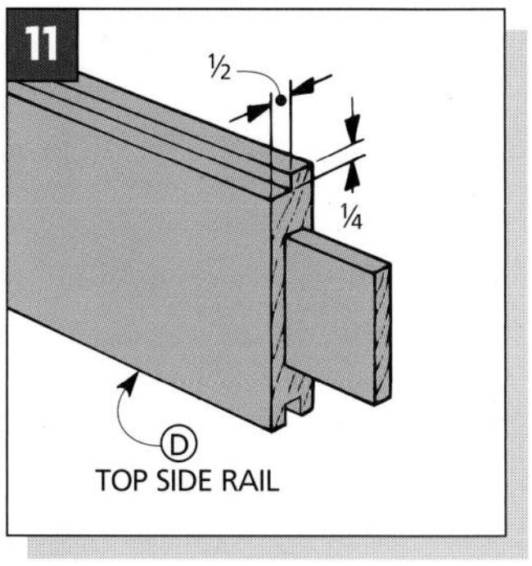

11
½
¼
Ⓓ TOP SIDE RAIL

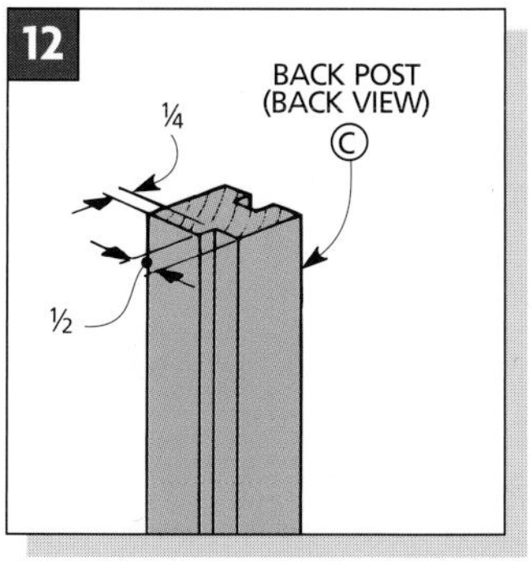

12
¼
BACK POST (BACK VIEW)
Ⓒ
½

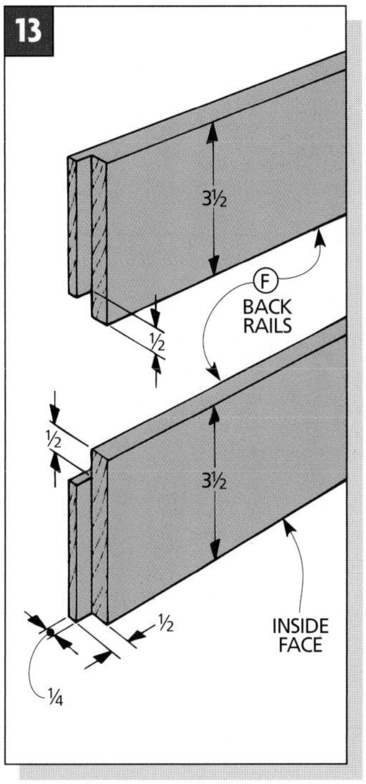

13
3½
½
Ⓕ BACK RAILS
½
3½
INSIDE FACE
¼
½

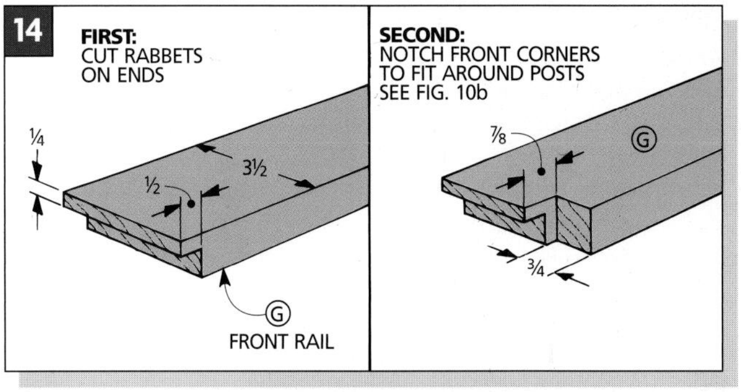

14
FIRST: CUT RABBETS ON ENDS
¼
3½
½
Ⓖ FRONT RAIL
SECOND: NOTCH FRONT CORNERS TO FIT AROUND POSTS SEE FIG. 10b
⅞
Ⓖ
¾

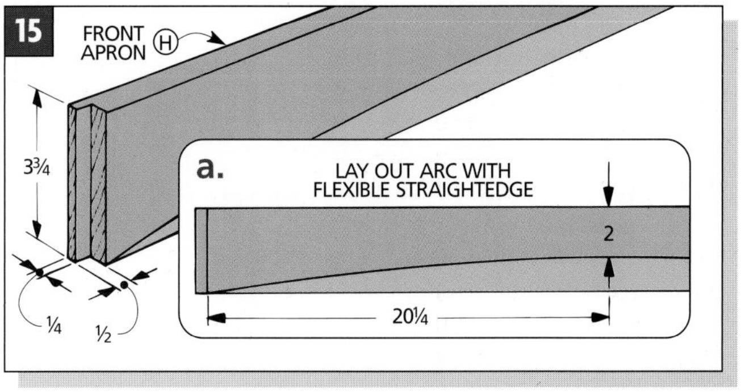

15
FRONT APRON Ⓗ
3¾
¼
½
a.
LAY OUT ARC WITH FLEXIBLE STRAIGHTEDGE
2
20¼

The bookcase is almost ready to be assembled. But first, I added some small details.

The first step is to fill the grooves at the bottom of the posts *(Fig. 16)*. To do this, I cut a plug (I) to fit each groove.

The top of the posts will be covered by the case top later.

Note: Make sure you don't cover the mortises already cut in the posts.

CHAMFERS. The next step is to rout $1/8$" chamfers on the bottoms of all the posts *(Fig. 17)*. This has two benefits. It gives the posts a finished look, and it also helps minimize splintering if the case should ever be dragged across the floor.

Another thing I did was to sand

chamfers on the ends of *all* the tenons. This "dresses up" the through tenons, giving them a finished look. And on the tenons that fit the blind mortises, the chamfers allow room for excess glue.

SANDING BLOCK. There are a number of ways to chamfer the tenons. I decided to make a simple sanding block that chamfers both edges at the same time *(Fig. 18)*.

To make the block, I cut a groove in a piece of scrap with the dado blade set $3/8$" deep. The width should equal the thickness of the tenon minus $1/8$". This will create a $1/16$" chamfer on both sides

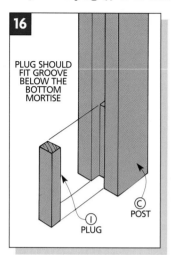

16
PLUG SHOULD FIT GROOVE BELOW THE BOTTOM MORTISE

Ⓘ PLUG
Ⓒ POST

17
POST Ⓒ

TO PREVENT CHIPOUT, USE BACKING BOARD

ROUT $1/8$" CHAMFER AROUND BOTTOM OF EACH POST

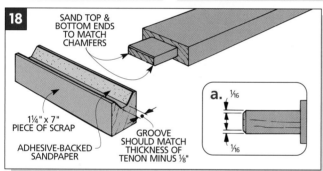

18
SAND TOP & BOTTOM ENDS TO MATCH CHAMFERS

$1 1/4$" x 7" PIECE OF SCRAP

ADHESIVE-BACKED SANDPAPER

GROOVE SHOULD MATCH THICKNESS OF TENON MINUS $1/8$"

a. $1/16$
$1/16$

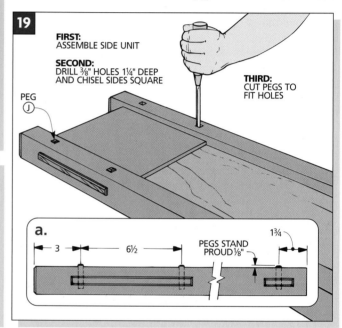

19
FIRST: ASSEMBLE SIDE UNIT

SECOND: DRILL $3/8$" HOLES $1 1/4$" DEEP AND CHISEL SIDES SQUARE

THIRD: CUT PEGS TO FIT HOLES

PEG Ⓙ

a.
3
$6 1/2$
PEGS STAND PROUD $1/8$"
$1 3/4$

SHOP TIP . . . . *Scraping and Sanding Corners*

Normally I like using a hand scraper and sanding block for scraping and sanding. But on a frame and panel, it can be hard to get right down into a corner with a scraper or typical sanding block.

Instead, I use two tools shaped for the job.

To scrape out a corner, I use a razor blade from a utility knife *(Fig. 1)*. It works great for scraping away glue smudges and dried beads of glue.

To use the razor blade, hold it at an angle and push

or pull it with the grain of the wood — just like a hand scraper. Never scrape *across* the grain. And always push or pull the

blade in the direction it's angled. (This way it won't cut into the workpiece.)

To sand a corner, I make a sanding block with

beveled ends and beveled sides *(Fig. 2)*. The pointed ends allow me to get the sandpaper right up against the corner.

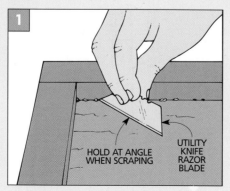

1
HOLD AT ANGLE WHEN SCRAPING
UTILITY KNIFE RAZOR BLADE

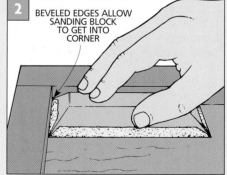

2
BEVELED EDGES ALLOW SANDING BLOCK TO GET INTO CORNER

SHOP TIP . . . . Adding Decorative Pegs

Once, a long tenon needed to be pinned in a mortise. But with improved wood glues, a peg just has to look good. Careful work is the key to this decoration.

The procedure is similar to cutting a mortise and tenon. Lay out the mortise on the outside face of the stile *(Fig. 1)*. Then drill inside the marks to a consistent depth, and square up the corners of the mortise with a chisel *(Fig. 2)*.

For the pegs, cut a long strip about $^1/_{32}$" thicker than the width of the mortise. (You want a tight fit.) Then cut the pegs from it *(Fig. 3)*.

Sand the buried end of each peg to a taper, and sand a decorative chamfer

around the top end.

The pegs look best if they stick out $^1/_8$" beyond the face of the frame. To

set the pegs at a consistent height automatically, I made a depth stop with a hole from $^3/_4$"-thick

hardwood *(Fig. 4)*. Then I spread glue in the holes, and used the stop to finish tapping in the pegs.

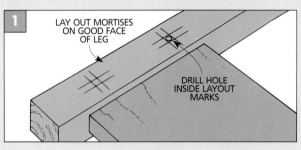

1 LAY OUT MORTISES ON GOOD FACE OF LEG

DRILL HOLE INSIDE LAYOUT MARKS

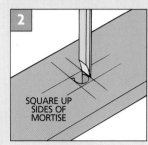

2 SQUARE UP SIDES OF MORTISE

3 CUT PEG TO FIT SNUGLY IN MORTISE

4 DRILL $^1/_8$"-DEEP HOLE

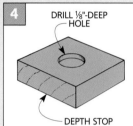

DEPTH STOP

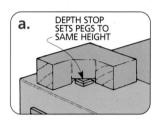

a. DEPTH STOP SETS PEGS TO SAME HEIGHT

---

of the tenon *(Fig. 18a)*. Next, I tilted the blade to 45° and beveled both sides of the groove.

To use the sanding block, stick adhesive-backed sandpaper on the beveled edges (or use standard sandpaper and rubber cement).

Then sand the tenons. Check them often to make sure the chamfers are consistent. After the tenon "bottoms out" on the block, sand the top and bottom ends to match, using a regular sanding block.

ASSEMBLE THE SIDE UNITS. To assemble the case, I began by gluing up the side units *(Fig. 19)*.

PIN TENONS. After both side units are assembled, their tenons can be pinned *(Fig. 19a* and the Shop Tip box above)*. First, drill and square up the holes. Next, cut pegs (J) to fit them. Then glue the pegs in place so they stand $^1/_8$" proud of the faces of the posts.

ASSEMBLE THE CASE. To connect the two side units, glue the front apron (H) between them and dry-assemble all the other rails *(Fig. 20)*. After the front apron dries, remove each of the rails and drill shank holes and pilot holes. Then glue and screw them back in place (refer to *Figs. 10b* and *20a)*.

BACK PANEL. After the case is assembled, I cut a back panel (K) from $^1/_4$" cherry plywood to fit in the rabbets in

the back of the case *(Fig. 20)*. But don't nail the panel in yet. It's easier to work on the inside if it's not in place.

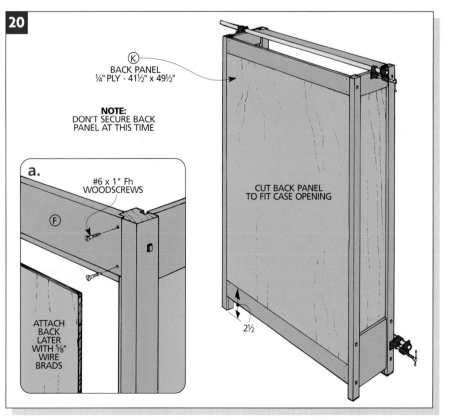

20

K
BACK PANEL
$^1/_4$" PLY - 41$^1/_2$" x 49$^1/_2$"

NOTE:
DON'T SECURE BACK PANEL AT THIS TIME

CUT BACK PANEL TO FIT CASE OPENING

2$^1/_2$

a.
#6 x 1" Fh WOODSCREWS

F

ATTACH BACK LATER WITH $^5/_8$" WIRE BRADS

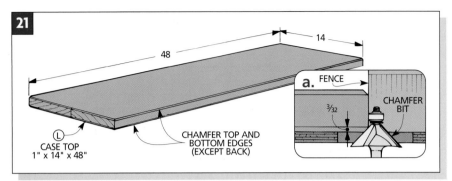

21

48
14

L
CASE TOP
1" x 14" x 48"

CHAMFER TOP AND
BOTTOM EDGES
(EXCEPT BACK)

a. FENCE

$^3/_{32}$

CHAMFER
BIT

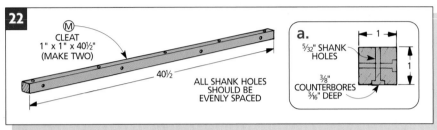

22

M
CLEAT
1" x 1" x 40½"
(MAKE TWO)

40½

ALL SHANK HOLES
SHOULD BE
EVENLY SPACED

a. $^5/_{32}$" SHANK
HOLES

1

1

$^3/_8$"
COUNTERBORES
$^3/_{16}$" DEEP

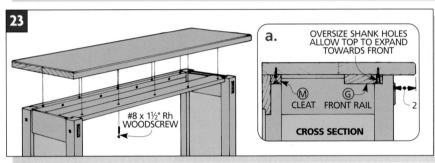

23

a. OVERSIZE SHANK HOLES
ALLOW TOP TO EXPAND
TOWARDS FRONT

#8 x 1½" Rh
WOODSCREW

M
CLEAT

G
FRONT RAIL

2

CROSS SECTION

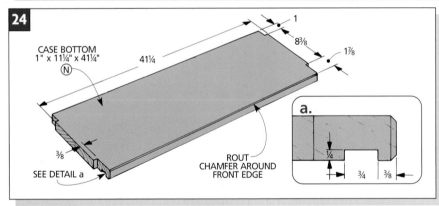

24

1

8$^3/_8$

1$^7/_8$

CASE BOTTOM
1" x 11¼" x 41¼"
N

41¼

$^3/_8$

SEE DETAIL a

ROUT
CHAMFER AROUND
FRONT EDGE

a.

¼

$^3/_4$ $^3/_8$

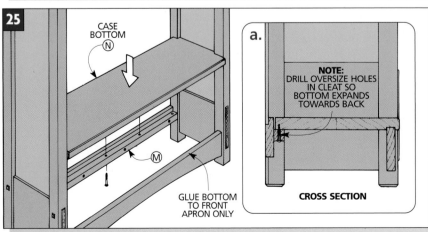

25

CASE
BOTTOM
N

M

GLUE BOTTOM
TO FRONT
APRON ONLY

a.

NOTE:
DRILL OVERSIZE HOLES
IN CLEAT SO
BOTTOM EXPANDS
TOWARDS BACK

CROSS SECTION

CASE TOP

The next step is to add the case top and bottom. First, glue up enough 1"-thick stock to make both panels (*Figs. 21 and 24*). Now, cut the case top (L) 4" longer and 2" wider than the case (*Fig. 21*). Rout chamfers on the top and bottom edges (except the back) (*Fig. 21a*).

In the front, the case top is screwed to the front rail (refer to *Fig. 23a*). In the back it's secured with a cleat.

CLEAT. First, cut the cleat (M) to fit between the back posts (*Fig. 22*). (Make two — you'll use one for the bottom shelf later.) Then drill two sets of counterbored shank holes in the top cleat (*Fig. 22a*). One set is used to attach the cleat flush with the top edge of the back rail. The other will secure the top.

A 14"-wide top will expand and contract quite a bit with seasonal changes in humidity. So rather than fight it, I decided to allow the panel some freedom to move by drilling oversize shank holes in the front rail. This way, the case top stays flush with the back of the case, but it can still expand toward the front without splitting.

BOTTOM

The bottom of the case involves a bit more work than the top. Begin by cutting the case bottom (N) to fit between the side panels (A) (*Figs. 24 and 25*).

NOTCHES. To fit in the case, each corner must be notched (*Fig. 25*). The notches at the front corners are $^1/_8$" wider (1$^7/_8$") than the posts (*Fig. 24*).

The notches at the back are only 1" wide (*Fig. 24*). This creates a tiny gap so the bottom can expand toward the back (refer to *Fig. 25a*).

Note: To get a clean cut, I first scored the notches with a razor knife. Then I used the miter gauge with an auxiliary fence and cut them with the panel standing on edge.

GROOVE. The next step is to cut a groove on the case bottom to fit over the front apron (*Fig. 24a*). Then, rout a chamfer around the front edge.

CLEAT. Like the case top, the bottom requires a cleat (M) (*Figs. 22 and 25*). But there are two differences. First, the cleat isn't flush with the back rail. It's 1" down from the top.

Also, the shank holes should be slightly oversized to allow for movement (*Fig. 25a*).

You might want to add the shelves next. But to position the top shelf so it hides behind the dividers in the doors, it makes sense to build the doors first.

FRAMES. To begin, cut 1"-thick door stiles (O) and upper (P) and lower door rails (Q) to fit the case opening *(Fig. 26)*.

Note: The final size of both doors should allow a $^1/_{16}$" gap between the case and the doors on all four sides.

The door frames are joined together with mortises and tenons *(Fig. 26)*.

After each frame is assembled, rabbet the back for the glass *(Fig. 27)*. Then chisel the corners square.

DOOR DIVIDERS. All the dividers in the doors are more for appearance than anything else. That's because the glass for each door is installed in one large piece — not individual panes.

To make the door dividers, first cut the $^1/_2$"-thick horizontal dividers (R) and long vertical dividers (S) to fit between the rabbets in the frames *(Figs. 28 and 29)*. Then cut the short vertical dividers (T).

HALF LAPS. The dividers are joined to the door frame and to each other with half laps *(Figs. 28a and 28b)*. So first, I rabbeted the ends of all the pieces.

Note: Just rabbet one end of the short vertical dividers.

Next, I cut half laps in the horizontal dividers *(Fig. 28b)*. Then I cut the mating half laps in the vertical pieces (on the face opposite the rabbet).

DIVIDER ASSEMBLY. Now, glue the dividers together. Then set the assembly in the rabbets in the door frame and mark the location of each divider *(Fig. 29)*.

To get the assembly flush with the front of the door, you'll need to cut mortises in the rabbets *(Fig. 29a)*. Once they fit, glue them in place.

PEGS. To complete the doors, pin each tenon with two door pegs (U) *(Fig. 26)*. These are shorter than the side pegs, but still extend out $^1/_8$".

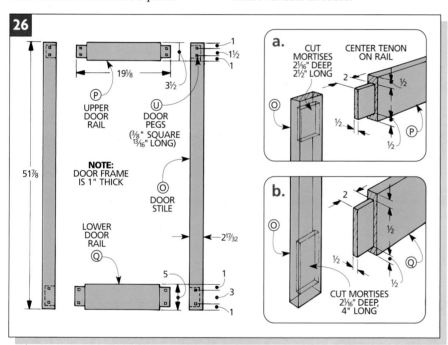

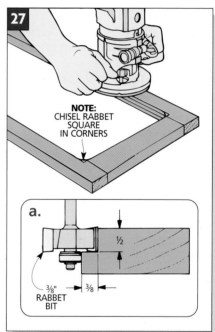

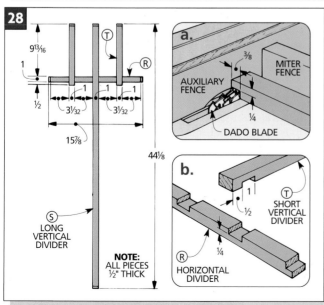

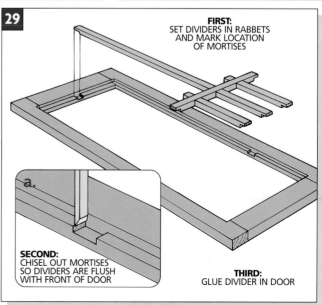

At this point, the doors should fit with a $^1/_{16}$" gap between the case and each door. The doors still need to be trimmed though — I didn't allow for any gap between them yet. I found it easier to mount the doors first. Then come back later and remove and trim them to create the center gap.

MOUNT HINGES. The ball-tipped hinges I used created a $^1/_{16}$" gap when mortised and mounted flush with the posts and the doors.

To mount the hinges, first lay out their locations on the posts and the doors *(Fig. 30)*. Then cut out most of the waste with a router. And clean up the shoulders with a chisel.

After drilling pilot holes, you can install the hinges and mount the doors in place *(Fig. 30b)*.

TRIM DOORS. Now the center stiles of each door can be trimmed. To do this, determine how much needs to be trimmed to create a $^1/_{16}$" gap. Then, to keep the doors identical, I removed them and planed the same amount off each door. (I used a hand plane, but a jointer will also work.)

ADD CATCHES. Next, reattach the doors and mount the catches to hold them closed. Since any door can have a tendency to twist, I installed double-ball catches at both the top and bottom of each door *(Figs. 30a and 30c)*.

REMOVE DOORS. To add the door pulls and the glass, I found it easiest to remove the doors once again. But first, I marked the position of the horizontal dividers on the inside faces of the corner posts *(Fig. 30)*. (Later, these marks will show you where to position the top shelf.)

ADD DOOR PULLS. At this point I added the door pulls. To do this, first I cut a mortise in the front of each door to accept a pull *(Fig. 31a)*. Then I made my own door pulls (V) (see the Shop Tip box on the opposite page) and glued them into the mortises.

GLASS STOPS. All that's left to add to the doors is the glass. Of course you don't want to add the glass until after the case has been finished, but now is a good time to cut the glass stops (W).

The glass stops are cut to finished dimensions of $^3/_8$" x $^3/_8$". Then a 45° chamfer is cut along one corner to provide a flat face to nail $^5/_8$"-long wire brads into *(Fig. 32a)*.

The safest way to make these glass stops is to start with an extra-wide ($1^1/_2$") blank and rout the chamfer first. Then come back and rip the pieces to final width ($^3/_8$") off the waste side of the blade.

The glass stops are mitered at the corners *(Fig. 32)*. It's tougher to remove mitered stops later, but they look better than butt joints. To determine the correct lengths, I find it's easiest to measure for each one individually and then creep up on the final cut until they just fit.

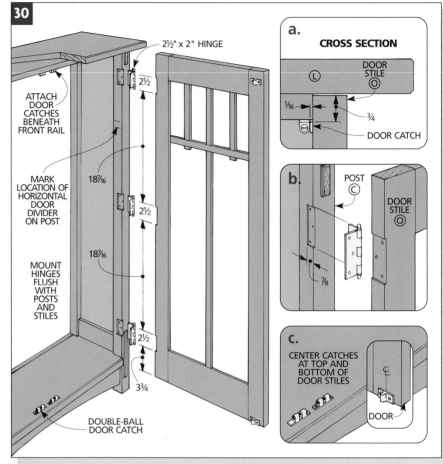

30

2½" x 2" HINGE

ATTACH DOOR CATCHES BENEATH FRONT RAIL

MARK LOCATION OF HORIZONTAL DOOR DIVIDER ON POST

MOUNT HINGES FLUSH WITH POSTS AND STILES

DOUBLE-BALL DOOR CATCH

2½

18⅞₆

2½

18⅞₆

2½

3¾

a. CROSS SECTION

DOOR STILE Ⓛ Ⓞ

$^1/_{16}$ ¾

DOOR CATCH

b. POST Ⓒ

DOOR STILE Ⓞ

⅞

c. CENTER CATCHES AT TOP AND BOTTOM OF DOOR STILES

DOOR

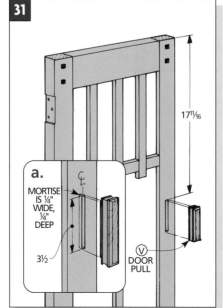

31

17¹¹⁄₁₆

a. MORTISE IS ¼" WIDE, ¼" DEEP

3½

Ⓥ DOOR PULL

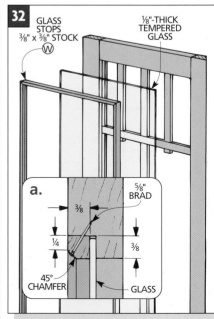

32

GLASS STOPS $^3/_8$" x $^3/_8$" STOCK Ⓦ

⅛"-THICK TEMPERED GLASS

a. ⅜

⅝" BRAD

¼ ⅜

45° CHAMFER GLASS

STANDARDS & SHELVES

At this point, you're almost done with the bookcase. The shelves are all that are left. They rest on spoon-style shelf pins that fit into shelf standards.

SHELF STANDARDS. To make the standards, start by cutting four $^5/_8$"-thick shelf standards (X) to fit between the top and bottom side rails *(Fig. 33)*.

Note: Add 2" for the rabbets that will be cut on the ends.

Now, cut a 1"-long rabbet on both ends of each standard *(Fig. 33a)*. Set the standards in place and mark the position of the top shelf *(Fig. 34)*. (It should line up behind the horizontal door dividers.)

SHELF PIN HOLES. Before attaching the standards to the sides, drill the holes for the shelf pins *(Fig. 33)*. (You can drill additional holes if you want. This will allow you to adjust the positions of the shelves later.)

SHELVES. For the shelves (Y), glue up three 1"-thick shelf blanks and cut them to length so they fit loosely between the corner posts ($^1/_{16}$" less) *(Fig. 34)*.

To determine the width of the

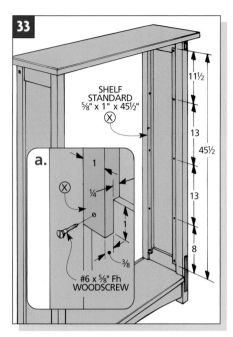

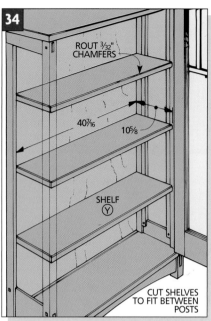

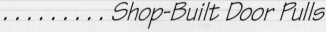

shelves, measure from the rabbet for the back panel to the back of the door. Then subtract $^1/_8$". In my case, this came out to be $10^5/_8$".

Note: The important thing is that the shelves aren't tight against the back of the door.

Finally, chamfer the top and bottom edges of the shelves and set each of them in place.

BACK PANEL. The last step on the bookcase before finishing is to install the back panel that you cut earlier. To do this, I used $^5/_8$" wire brads. ∎

SHOP TIP . . . . Shop-Built Door Pulls

Stickley's furniture company made all of its own hardware. While I didn't make my own hinges or door catches for the bookcase, I did make the wooden door pulls.

The pulls are cut from an extra-long blank of $^3/_4$"-thick cherry *(Fig. 1)*. The extra length makes the blank safer to work with.

The first step in shaping the pulls is to rout a chamfer around each end of the blank *(Fig. 2)*.

Next, rout a cove around each end using a $^1/_2$"-dia. core box bit *(Fig. 3)*.

Now, before cutting the pulls from the blank, form tenons to fit the mortises in the doors *(Fig. 31a on the opposite page)*.

Since the tenon is in the middle of the blank and not at the end, this cut looks a little odd. Just cut or rout dadoes around the blank *(Fig. 4)*.

All that's left now is to sand the pulls smooth and cut them from the blank.

Then glue them into the mortises in the doors.

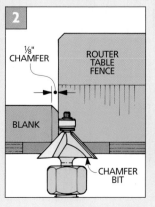

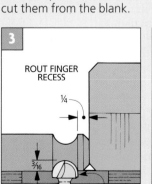

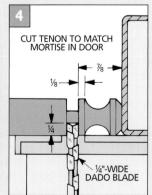

JOINERY ... . Through Mortise and Tenon

One of the strongest joints you'll find on a project is a mortise and tenon. And a *through* mortise and tenon joint not only gives you a strong joint, but a decorative one as well.

When the tenon is glued into the mortise, the two fit together like the handle in the head of a hammer (see photo). The end grain on the tenon is a decorative contrast to the long grain on the sides of the mortise.

PERFECT FIT. The main reason for gluing a long tenon into an open mortise is usually appearance. And for the best appearance, the parts of the joint have to be cut perfectly.

If there are any gaps where the tenon comes out of the mortise, it will be apparent — but it probably won't be the look you were expecting. That's why I follow a specific sequence when cutting a through mortise and tenon.

SEQUENCE. Does that mean a through mortise and tenon joint is made differently than a traditional blind mortise and tenon? Not exactly. The mortise is usually cut first, then the tenon is cut to fit the mortise. So far, no difference. But because the fit of the joint is so important, I take a couple extra steps as is explained on the following pages.

Note: Sometimes there's a good reason to reverse the sequence and cut the *tenon* first. (The Mission bookcase is an example. Refer to page 76.) But the cutting operation is the same.

OPTIONS. Like an ordinary mortise and tenon joint, a through mortise and tenon joint has some options. For one, the leg is often thicker than the rail (see photo above and the drawing at right).

But this is primarily a design decision — the parts could just as well be the same thickness.

And how far beyond the leg should the tenon stick out? It could be flush to the outside of the leg (right in photo) or stand a little proud with chamfered edges (left in photo). Again, it's mostly a design decision.

Finally, a through mortise and tenon joint is often pinned with small wood pegs through the cheeks of the tenon (left in photo). In the past this was done to lock the tenon in the mortise to create a stronger joint. But with the improved glues available today, the

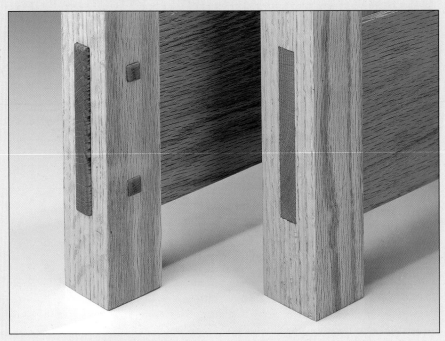

pegs are mostly for appearance. (See page 79 for more on installing pegs.)

HOW THE JOINT WORKS

There's more to a through mortise and tenon joint than one piece of wood sticking through another. If the parts fit together properly, the joint is strong in several directions. And of course, it looks good too.

The load-bearing strength of the joint comes from the bottom edge of the tenon resting in the bottom of the mortise (see drawing). It's what supports a panel in a frame or a top on a table.

The shoulders around the tenon give the joint resistance to racking and twisting — and hide imperfections.

Probably the strongest part of a through mortise and tenon joint is the fit between the cheeks of the tenon and the cheeks of the mortise. When properly glued, the bond between the cheeks of the two pieces will produce a joint that's practically unbreakable.

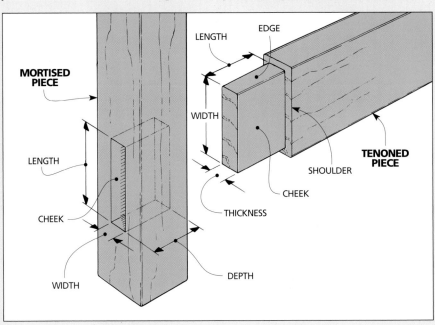

The key to cutting a perfect through mortise is uniformity. The tenon opening should have very straight edges to fit tight around the tenon.

Here are a couple tips — and a guide — to make cutting a perfect mortise easier.

LAY OUT ENDS. I start by laying out (marking) the mortise on the *outside* face of the workpiece (*Step 1*). To do this, first use a try square and a sharp pencil to draw a line indicating the top and bottom edges of the mortise. Then use a square to extend these lines around to the opposite (inside) face.

MARK SIDES. Next, I mark the sides of the mortise. And for the most accuracy on the sides, I don't use a pencil. Instead, I make the marks using a chisel, a mallet and a shop-made guide block (*Step 1*). (Again, make the marks on the face of the workpiece where the end of the tenon will show.)

The guide block I use is simply a squared-up wood block with a shallow rabbet cut along one edge. As simple as it is, the block is surprisingly helpful.

The block helps to mark a perfectly straight line for the sides of the mortise. And after the mortise has been roughed out with a drill bit, it helps hold a chisel straight up for cleaning up the mortise.

SETTING OUT. There's a trick I use to help ensure crisp, clean edges on a through mortise. The trick is called "setting out."

To set out a mortise, first chop straight down on the chisel holding the back of the chisel tight to the guide block (*Step 1*).

After marking the perimeter of the mortise, remove the guide block and make a second angled chisel cut that intersects with the first (*Step 2*).

Then remove all the little three-sided slivers from the edges of the mortise.

Now you should be able to see the outline of a perfect through mortise. All that's left is to clean out the waste.

BORE HOLES. At this point the mortise could be chopped out by hand. But it saves a lot of time (especially for deep mortises) to rough out most of the waste using the drill press (*Step 3*).

To rough out the mortise, I use a Forstner bit *smaller* than the width of the mortise and drill a series of overlapping holes between the score marks.

Note: For the cleanest mortise, bore halfway from each side (*Step 4*).

CHISEL CLEAN. The overlapping holes will leave a series of "ripples" in the mortise. To remove these ripples and also complete the mortise, I use a chisel and the guide block to pare the sides of the mortise (*Step 5*). (Again, work from both sides.)

Finally, to insert the tenon more easily, I like to "back cut" the mortise slightly (*Step 5a*).

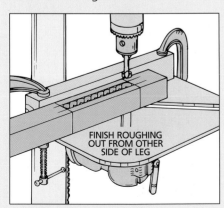

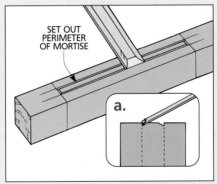

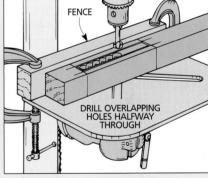

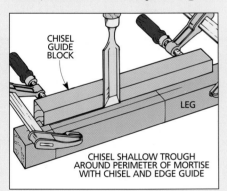

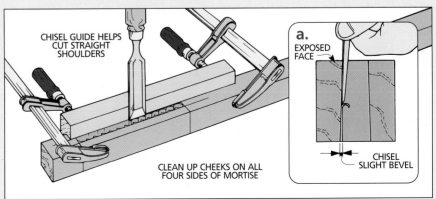

1 First mark ends of the mortise using a try square and pencil. Then make a block for marking the sides with a chisel.

2 After scoring sides with a chisel, "set out" the mortise by chiseling a slight bevel inside score lines. Set out ends too.

3 Rough out mortise by drilling a series of holes inside the score lines. Use a Forstner bit smaller than the mortise.

4 Finish roughing out the mortise from the opposite side of the workpiece. But keep the same face against the fence.

5 Complete the mortise by chiseling the sides of the mortise smooth and flat. Use the guide block to keep the chisel straight up and down. After cutting from both sides of the mortise, chisel a slight bevel from the good face.

A tenon can come in any shape or size. But there's only one thing that counts — how well it fits in a mortise.

One of the easiest ways to cut a tenon is to use a dado blade in the table saw. And to help set up the saw just right, I start by cutting a tenon on a test piece. (Use a piece of wood that's the same thickness and width as the actual workpiece.)

TEST THICKNESS. To begin work on the tenon, raise the dado blade and make a shallow cut across one end *(Step 1)*. Then flip the piece and make a second pass on the opposite face.

Note: For the most control — and the cleanest cut — I cut tenons using the miter gauge with an auxiliary fence attached. This helps prevent chipout as the blade exits the workpiece.

Now check the test tenon in one of the completed mortises *(Step 2)*. The idea is to sneak up on the height of the blade until the end of this short tenon fits the mortise perfectly — not too tight and not too loose.

CUT CHEEKS. When the thickness of the tenon is set, the tenon can be cut to length *(Step 3)*. To do this, I again use the miter gauge and auxiliary fence. But this time the rip fence on the table saw is used as a stop.

Position the rip fence so the distance between the outside of the dado blade and the fence equals the desired length of the tenon. Now, cut the tenon by making several passes over the dado blade for each cheek.

CUT SHOULDERS. The last thing to do is cut the tenon to the desired width. You may have to change the height of the dado blade to determine this width.

Note: Again, I test the height first by making cuts near the end of a test piece of the same width.

To keep the position of the tenon shoulder consistent all the way around the workpiece, I used the same fence setup as I did when cutting the tenon cheeks. The only difference is that the workpiece is stood on edge now as it passes over the blade *(Step 4)*.

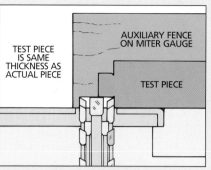

1 *Begin cutting the tenon on a test piece. Sneak up on thickness of tenon by adjusting height of the dado blade.*

2 *Test the fit of the tenon in a mortise. If the tenon is too tight, raise the height of the dado blade and cut again.*

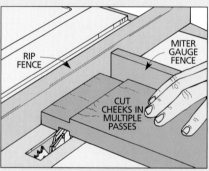

3 *When the blade is adjusted for the correct thickness, cut the tenon to the desired length. Use the fence as a stop.*

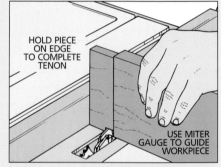

4 *Now the tenon can be cut to width. Don't move the fence, but the height of the blade may need to be adjusted.*

DESIGNER'S NOTEBOOK

Removing the doors and using blind mortise and tenon joints makes for a simpler version of the Mission Bookcase. The one shown here is also shorter than the original.

CONSTRUCTION NOTES:

■ The basic construction of this short open version is virtually the same as for the full Mission Bookcase. The main difference is that the size and number of some of the parts differ, and none of the hardware or parts for the doors are needed (see Materials List).

   Note: The width and depth of this bookcase will remain the same, but the overall height will be 11" shorter (48").

■ First, the side panels (A) and panel cores (B) are cut to a length of $33^3/_{16}$" *(Fig. 1)*. (Their width is the same.)

■ To make this version simpler, you can use blind tenons on the fronts of the rails (D, E) identical to the ones on their backs *(Fig. 1)*. This makes each rail slightly shorter (11").

■ The posts (C) also need to be shortened for this design. They are now cut to a length of 47" *(Fig. 1)*. And their mortises are shallower ($1^5/_{16}$" deep) to accept the shorter tenons on the rails.

■ The back panel (K) is once again cut to fit the rabbets in the back of the case. (Mine ended up $38^1/_2$" high.)

■ Finally, since there are no doors, the front rail (G) and shelves (Y) are made wider to extend to the front of the bookcase *(Fig. 2)*. The shelves will need notches on their front and back corners (similar to those on the front rail) because the shelf standards (X) are removed *(Fig. 1)*. Now you can drill shelf pin holes directly into the posts.

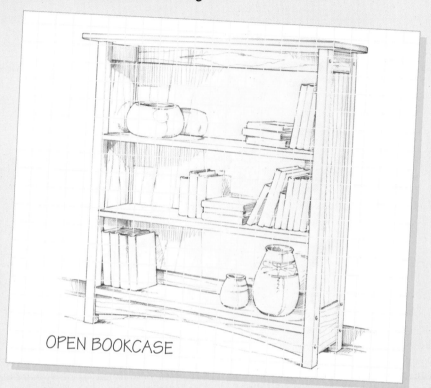

OPEN BOOKCASE

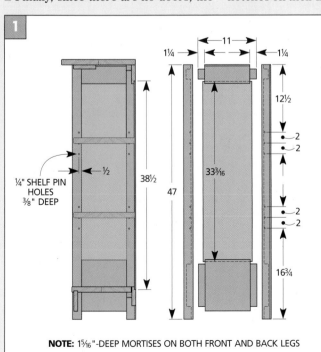

1

¼" SHELF PIN HOLES ⅜" DEEP

½

38½

47

11

1¼   1¼

12½

2
2

$33^3/_{16}$

2
2

16¾

NOTE: 1⁵⁄₁₆"-DEEP MORTISES ON BOTH FRONT AND BACK LEGS

MATERIALS LIST

CHANGED PARTS

A	Side Panels (4)	¼ ply - 9³/₁₆ x 33³/₁₆	Note: Do not need
B	Panel Cores (2)	⅛ hdbd. - 9³/₁₆ x 33³/₁₆	parts O, P, Q, R, S, T,
C	Posts (4)	1³/₄ x 1³/₄ - 47	U, V, W, X, hinges,
D	Top Side Rails (2)	1 x 3½ - 11	door catches, or
E	Btm. Side Rails (2)	1 x 9½ - 11	glass panes.
G	Front Rail (1)	¾ x 4¼ - 42¼	
K	Back Panel (1)	¼ ply - 41½ x 38½	
Y	Shelves (2)	1 x 11½ - 41½	

2

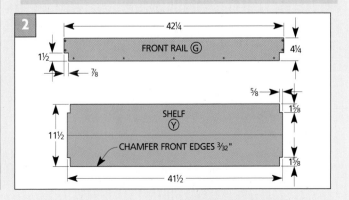

42¼

FRONT RAIL ⓖ

1½

⅞

4¼

⅝

1⅝

11½

SHELF ⓨ

CHAMFER FRONT EDGES ³/₃₂"

41½

1⅝

COUNTRY PROJECTS

The term "country" suggests a straightforward, practical style of furniture. Typically made from pine boards, it has a "down-home" feel.

So it may be surprising to see a coat rack made from oak. Its simple, decorative curves and traditional pegs give it a distinctly country look. There's also a painted pine version.

Knotty pine is the perfect material for the high back bench and jelly cupboard. Both projects offer options that let you change the look without changing their charm.

But not all pine is knotty. Using clear pine for the dovetail chest highlights the hand-cut dovetails. Or for a different look, try the frame-and-panel version.

Coat and Glove Rack   90

Designer's Notebook: Square Pegs 92
Shop Tip: Hanging System 94
Designer's Notebook: Milk Paint/Aging 95

High-Back Bench   96

Shop Tip: Spacing Slats 98
Designer's Notebook: Heart Cutout 99
Shop Tip: Mortises With a Jig Saw 100
Designer's Notebook: Under-Seat Storage 102
Finishing: Milk Paint 104

Jelly Cupboard   106

Shop Tip: Routing Custom-Fit Dadoes 108
Shop Tip: Clamping with Wedges 109
Designer's Notebook: Wood Raised Panels 113

Dovetail Chest   114

Shop Tip: Sanding Flush 117
Shop Jig: Flush Trim Jig 117
Finishing Tip: Shellac 119
Joinery: Hand-Cut Dovetails 120
Designer's Notebook: Frame and Panel Chest 124

Coat and Glove Rack

Hang coats and mittens or cups and linens on this rack that features additional storage behind its door. Choose a finish that highlights the wood, or try one that turns your rack into an "instant antique."

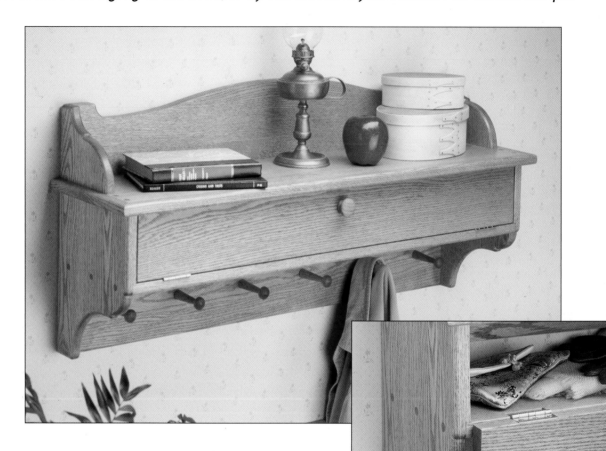

When I started building this project, I never considered hanging anything more than my coats and hats on it. But when a friend saw it, she insisted I build one for her. And she wanted to know if I could make it look like a well-used antique (more about that in a moment).

JOINERY. The construction of the coat and glove rack is very simple. The shelves both sit in dadoes in the sides and are then screwed in place. And the back pieces are screwed to the shelves.

DOOR. The only trick to this country coat rack is fitting the door. How do you get a uniform gap around each side? I started with the gap at the bottom — it's determined by the depth of the hinge mortises. Then after the bottom

gap is set, creating the other gaps is just a matter of trimming the door to size.

HANGING SYSTEM. The rack itself doesn't weigh that much, but when it's full of coats you want to know it will stay put. So the back is beveled and this bevel then locks into a mating cleat screwed to the wall (refer to the Shop Tip on page 94). It's strong and makes it easy to position the rack.

FINISHES. On the oak version shown here, I used an oil/varnish combination to let the wood grain show through.

My friend wanted a more "country" look, so I built hers out of pine. And to make it a bit more rustic, I tried milk paint for a finish. (The Technique box

on page 104 tells you how to use milk paint.) Then, to make it look like it had seen years of use, I distressed the wood and finish. You can see the results (and learn more about doing this) in the Designer's Notebook on page 95.

HARDWARE AND PATTERNS. A hardware kit, as well as full-size patterns for the sides and the back, are available from *Woodsmith Project Supplies*. For more information, other sources, and finishing supplies, see page 126.

EXPLODED VIEW

OVERALL DIMENSIONS:
36W x 9D x 16H

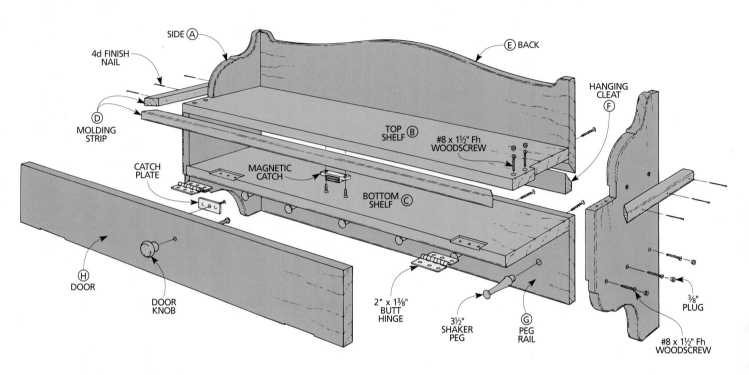

SIDE Ⓐ

4d FINISH NAIL

Ⓓ MOLDING STRIP

CATCH PLATE

MAGNETIC CATCH

TOP SHELF Ⓑ

#8 x 1½" Fh WOODSCREW

Ⓔ BACK

HANGING CLEAT Ⓕ

BOTTOM SHELF Ⓒ

DOOR Ⓗ

DOOR KNOB

2" x 1⅜" BUTT HINGE

3½" SHAKER PEG

PEG RAIL Ⓖ

⅜" PLUG

#8 x 1½" Fh WOODSCREW

MATERIALS LIST

WOOD

A	Sides (2)	¾ x 8¼ - 16
B	Top Shelf (1)	¾ x 7½ - 34½
C	Bottom Shelf (1)	¾ x 7½ - 33½
D	Molding Strip (1)	¾ x ¾ - 60 rough
E	Back (1)	¾ x 7¼ - 33½
F	Hanging Cleat (1)	¾ x 1⅞ - 32
G	Peg Rail (1)	¾ x 6¼ - 33½
H	Door (1)	¾ x 4⅛ - 32⅞

HARDWARE SUPPLIES

(24) No. 8 x 1½" Fh woodscrews
(2) 2" x 1⅜" butt hinges w/ screws
(1) Magnetic catch and plate w/ screws
(6) 3½" Shaker pegs
(1) 1" oak door knob w/ screw
(10) ⅜" oak flat-top plugs
(14) 4d (1½") finish nails

CUTTING DIAGRAM

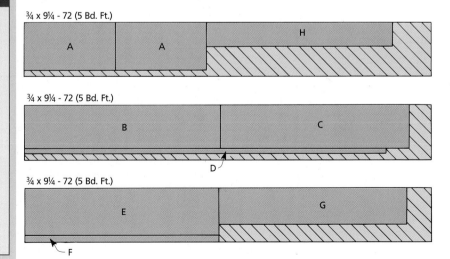

¾ x 9¼ - 72 (5 Bd. Ft.)

A   A   H

¾ x 9¼ - 72 (5 Bd. Ft.)

B   C

D

¾ x 9¼ - 72 (5 Bd. Ft.)

E   G

F

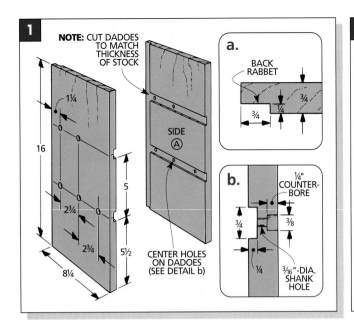

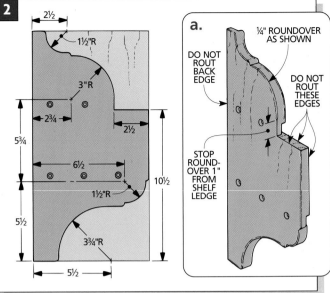

SIDES

The country coat rack is held together by the sides (A). Start by cutting two blanks roughly 8½" wide. Then cut them to a finished length of 16" (*Fig. 1*).

CUT DADOES. The shelves fit into ¼"-deep dadoes cut in the blanks (*Fig. 1b*). Position the first dado 5½" from the bottom edge, the second 10½".

CUT RABBETS. After cutting the dadoes, cut the rabbets for the back pieces. They're cut along the inside back edge of each blank (*Fig. 1a*).

Next, cut the side blanks to finished width (8¼") (*Fig. 1*). Doing this after cutting the dadoes cleans up any chipout. Just be sure to trim off the front edges — not the rabbeted edges.

SCREW HOLES. To screw the shelves to the sides, you'll need to drill ⅜"-dia. counterbores. They're centered on the width of each dado (*Figs. 1 and 1b*). (The counterbores are filled with plugs later.) Then, drill a ³⁄₁₆"-dia. shank hole through each counterbore.

CUT SHAPE. To cut an identical shape on both sides (A), tape them together with carpet tape (dadoes facing in).

Now lay out the curved pattern on one face and cut just outside the lines (*Fig. 2*). Then I used a drum sander and file to finish the shape.

ROUND OVER EDGES. To complete the sides, I routed ¼" roundovers on all the exposed edges except the back.

Note: To prevent gaps, don't round over the edges where noted in *Fig. 2a*.

SHELVES

With the sides complete, I began on the shelves. To make the top shelf look as if it extends through the sides, I added molding strips on the front and sides.

DESIGNER'S NOTEBOOK

SQUARE PEGS

■ If you want to add another interesting detail to the coat rack, try using square pegs instead of round plugs to fill the screw counterbores. The square plugs stand a bit "proud" of the surface.
■ To make square pegs, first cut a ⅜"-square blank to a rough length of 18".
■ Next, using a disc sander, shape each end of the blank to a slight pyramid (*Fig. 1*). Then cut off a peg about ⅜" long from each end.
■ Repeat this procedure until you have enough pegs to fill all the holes.
■ The pegs will fit easier if you round their bottom edges with sandpaper.
■ Next, carefully square up the screw

holes using a small chisel (*Fig. 2*).
■ Finally, place a drop of glue in each hole and spread it around the sides of the hole. (A straightened paper clip works well for this.) Then gently tap the pegs in place.

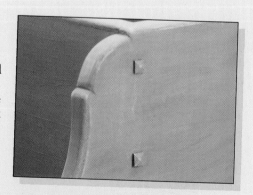

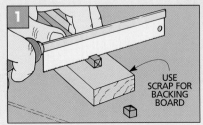

CUT TO SIZE. To begin, rip the top shelf (B) and bottom shelf (C) to width. To find the width, measure the length of the lower dado on a side (A) *(Figs. 3 and 4)*. Start from the shoulder of the back rabbet. (Mine were 7½" wide.)

Next, cut the bottom shelf (C) to length (33½") *(Fig. 4)*. Then clamp the shelf between the two sides (A) and measure from the outside face of one side to the outside of the other. This will be the length of the top shelf (C) (34½" in my case) *(Fig. 3)*.

TOP SHELF. The top shelf extends across the front edge of each side, so cut a notch out of each back corner *(Fig. 3)*. The length of this notch equals the length of the top dado in the sides (A). (Again, measure from the shoulder of the back rabbet.)

At this point, I drilled pilot holes for the door catch *(Fig. 3)*. Inset the door catch a distance equal to the thickness of the door *plus* the catch plate. I attached the plate to the catch and positioned them ¾" in from the front edge.

BOTTOM SHELF. Next, I went back to the bottom shelf. First, lay out the locations of the hinge mortises *(Fig. 4)*.

I wanted a uniform 1/16" gap around the door. If the hinges were mounted flush with the surface, the gap between the shelf and the door would be about 1/8". So I cut the mortise on the shelf a little deeper — to half the thickness of the hinge barrel *(Fig. 4a)*.

After the mortises are cut, drill pilot holes for the screws. Then, round over the front bottom edge *(Fig. 4a)*.

ASSEMBLY. At this point, dry-assemble the shelves (B, C) and sides (A), and drill pilot holes into the shelves *(Fig. 5)*. Then glue and screw the shelves between the sides.

To prevent the top shelf from cupping at the front, I also drilled and screwed the shelf to the sides from the top *(Figs. 5 and 5a)*. Then I plugged all the screw holes except those covered by the molding strips.

MOLDING. The molding strips cover the edges of the top shelf. (The thicknesses of each should match.) I started by rounding over the front edges of the

¾"-wide molding strips (D) *(Fig. 6)*. Then I cut one 40"-long strip, plus two 10"-long strips.

For the best fit at the mitered corners, I cut the front piece first so the distance between the short points equals the length of the top shelf *(Fig. 6)*.

After the front strip is glued on, miter the other strips to fit on the sides. But glue the strips only to the shelf, not the sides. Then nail the strips on with 4d (1½") finish nails *(Fig. 6)*. This allows the sides to expand and contract.

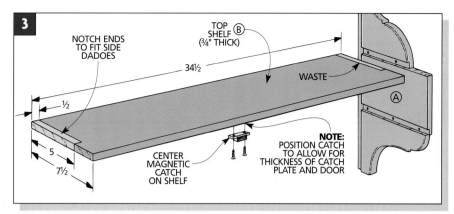

3
NOTCH ENDS TO FIT SIDE DADOES
TOP SHELF (B) (¾" THICK)
34½
WASTE
½
5
7½
CENTER MAGNETIC CATCH ON SHELF
NOTE: POSITION CATCH TO ALLOW FOR THICKNESS OF CATCH PLATE AND DOOR

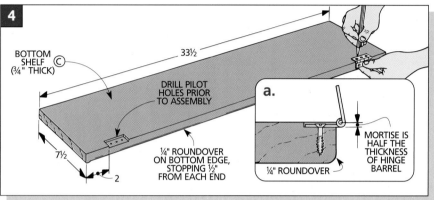

4
BOTTOM SHELF (C) (¾" THICK)
33½
DRILL PILOT HOLES PRIOR TO ASSEMBLY
a.
7½
2
¼" ROUNDOVER ON BOTTOM EDGE, STOPPING ½" FROM EACH END
MORTISE IS HALF THE THICKNESS OF HINGE BARREL
¼" ROUNDOVER

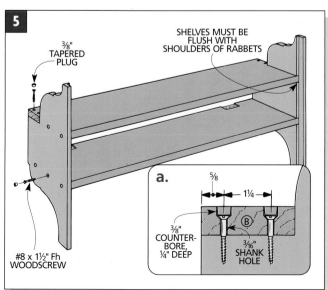

5
⅜" TAPERED PLUG
SHELVES MUST BE FLUSH WITH SHOULDERS OF RABBETS
a.
⅝
1¼
⅜" COUNTER-BORE, ¼" DEEP
(B)
3/16" SHANK HOLE
#8 x 1½" Fh WOODSCREW

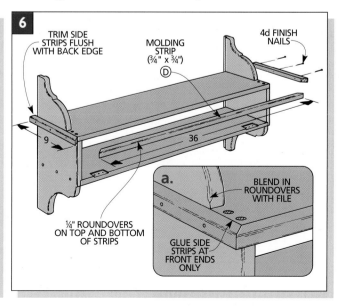

6
TRIM SIDE STRIPS FLUSH WITH BACK EDGE
MOLDING STRIP (¾" x ¾") (D)
4d FINISH NAILS
9
36
a.
BLEND IN ROUNDOVERS WITH FILE
¼" ROUNDOVERS ON TOP AND BOTTOM OF STRIPS
GLUE SIDE STRIPS AT FRONT ENDS ONLY

Instead of one wide back for the coat rack, it's two separate pieces. The gap between the pieces allows the coat rack to hang on a beveled cleat. See the Shop Tip at right for details.

BACK. The hanging cleat (F) is originally part of the back (E). Start by ripping the piece to a rough width of $9^1/_4$". Next, cut it to length to fit between the rabbets in the sides (A). Then tilt the table saw blade to 45° and rip the back to a width of $7^1/_4$" *(Fig. 8)*. The waste piece is used for the hanging cleat.

CURVES. The next step is to lay out the curve on the *back* side of the back (E) *(Figs. 7 and 8)*. Then rough out the curve with a band saw or jig saw. I used a drum sander to smooth up to the line.

PEG RAIL. The peg rail (G) makes up the lower half of the back *(Fig. 10)*. To determine the width of this piece, measure from the top edge of the bottom shelf to the bottom of the side pieces ($6^1/_4$") *(Fig. 9)*. Like the back, it fits between the rabbets ($33^1/_2$" long).

DRILL PEG HOLES. After the peg rail is cut to size, drill holes for the coat pegs *(Fig. 9)*. Center these holes on a line drawn $2^3/_4$" from the bottom edge. Begin with a hole centered 3" from the end of the piece. Then drill the remaining five holes at $5^1/_2$" intervals (center to center).

ROUT BACKS. Next, I routed a $^1/_4$" roundover along the *upper* front edge of the back (E) *(Fig. 8a)* and the *lower* front edge of the peg rail (G) *(Fig. 9)*.

Note: To prevent any gaps where the back pieces fit into the rabbets, stop the roundovers $^1/_2$" from the ends of each piece.

ATTACH BACKS. Now, drill countersunk screw holes through the back pieces and into the shelves *(Fig. 10)*. Then screw the top and bottom into the shelves. To hold the backs in tight, I nailed them into the rabbets as well.

SHOP TIP ...... Hanging System

Here's how the hanging system works. First, the back is cut to finished length. Next, a beveled cleat is ripped from one edge of the back. Then screw the cleat to a pair of studs in the wall.

After it's finished, hang the shelf on the cleat so the mating bevels interlock.

Note: This same system can be easily adapted for other styles of shelves or wall-hung cabinets.

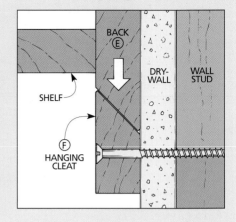

7

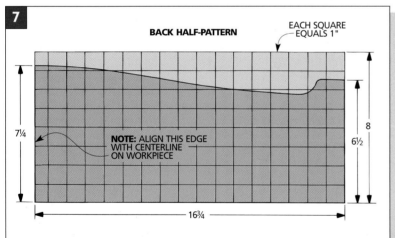

BACK HALF-PATTERN

EACH SQUARE EQUALS 1"

NOTE: ALIGN THIS EDGE WITH CENTERLINE ON WORKPIECE

$7^1/_4$

8

$6^1/_2$

$16^3/_4$

8

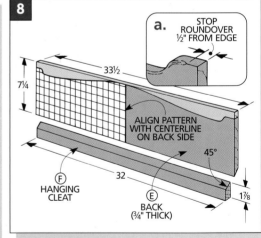

a. STOP ROUNDOVER $^1/_2$" FROM EDGE

$33^1/_2$

$7^1/_4$

ALIGN PATTERN WITH CENTERLINE ON BACK SIDE

45°

F HANGING CLEAT

32

E BACK ($^3/_4$" THICK)

$1^7/_8$

9

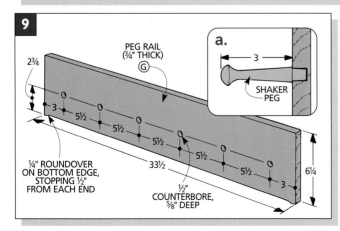

PEG RAIL ($^3/_4$" THICK) G

a.

3

SHAKER PEG

$2^3/_4$

3

$5^1/_2$

$5^1/_2$

$5^1/_2$

$5^1/_2$

$33^1/_2$

$5^1/_2$

3

$6^1/_4$

$^1/_4$" ROUNDOVER ON BOTTOM EDGE, STOPPING $^1/_2$" FROM EACH END

$^1/_2$" COUNTERBORE, $^5/_8$" DEEP

10

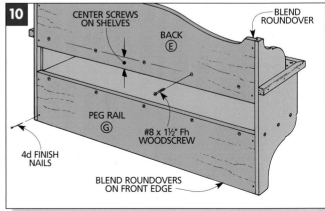

CENTER SCREWS ON SHELVES

BACK E

BLEND ROUNDOVER

PEG RAIL G

#8 x $1^1/_2$" Fh WOODSCREW

4d FINISH NAILS

BLEND ROUNDOVERS ON FRONT EDGE

Note: To avoid splitting the wood, I drilled pilot holes and used 4d finish nails, angling them slightly.

BLEND ROUNDOVERS. Some of the roundovers on the sides (A) and the backs (E, G) were stopped short so there wouldn't be gaps at the joints. Now that these pieces are assembled, you can finish rounding them over with a file *(Figs. 6a and 10)*.

DOOR

All that's left is the door. It should have a consistent gap around each side. To get this, I cut the door to fit tight and trimmed it for an even gap later.

CUT DOOR. Start by measuring the opening and cut the door (H) to fit. Then rip it $1/16''$ narrower than the height of the opening so you can close the door when the hinges are mounted.

Now, screw the hinges to the bottom shelf. Then, clamp the door to them and mark their position *(Fig. 11)*.

Note: The door should be centered across the opening.

CUT MORTISES. Next, cut the hinge mortises on the door edge *(Fig. 11a)*. These mortises can be cut to the thickness of the hinge leaf.

TRIM DOOR. After mounting the door, measure the gap along the bottom and mark the door's top and sides so they'll have uniform gaps. Next, remove

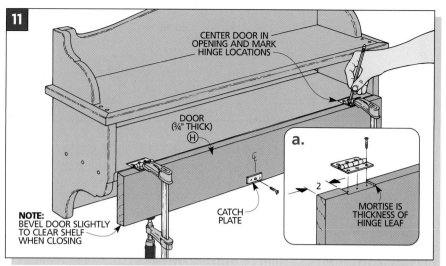

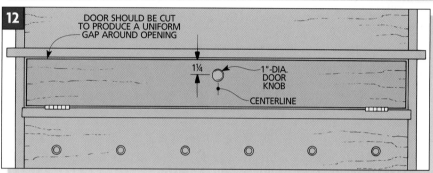

the door and trim its top and sides. Then soften the edges with sandpaper.

Note: When trimming the top edge, cut a slight bevel so the inside edge of the door will clear the shelf.

DOOR KNOB AND CATCH. Finally, drill pilot holes for the catch plate and door knob *(Figs. 11 and 12)*. Then apply a finish to the coat rack and mount the catch, pegs, and door knob. ■

DESIGNER'S NOTEBOOK

AGING/MILK PAINT

■ For tips on applying milk paint, see the Finishing article on pages 104-105.

■ To give the coat rack a worn appearance, sand some of the edges after painting, and round the corners that would get the most wear.

■ To distress the wood and finish more, add dings and scratches. But do a little bit at a time — it can be overdone.

High-Back Bench

Choose from several options to make the bench you want. It can be built with or without storage under the seat, with your choice of designs in the back, and finished with a stain or milk paint.

Probably the first thing you notice about this bench is all the curves. And you may wonder how to cut these on such large panels. Actually, it's easy to do with a pattern, a jig saw, and a bit of sanding.

V-GROOVE. But there's another feature that helps give this high back bench its old-fashioned look. That's the V-groove between the boards in each panel. It highlights all of the joints — instead of hiding them.

I used two techniques to cut these grooves. Since the back of the bench is made up of individual boards that aren't glued together, the edges of the boards

are chamfered before assembly. Then they're held together with cleats.

But the seat and sides are glued-up panels. It's easier to cut these grooves after gluing up each panel. I did this on a table saw with the blade tilted to 45°.

WOOD. I used ³⁄₄"-thick No. 2 Ponderosa pine for most of the bench, and straight-grained 1¹⁄₂"-thick stock for the supports under the seat.

FINISH OPTIONS. I actually built two benches just so I could try out a different finish on each of them.

The first bench (shown above) was stained to give the deep color that a hundred-year-old bench would have

acquired over time. To do this, I first applied a sealer to help the pine absorb the stain evenly. Then I used a 50/50 blend of a golden oak color mixed with a maple stain. For the top coat, I used two coats of a satin finish clear sealer.

On the second bench, I used milk paint, a finish that's been used since colonial times. (You can see this bench on page 104.) After a bit of "distressing," this finish helps the bench look like an authentic antique.

DESIGN OPTION. To make your bench even more useful, the Designer's Notebook on page 102 shows how to build it with under-seat storage.

EXPLODED VIEW

OVERALL DIMENSIONS:
52W x 20D x 47H

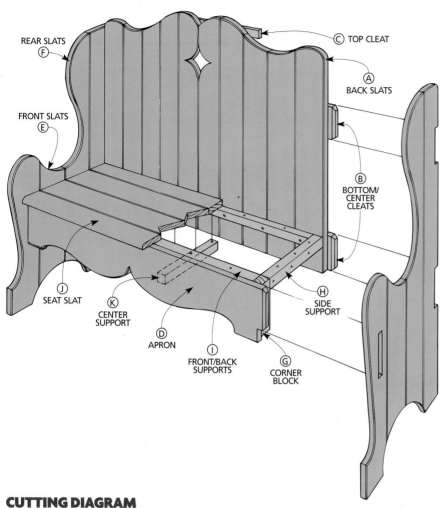

REAR SLATS
(F)

FRONT SLATS
(E)

© TOP CLEAT

(A)
BACK SLATS

(B)
BOTTOM/
CENTER
CLEATS

(J)
SEAT SLAT

(K)
CENTER
SUPPORT

(D)
APRON

(I)
FRONT/BACK
SUPPORTS

(G)
CORNER
BLOCK

(H)
SIDE
SUPPORT

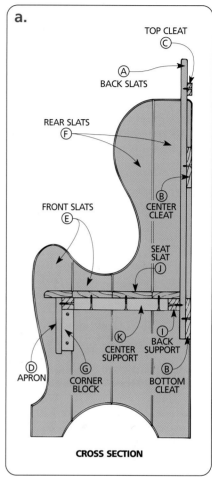

a.

TOP CLEAT
©

(A)
BACK SLATS

REAR SLATS
(F)

(B)
CENTER
CLEAT

FRONT SLATS
(E)

SEAT
SLAT
(J)

(D)
APRON

(G)
CORNER
BLOCK

(K)
CENTER
SUPPORT

(I)
BACK
SUPPORT

(B)
BOTTOM
CLEAT

CROSS SECTION

CUTTING DIAGRAM

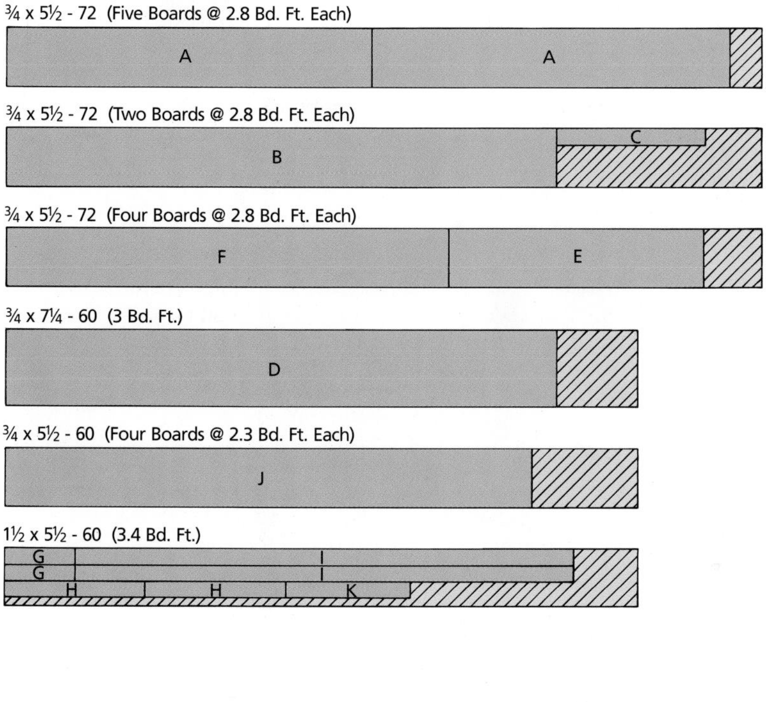

¾ x 5½ - 72 (Five Boards @ 2.8 Bd. Ft. Each)

A	A

¾ x 5½ - 72 (Two Boards @ 2.8 Bd. Ft. Each)

B	C

¾ x 5½ - 72 (Four Boards @ 2.8 Bd. Ft. Each)

F	E

¾ x 7¼ - 60 (3 Bd. Ft.)

D

¾ x 5½ - 60 (Four Boards @ 2.3 Bd. Ft. Each)

J

1½ x 5½ - 60 (3.4 Bd. Ft.)

G
G
H   I   H   K

MATERIALS LIST

WOOD
A	Back Slats (10)	¾ x 5 - 34¾
B	Btm./Ctr. Cleats (2)	¾ x 5 - 52
C	Top Cleat (1)	¾ x 1½ - 14
D	Apron (1)	¾ x 7 - 52
E	Front Slats (4)	¾ x 5 - 24
F	Rear Slats (4)	¾ x 5 - 42
G	Corner Blocks (2)	1½ x 1½ - 6¾
H	Side Supports (2)	1½ x 1½ - 13¼
I	Fr./Bk. Supports (2)	1½ x 1½ - 47
J	Seat Slats (4)	¾ x 5 - 50
K	Center Support (1)	1½ x 1½ - 11¾

HARDWARE SUPPLIES
(46) No. 8 x 1¼" Fh woodscrews
(69) No. 8 x 2" Fh woodscrews

I started work on the bench by building the back. The back consists of ten slats supported by two cleats — much like a picket fence.

BACK SLATS. I ripped the ten back slats (A) to width from $^3/_4$"-thick boards *(Fig. 1)* and cut them $34^3/_4$" long.

Next, to give the bench a traditional look, I routed $^1/_8$" chamfers on the long edges of each slat *(Fig. 2a)*. (Don't chamfer the ends.)

BOTTOM AND CENTER CLEATS. To make the bottom and center cleats (B), first rip two boards 5" wide *(Fig. 1)*. Then, cut them to length.

Note: The cleats are 2" longer than the combined width of all the back slats. In my case, they were 52" long.

The ends of the cleats serve as through tenons. To dress them up a little, I routed a $^1/_4$" chamfer around both ends of each cleat *(Fig. 2a)*.

BACK ASSEMBLY. Once the cleats are chamfered, the back can be assembled. To ensure the proper distance across the back, first position the two *outside* slats 50" apart measured from outside edge to outside edge *(Fig. 2)*.

Next, place the bottom cleat on top of the two slats *(Fig. 2)*. Then, adjust the position of the cleat so it overhangs the side of each slat by 1", and is flush with the bottom end of each slat.

Use only one screw at each cleat/slat point for now — you'll drive the second screw after the frame is square.

The center cleat can be attached the same way. Position it $13^3/_4$" up from the *top* edge of the bottom cleat *(Fig. 2)*.

Now, square up the frame and install a second screw at each joint. Then attach the remaining slats, working from the outside in. See the Shop Tip at right for a tip on doing this.

TOP CLEAT. Finally, cut a small top cleat (C) to size *(Fig. 1)*. Later, this cleat helps support the two center slats after you've cut a design in the back. But before the cleat is screwed in place, the patterns in the back are laid out and cut.

SHAPING BACK

To add a bit of country flair to the back, I cut a double curve along the top edge and a diamond in the center of the back. (An alternate heart-shaped cutout is shown in the Designer's Notebook on the opposite page.)

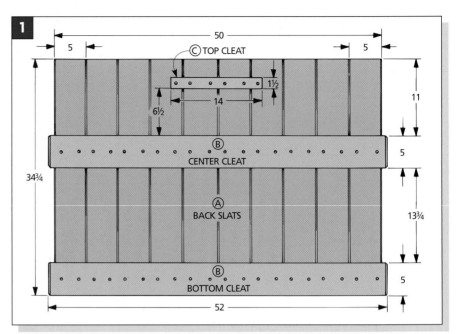

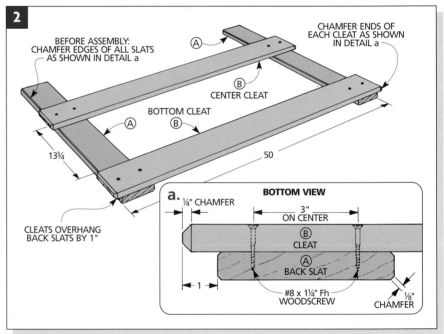

SHOP TIP .... *Spacing Slats*

If you build the bench in a dry shop, each 5"-wide slat may swell across its width by about 1%, or as much as $^3/_{64}$" as the humidity increases. So attach them to the cleats with a gap this size between them.

To space the slats evenly and consistently, I used playing cards as spacers. The thickness of three cards is just about the right amount of space.

Note: You may have to trim the width of a few of the inside slats and rechamfer the edges.

BACK PATTERN. To shape the back as symmetrically as possible, first draw the half-pattern full size on a piece of ⅛"-thick hardboard to be used as a template *(Fig. 3)*. Then cut and sand the hardboard template to finished shape.

SHAPING THE BACK. Now the pattern can be traced onto the back side of the back. To do this, trace around the template onto one half of the back. Flip the template over to the opposite half and trace it again.

Note: I worked from the back side because my jig saw cuts on the upstroke. This way, any splintering is hidden in the back.

CHAMFER EDGES. After the curved top edge and cutout have been cut, sand the edges. Next, rout a ⅛" chamfer on the front and back of the top edge and inside the cutout *(Figs. 4 and 4a)*.

Because the router bit can't reach into the tight corners, I completed the chamfers with a file.

After you're through chamfering the edges, attach the top cleat (C) to the rear of the back, just above the cutout.

APRON

The next step is to cut an apron (D) that fits below the seat and between the sides. Cut the apron 7" wide from a ¾"-thick board *(Fig. 5)*. Then, cut the apron the same length as the back cleats (B). (In my case, 52" long.)

TENONS. Next, cut the notches to form a tenon on each end of the apron *(Fig. 5a)*. These tenons will fit into mortises that are cut later into the side panels of the bench. To cut the notches, I raised the table saw blade 2" high and made a cut 1" from each end. Then, I removed the waste with a back saw.

After the tenons are formed, the end of each tenon is chamfered the same as the ends on the cleats *(Fig. 5a)*.

Note: Chamfer the bottom edge of the tenon with a back saw or file.

PATTERN. The apron can be shaped in

DESIGNER'S NOTEBOOK

HEART CUTOUT

■ Drill 2½"-dia. holes to make the curved top portion of the heart.
■ Cut out the lower portion with a jig saw. Chamfer the edges. Complete the chamfer on the bottom point with a file.

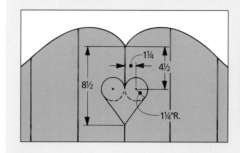

3
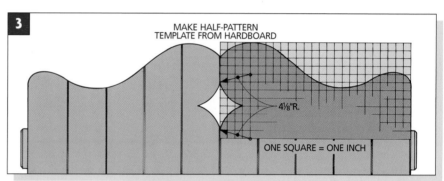
MAKE HALF-PATTERN TEMPLATE FROM HARDBOARD
4⅛"R.
ONE SQUARE = ONE INCH

4
NOTE: CHAMFER FRONT AND BACK EDGES
COMPLETE CHAMFERS INTO CORNERS WITH FILE
a.
CHAMFER BIT
⅛

the same manner as the back. First, make a hardboard template *(Fig. 5)*. Then trace the template onto the apron, cut out the shape, and sand it smooth. Finally, rout ⅛" chamfers along the bottom edges of the apron.

5
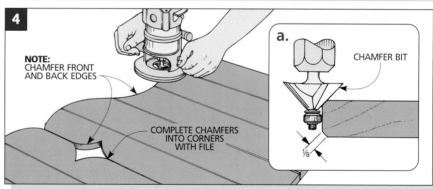
52
MAKE HALF-PATTERN TEMPLATE FROM HARDBOARD
ONE SQUARE = ONE INCH
5
2
1
4
21
D APRON
⅛" CHAMFER ON BOTTOM EDGE
a.
D
¼" CHAMFERS ON ALL EDGES OF TENON
NOTCH

SIDES

Next, work can begin on the two glued-up side panels.

SIDE PANELS. Start by ripping enough $3/4$"-thick stock to width for four front slats (E) and four rear slats (F) *(Fig. 6)*. Then, rough cut the front slats 25" long and the rear slats 43" long.

Now, form each "L"-shaped side by gluing two front and two rear slats together *(Fig. 6)*. Once the glue dries, sand them flat and cut them to final size.

NOTCHES. Now, lay out notches on the back edge of each panel for the back cleats *(Fig. 6)*. I used a jig saw to cut the three edges on each notch a little short. Then I used a chisel to sneak up on their final size until the notches fit the cleats.

MORTISES. Next, lay out the location for each mortise to attach the apron (D) *(Fig. 6)*. Then, cut each mortise to fit the apron tenons. (See the Shop Tip below for one way to do this.)

CUT V-GROOVES. To make the joints on the side panels look like those on the back, I cut V-grooves along each one.

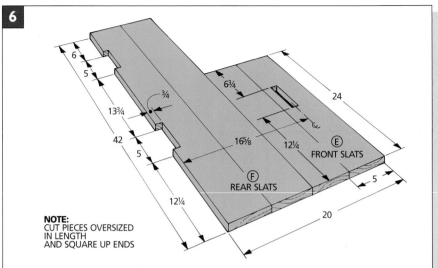

6

6
5
$13\frac{3}{4}$
$3/4$
$6\frac{3}{4}$
24
42
5
$16\frac{5}{8}$
$12\frac{1}{4}$
E FRONT SLATS
5
F REAR SLATS
$12\frac{1}{4}$
20

NOTE: CUT PIECES OVERSIZED IN LENGTH AND SQUARE UP ENDS

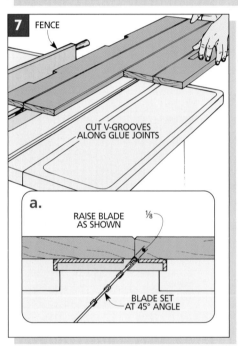

7 FENCE

CUT V-GROOVES ALONG GLUE JOINTS

a.

RAISE BLADE AS SHOWN
$1/8$

BLADE SET AT 45° ANGLE

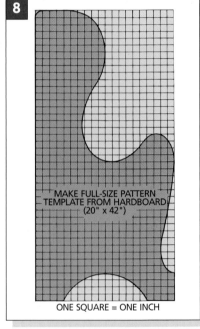

8

MAKE FULL-SIZE PATTERN TEMPLATE FROM HARDBOARD (20" x 42")

ONE SQUARE = ONE INCH

SHOP TIP . . . . *Mortises With A Jig Saw*

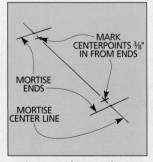

MARK CENTERPOINTS $3/8$" IN FROM ENDS

MORTISE ENDS

MORTISE CENTER LINE

1 Lay out the mortise centerline, ends, and pilot holes $3/8$" from each end.

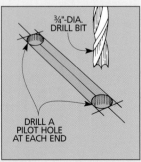

$3/4$"-DIA. DRILL BIT

DRILL A PILOT HOLE AT EACH END

2 Drill a $3/4$" hole at each end. Use these holes to lay out edge of mortise.

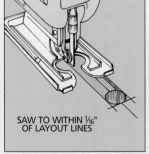

SAW TO WITHIN $1/16$" OF LAYOUT LINES

3 Remove waste using a jig saw (or chisel). Cut to within $1/16$" of all layout lines.

CHISEL HALFWAY THROUGH EACH SIDE TO CLEAN OUT MORTISE

4 Chisel up to layout lines. To help prevent chipout, work from both faces.

To do this, I used a rip blade (because of the blade's flat-top profile) tilted to 45° *(Fig. 7a).* Before moving the rip fence to cut the next groove, flip the panel over to cut the opposite side of the joint.

CUT TO SHAPE. To complete the sides, make a pattern as you did for the back and apron *(Fig. 8).* Then chamfer all the edges *except* inside the notches (refer to *Fig. 4a* on page 99).

ASSEMBLY

Before making the bench seat, the side panels are glued to the back and apron.

To do this, first spread glue around the edges of the apron tenons. Then, insert the tenons into the mortises in the sides and clamp the assembly together *(Fig. 9).*

Note: Make sure the tenon shoulders are tight against the sides.

Now, lift the back into place, and slip the cleats into the side panel notches *(Fig. 9).* Then, drill and screw the cleats into the notches *(Fig. 9a).*

SEAT

Once the glue has dried, the final steps are building the seat support and seat.

SEAT SUPPORT. The seat support consists of a frame and center support made from $1\frac{1}{2}$" x $1\frac{1}{2}$" boards *(Fig. 10).* Begin by cutting two corner blocks (G) to a length of $6\frac{3}{4}$". Then, glue and screw them in place.

Next, cut two side supports (H) to fit between the back slats (A) and the corner blocks (G) *(Fig. 10).* Now, drill and screw (don't glue) the supports in place. The sides must be able to shrink and swell during changes in humidity.

Now, cut the front and back supports (I) to length *(Fig. 10).* Then, drill and screw them to the apron and back slats.

SEAT. To make the seat, first rip four $\frac{3}{4}$"-thick boards for the seat slats (J) to a width of 5" and slightly over 50" long *(Fig. 11).* Then, glue and clamp the boards together for the seat blank.

Once the glue has dried, cut the panel to fit between the sides. Next, cut V-grooves along all three glue joints. Then, rip the front and back slats to width until the V-grooves in the seat align with the side grooves *(Fig. 11).*

Next, rout a $\frac{1}{2}$" roundover on the front edge of the seat *(Fig. 11a).* Then chamfer the top outside ends, and complete the chamfer with a file *(Fig. 11b).*

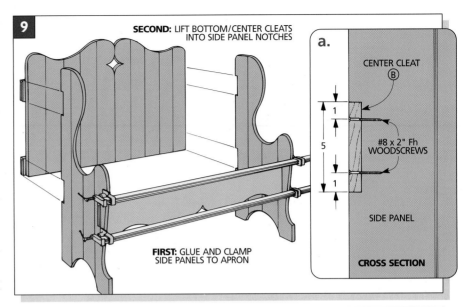

9

SECOND: LIFT BOTTOM/CENTER CLEATS INTO SIDE PANEL NOTCHES

FIRST: GLUE AND CLAMP SIDE PANELS TO APRON

a.

CENTER CLEAT (B)

1

5

1

#8 x 2" Fh WOODSCREWS

SIDE PANEL

CROSS SECTION

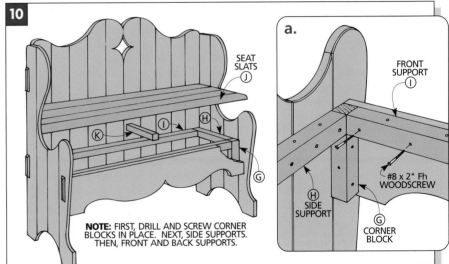

10

SEAT SLATS (J)

(K) (I) (H)

(G)

NOTE: FIRST, DRILL AND SCREW CORNER BLOCKS IN PLACE. NEXT, SIDE SUPPORTS. THEN, FRONT AND BACK SUPPORTS.

a.

FRONT SUPPORT (I)

#8 x 2" Fh WOODSCREW

(H) SIDE SUPPORT

(G) CORNER BLOCK

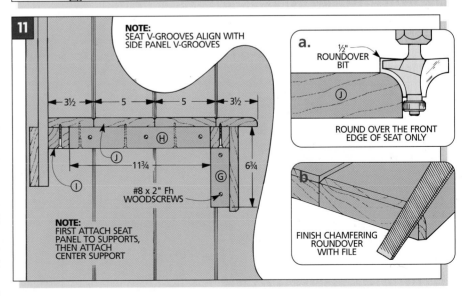

11

NOTE: SEAT V-GROOVES ALIGN WITH SIDE PANEL V-GROOVES

$3\frac{1}{2}$ 5   5 $3\frac{1}{2}$

(H)

(J)

$11\frac{3}{4}$

$6\frac{3}{4}$

(I)

(G)

#8 x 2" Fh WOODSCREWS

NOTE: FIRST ATTACH SEAT PANEL TO SUPPORTS, THEN ATTACH CENTER SUPPORT

a.

$\frac{1}{2}$" ROUNDOVER BIT

(J)

ROUND OVER THE FRONT EDGE OF SEAT ONLY

b.

FINISH CHAMFERING ROUNDOVER WITH FILE

ATTACH SEAT. Now, drill and screw the seat supports to the seat *(Fig. 11).*

Finally, screw a center support (K) to the bottom of the seat between the front and back supports (refer to detail 'a' in Exploded View on page 97). ■

DESIGNER'S NOTEBOOK

You can make the high-back bench more versatile by building a hidden storage area under the seat. To allow access to this compartment, the seat panel doubles as a hinged lid.

CONSTRUCTION NOTES:

■ For this bench, the back is built the same, except it's a bit longer (taller). So first cut the back slats (A) to width (5") and to a length of 37³/₄" (*Fig. 1*).

■ Assemble the back with the bottom cleat (B) flush with the bottom edges of the back slats. Then position the bottom edge of the center cleat (B) 16³/₄" from the top of the bottom cleat (B) (*Fig. 1*).

■ Now complete the back the same as for the regular bench.

■ Next, glue up two 5¹/₂"-wide boards to make a panel for the apron (D) (*Fig. 2*).

■ After cutting the apron to length (52"), a tenon is cut on each end, centered on the width of the apron (*Fig. 2*). To do this, first raise the table saw blade to just under 3". Then set the rip fence 1" from the *outside* of the blade as a stop. With the workpiece standing *on edge* against the miter gauge, make a pass on each end.

Sneak up on the final blade height, making a pass on each edge until the distance between the kerfs is 5". If your saw blade won't go high enough, use a hand saw to finish the cuts. Then remove the waste with a back saw.

■ Rout ¹/₄" chamfers on all the edges of the tenons.

■ Cut a V-groove along the joint line as shown in *Fig. 7a* on page 100.

■ To accept the bottom panel (added later) cut a ³/₄"-wide groove ³/₈" deep on the back face of the apron (*Fig. 2*). The top edge of the groove should align with the bottom of the tenon.

■ The apron pattern on this bench has shallower curves (*Fig. 2*). Lay out the pattern so it's below the groove.

■ The side panels have two differences from the regular bench. The mortises

for the apron and the notches for the bottom cleat are cut so their bottom edges are 9¹/₄" from the bottom edge of each side panel (*Fig. 3*).

■ Once the remaining notch and the V-grooves are cut in each side panel, you can assemble the sides with the back panel and apron.

■ Next, cut the side supports (H) to fit between the back panel and the apron (*Fig. 4*). Screw (don't glue) them to the sides. Then cut the corner blocks (G) to length to fit between the side supports and the top of the groove in the apron. Finally, add the back support (I).

Note: There is no front support.

■ Now you can glue up a panel for the bottom (M). When the glue is dry, cut it to length to fit between the side panels. Its width will be the distance from the back face of the bottom cleat (B) to the back of the apron, plus ¹/₄" (*Fig. 7*).

■ Slide the bottom panel into the groove in the apron. Align its rear edge with the

back face of the bottom cleat and screw and glue it to the bottom cleat (*Fig. 7*).

■ Cut two bottom supports (N) 14³/₄" long. Butt them against the underside of the bottom (M), then screw (don't glue) them to the side panels (*Fig. 7*).

■ Cut three seat slats (J) and a hinge slat (L) to width (5") and to rough length.

■ Glue up the three seat slats (J) to make the seat panel. When it's dry, cut it to finished length so it will fit between the side panels, less ¹/₄".

■ Cut V-grooves along the glue joints and complete the edges of the seat as shown in *Figs. 11a* and *11b* on page 101.

■ To match the seat panel, chamfer the *front* and *side* edges of the hinge slat and *rear* edge of the seat panel.

■ To position the hinges on the hinge slat (L), measure 3⁵/₈" from each end (*Fig. 5*). Center the third hinge on the slat's length. At these positions, cut mortises the full depth of the hinges.

■ Center the hinge slat between the

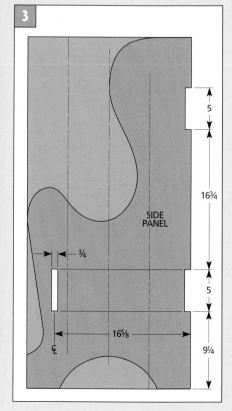

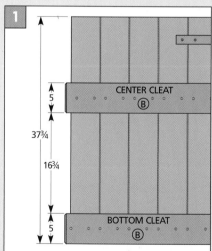

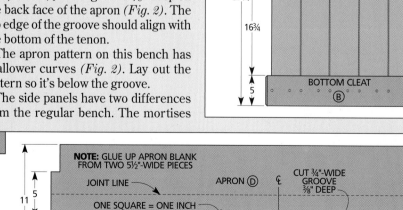

CHANGED PARTS

A Back Slats (10) $3/4$ x 5 - $37^3/4$
D Apron (1) $3/4$ x 11 - 52
G Corner Blocks (2) $1^1/2$ x $1^1/2$ - $6^1/2$
H Side Supports (2) $1^1/2$ x $1^1/2$ - $14^3/4$
I Back Support (1) $1^1/2$ x $1^1/2$ - 47
J Seat Slats (3) $3/4$ x 5 - $49^3/4$

NEW PARTS

L Hinge Slat (1) $3/4$ x 5 - $49^3/4$
M Bottom (1) $3/4$ x $16^5/8$ - 50
N Btm. Supports (2) $1^1/2$ x $1^1/2$ - $14^3/4$
O Seat Cleats (3) $3/4$ x 2 - 11
Note: Don't need part K, only one part I

HARDWARE SUPPLIES

(3) $1^3/8$" x $2^1/2$" butt hinges
(55) #8 x $1^1/4$" Fh woodscrews
(42) #8 x 2" Fh woodscrews

STORAGE BENCH

sides. Glue it to the back support (I), tight against the bench back *(Fig. 5)*. (Do not glue the slat to the back panel.)

■ Now cut three seat cleats (O). Their length is the distance from the front edge of the hinge slat to the inside edge of the apron, less $1/4$". Cut a $3/8$" chamfer across each end *(Fig. 6)*.

■ Mount a seat cleat $3^7/8$" from each end of the seat *(Fig. 6)*. Mount the third cleat centered on the seat's length. The cleats should be flush with the rear edge of the seat panel.

■ Screw the hinges to the rear hinge slat and then screw the seat panel in place.

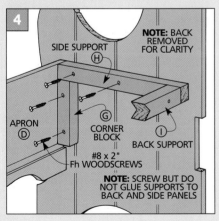

4

SIDE SUPPORT Ⓗ

NOTE: BACK REMOVED FOR CLARITY

APRON Ⓓ

Ⓖ

CORNER BLOCK

Ⓘ

BACK SUPPORT

#8 x 2" Fh WOODSCREWS

NOTE: SCREW BUT DO NOT GLUE SUPPORTS TO BACK AND SIDE PANELS

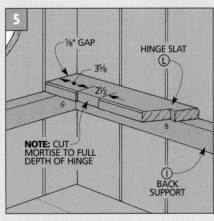

5

$1/8$" GAP

$3^5/8$

$2^1/2$

HINGE SLAT Ⓛ

NOTE: CUT MORTISE TO FULL DEPTH OF HINGE

Ⓘ BACK SUPPORT

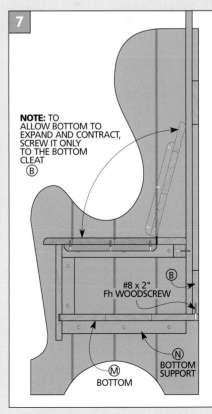

7

NOTE: TO ALLOW BOTTOM TO EXPAND AND CONTRACT, SCREW IT ONLY TO THE BOTTOM CLEAT Ⓑ

Ⓑ

#8 x 2" Fh WOODSCREW

Ⓝ BOTTOM SUPPORT

Ⓜ BOTTOM

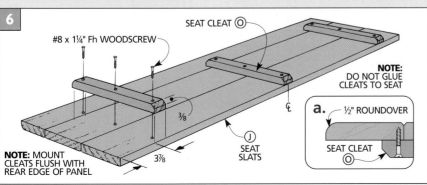

6

#8 x $1^1/4$" Fh WOODSCREW

SEAT CLEAT Ⓞ

NOTE: DO NOT GLUE CLEATS TO SEAT

$3/8$

Ⓙ SEAT SLATS

℄

a. $1/2$" ROUNDOVER

SEAT CLEAT Ⓞ

NOTE: MOUNT CLEATS FLUSH WITH REAR EDGE OF PANEL

$3^7/8$

FINISHING .... *Milk Paint*

How do you add 150 years of age and wear to a project in just a short time? Part of the secret is knowing what finish might have been used that long ago. A good guess would be milk paint.

PRE-MIXED POWDER. It's called milk paint because milk was one of the materials farmers used when they had to make their own paint. But that doesn't mean you can run down to the grocery store and get a quart of 2%, then add a few ingredients to end up with milk paint. The pigments and ingredients can be found, but to be honest, it's a lot more convenient just to buy pre-mixed powder. (For sources, see page 126.)

MIXING PRE-MIX. All you have to do with the pre-mix is add together equal parts (by volume) of water and powder. I use a large, clean jar to mix in. A vigorous shaking (with the lid on) helps dissolve most of the powder.

To remove any powder clumps that weren't completely dissolved during the mixing, strain the solution through cheesecloth. If the clumps are left in the mixture, they will break open during brushing and powder will be smeared across the wood.

DIFFERENT RESULTS. One of the neat things about using milk paint is you can get different results by using different techniques as shown below. You can just brush it on and be done, or use antiquing steps to make a project look old and worn. (For the bench shown above, I used the "Aging" technique.)

APPLYING MILK PAINT

The easiest way to use milk paint is to simply brush on a couple of coats over bare wood. The result is a flat, dull color that has a rough texture once it's dried.

PREPARATION. Milk paint doesn't require a primer. After you've mixed up a batch of milk paint, just wipe the workpiece down with a damp sponge. This prevents the wood from drawing water out of the first coat of paint, and it allows the paint to cure as it's drying.

PAINTING. With the wood still damp, brush on the first coat of milk paint with a stiff bristle brush. (Foam brushes can cause streaking.) Then allow the first coat to dry at least four hours.

If you want to completely cover the wood grain, apply a second coat of paint.

POLISHING. For a smoother, glossier surface, lightly rub out the finish with a nylon scouring pad. For a really polished surface, buff in a small amount of Danish oil with a soft rag.

Note: The oil will darken the milk paint, so it's a good idea to test it first on a hidden part of the project or on a sample piece of painted wood.

1. *Apply the first coat of milk paint on bare, dampened wood.*
2. *When the first coat is dry, apply the second coat.*
3. *Let paint dry overnight, then smooth by buffing with a nylon scouring pad.*
4. *Polish with a light coat of Danish oil.*

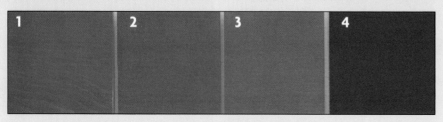

AGING

In Colonial days, a couple coats of milk paint were all that was required for a piece of furniture. With daily use, the paint slowly wore away and exposed some of the wood. And the more the piece was used, the more polished the paint and wood became.

AGED LOOK. To simulate this look, first apply a coat of stain over the bare wood. Once the stain has dried, apply two coats of milk paint. Let the first coat dry before adding the second coat.

The next step is to simulate years of daily use. On the bench, I sanded areas that would have been rubbed on, sat on, and even scuffed with boots and shoes.

Using 180 grit sandpaper, lightly sand the selected areas down to the stain — but don't sand through the stain to expose the bare wood. (If you do happen to sand through the stain, just touch up the area with more stain.)

POLISH. To remove the rough texture and flat, dull look of the milk paint, rub out the entire piece with a nylon scouring pad. Then buff in a coat of Danish oil to darken and polish it.

1. *To simulate aged wood, apply one coat of stain over the bare wood.*
2. *Apply two coats of paint. Let each coat dry thoroughly.*
3. *Lightly sand through the paint to expose the stained wood below.*
4. *Rub out and polish with Danish oil.*

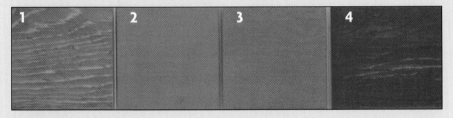

LAYERING PAINT

When a piece of furniture required a new coat of milk paint, sometimes a different color was used. And if the top layer was dinged or scratched, the underlying color would show through.

DINGS AND SCRATCHES. When layering milk paint, I like to give the piece a little "natural" wear first.

To do this, use the edge of a small file to make dings and scratches wherever they may have normally occurred. At first, there's a tendency to be cautious, but once you get started it's easy to get carried away — don't. When you're through distressing, stain the entire piece to simulate aged wood.

LAYERING. Once the stain is dry, apply the first coat of milk paint. When it's dry, apply the second color.

After the paint dries, rub out the entire piece with a nylon scouring pad to remove the paint's rough texture. Then create wear spots and polish the finish with Danish oil.

1. *Apply the first coat of milk paint (red) on stained wood.*
2. *Apply the second coat of paint (blue) over the first color.*
3. *Lightly sand through the top color to expose the bottom color.*
4. *Polish with a light coat of Danish oil.*

ANTIQUE CRACKLE FINISH

Milk paint left in the sun or elements would often dry out and "alligator."

CRACKLE FINISH. To simulate this look, a special crackle gel is used. (For sources, see page 126.)

First, I stained the bare wood. Then I applied the first coat of milk paint.

Note: Only apply stain if you're going to create wear spots later.

Once the milk paint is thoroughly dry, brush the crackle gel on the paint.

Note: You may want to simulate where sunlight took its toll by only applying the crackle gel on places that may have been directly hit by sunlight.

Once the crackle gel has dried for two hours, apply the next color of milk paint. Don't brush this coat of milk paint too much — the paint and gel may mix together into a messy sludge. Simply load the brush up with paint, then apply it in one smooth stroke. The "alligatoring" will appear as the paint dries.

POLISH. When the final coat of paint is dry, rub out the entire piece with a nylon scouring pad. Create wear spots (if desired) and buff with Danish oil.

1. *Apply the first coat of milk paint (red) on stained wood.*
2. *When the first coat is dry, apply crackle gel. Allow to dry two hours.*
3. *Apply the second coat of paint (green) over the gel.*
4. *Polish with a light coat of Danish oil.*

Jelly Cupboard

Back when jelly was made at home, a simple cupboard like this stored the finished product.
But even a simple cupboard can still offer some interesting joinery and several options to "dress it up."

Every fall, my grandma made home-made jelly. After each jar was sealed, it was set in a jelly cupboard similar to this one to cool.

I always liked the "down-home" look of that cabinet and tried to duplicate that appearance with this version.

JOINERY. The shelves in this cupboard could have been mounted on adjustable shelf brackets. But I did something different this time.

By gluing the shelves into dadoes in the cupboard sides, the shelves are permanently attached. This helps keep the cabinet from racking. So the shelves are both functional and structural.

The door frame is assembled with half-lap joints reinforced with dowel pins at the corners. This joint is easily cut on the table saw or router table.

TIN PANELS. The door holds four tin panels. The pattern punched in each one is decorative, but it also serves a practical purpose. The holes allowed air to circulate so moisture from the jelly wouldn't build up inside the cabinet.

And making these panels is easy. Just use a punch and follow a pattern. You can draw your own pattern or *Woodsmith Project Supplies* offers the patterns shown on the opposite page. See page 126 for more details.

The cupboard can also be built with wood raised panels instead of tin. The Designer's Notebook on page 113 shows how to make this option.

BACK SLATS. Ordinarily I use plywood for a cabinet back, but for a "country" project like this, plywood seemed out of place.

So I used solid pine — but not a glued-up panel. Instead, I cut rabbets on the slats for a "ship lap" joint. This allows them to expand and contract without pushing on the cupboard sides.

FINISH. To prevent a blotchy finish, I coated the pine with a sealer first. Then I stained it to make it look aged.

EXPLODED VIEW

OVERALL DIMENSIONS:
20W x 12¾D x 58H

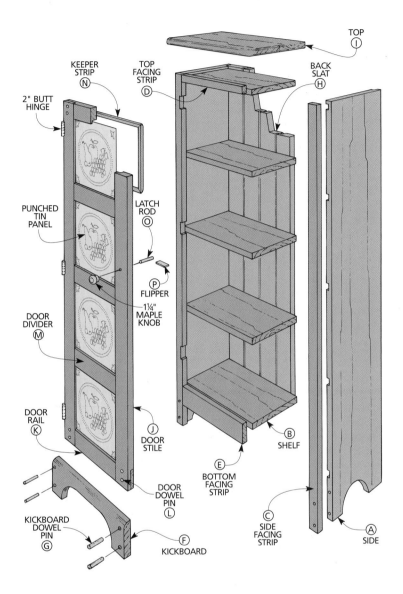

- 2" BUTT HINGE
- KEEPER STRIP (N)
- TOP FACING STRIP (D)
- TOP (I)
- BACK SLAT (H)
- PUNCHED TIN PANEL
- LATCH ROD (O)
- DOOR DIVIDER (M)
- FLIPPER (P)
- 1¼" MAPLE KNOB
- DOOR RAIL (K)
- DOOR STILE (J)
- DOOR DOWEL PIN (L)
- BOTTOM FACING STRIP (E)
- SHELF (B)
- SIDE (A)
- SIDE FACING STRIP (C)
- KICKBOARD DOWEL PIN (G)
- KICKBOARD (F)

PUNCHED TIN PATTERNS
(SEE SOURCES ON PAGE 126)

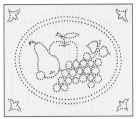

HARVEST FRUIT

GRANDMA'S PIE

HEARTS ON A BLANKET

FRUIT BASKET

SPRING FLOWERS

DAISY SWIRL

MATERIALS LIST

CASE

A	Sides (2)	¾ x 11¼ - 57¼
B	Shelves (5)	¾ x 10½ - 17¾
C	Side Facing Str. (2)	¾ x 1 - 57¼
D	Top Facing Strip (1)	¾ x 1 - 16½
E	Bot. Facing Strip (1)	¾ x 2 - 16½
F	Kickboard (1)	¾ x 5½ - 18½
G	Kickbd. Dwl. Pins (4)	¼ dowel - 2¼
H	Back Slats (4)	¾ x 4⅝ - 51¼
I	Top (1)	¾ x 12¾ - 20

DOOR

J	Door Stiles (2)	¾ x 2½ - 49⅝
K	Door Rails (2)	¾ x 2½ - 16⅜
L	Door Dowel Pins (8)	¼ dowel - ¾
M	Door Dividers (3)	¾ x 2½ - 12⅛
N	Keeper Strips (16)	¼ x ¼ - 13 rough
O	Latch Rod (1)	⅜ dowel - 1⅝
P	Flipper (1)	⅛ x ½ - 1¹¹⁄₁₆

HARDWARE SUPPLIES

(24) No. 8 x 1½" Fh woodscrews
(6) No. 8 x 1¾" Fh woodscrews
(3) 2" x 1⁹⁄₁₆" butt hinges w/ screws
(4 pieces) 10" x 14" tin (rough size)
(40) ½" wire brads
(1) 1¼"-dia. maple knob
(20) 4d (1½"-long) square cut finish nails (optional)

CUTTING DIAGRAM

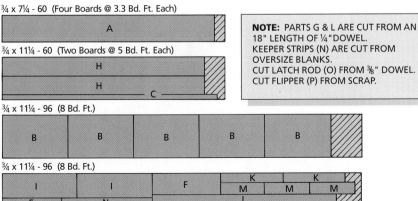

¾ x 7¼ - 60 (Four Boards @ 3.3 Bd. Ft. Each)
A

¾ x 11¼ - 60 (Two Boards @ 5 Bd. Ft. Each)
H
H
C

¾ x 11¼ - 96 (8 Bd. Ft.)
B B B B B

¾ x 11¼ - 96 (8 Bd. Ft.)
I I F K K
M M M
J
E D N J
N

NOTE: PARTS G & L ARE CUT FROM AN 18" LENGTH OF ¼" DOWEL. KEEPER STRIPS (N) ARE CUT FROM OVERSIZE BLANKS. CUT LATCH ROD (O) FROM ⅜" DOWEL. CUT FLIPPER (P) FROM SCRAP.

Back when cupboards like this were a common fixture in the kitchen or pantry, they would probably have been made of knotty pine. So to make this jelly cupboard look authentic, I used No. 2 common pine.

After letting the lumber dry out in the shop for two weeks, I started work on the sides of the cupboard.

CUT TO SIZE. In order to minimize the cupping that may occur with wide boards, I edge-glued each of the sides from two narrower boards. When the glue dried, I cut the sides (A) to a finished width of 11¼" and finished length of 57¼" *(Fig. 1)*.

SHELF DADOES. Five shelves hold the sides of the cupboard together. The shelves are held in dadoes spaced apart evenly *(Fig. 1)*. But there are a couple tricks to routing the dadoes in the sides and getting them to align after the cupboard is assembled.

First, I clamped both cupboard sides together with their top ends flush and the inside faces *up (Fig. 1)*. Then I laid out the positions of the dadoes by measuring down from the top end.

To follow the layout lines for the dadoes, I guided the router against a straightedge clamped to the workpiece. And because the pine for the shelves was slightly *less* than ¾" thick, I used a ½" straight bit in the router. I routed each dado to the correct width in two

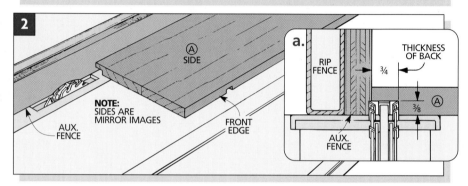

passes by using a removable spacer against the straightedge *(Fig. 1)*. (Refer to the Shop Tip below for details.)

BACK RABBET. After routing the dadoes for the shelves, a rabbet can be cut in each cupboard side for installing the back slats *(Figs. 2 and 2a)*.

Note: To make sure the rabbets are routed along the correct edges (the sides are "mirror" images), it helps to stand the sides up first and mark the edges to be rabbeted.

DECORATIVE CUTOUTS. The last cuts to make on the cupboard sides look simply to be decorative — but they also serve a purpose.

The semi-circular cutout at the bottom of each piece creates a pair of "feet." *(Fig. 3)*. This allows the cabinet to "bridge" uneven spots in the floor.

SHOP TIP.................Routing Custom-Fit Dadoes

When cutting a dado in a large panel, I find using a hand-held router is easier than wrestling with a large panel on my table saw or router table.

Since lumber is rarely the exact same thickness as the diameter of a router bit, I use a smaller bit and make two passes.

To do this, I set up a

fence with a spacer strip that determines the exact finished width of the dado. The width of the strip, plus the diameter of the router bit should equal

the finished width of the dado *(Fig. 1a)*. After the first pass, remove the spacer. Then make the second pass to complete the dado *(Fig. 2)*.

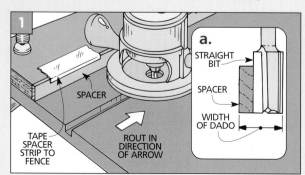

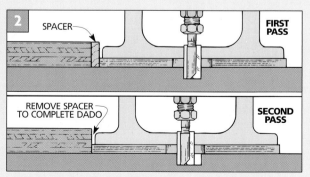

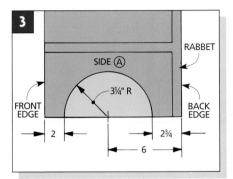

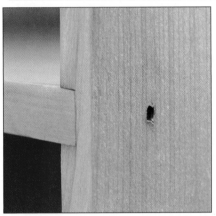

NOTE: IF 1x12 IS CUPPED, RIP SHELF INTO THIRDS AND REGLUE WITH MIDDLE PIECE UPSIDE DOWN, THEN PLANE FLAT

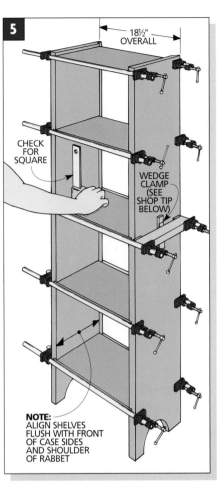

Note: Although the feet start out different widths, they'll end up the same after a facing strip is added to the front (refer to *Fig. 6* on page 110).

After laying out the arcs, I used a jig saw to cut just shy of the layout lines. Then I smoothed up to the line with a drum sander.

SHELVES. Next, I started on the shelves. I cut these from 1x12s. A single board this wide will often cup. If your stock is cupped, one way to flatten it is to rip each shelf blank into thirds. Then glue the blank together with the middle piece upside down. When the glue dries, plane the blank flat.

Now the shelves can be ripped to width so they're flush with the front edges of the sides and also the shoulders of the rabbets for the back slats *(Fig. 5)*. Then cut the shelves (B) to finished length *(Fig. 4)*. To determine this length, measure between the bottoms of the dadoes on the case sides.

ASSEMBLY. Finally, the case can be

Square-cut nails are an authentic detail. To prevent splitting the wood, drill pilot holes before driving the nails. Then "set" the heads just below the surface with a punch before sanding the side.

assembled with the shelves glued into the dadoes *(Fig. 5)*. The Shop Tip below shows one way to do this.

Note: Keep the shelves flush to the front edges of the sides (A).

If you don't have enough clamps (or for an authentic antique touch), you could assemble the case with square-cut nails (see the photo above). (For sources of these nails, see page 126.)

SHOP TIP .... *Clamping With Wedges*

While dry-assembling the jelly cupboard, I ran into a problem. When the shelves were clamped between the sides, the centers of the side panels cupped out *(Fig. 1)*.

I came up with a fix that uses opposing wedges. These wedges work against a clamping bar that "straddles" the sides *(Fig. 2)*. This bar is simply a 2x4 block with a ½"-thick

spacer glued on each end. I stuck the spacers to the side of the cabinet using carpet tape. Then I clamped the cupboard assembly together.

To force the center of

the side panel tight against the shelf, tap opposing wedges between the clamping bar and the sides until the shelf is completely seated in the dado *(Fig. 2)*.

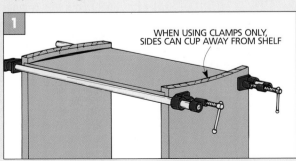

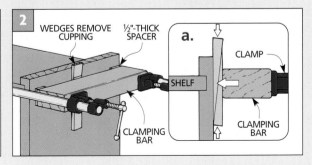

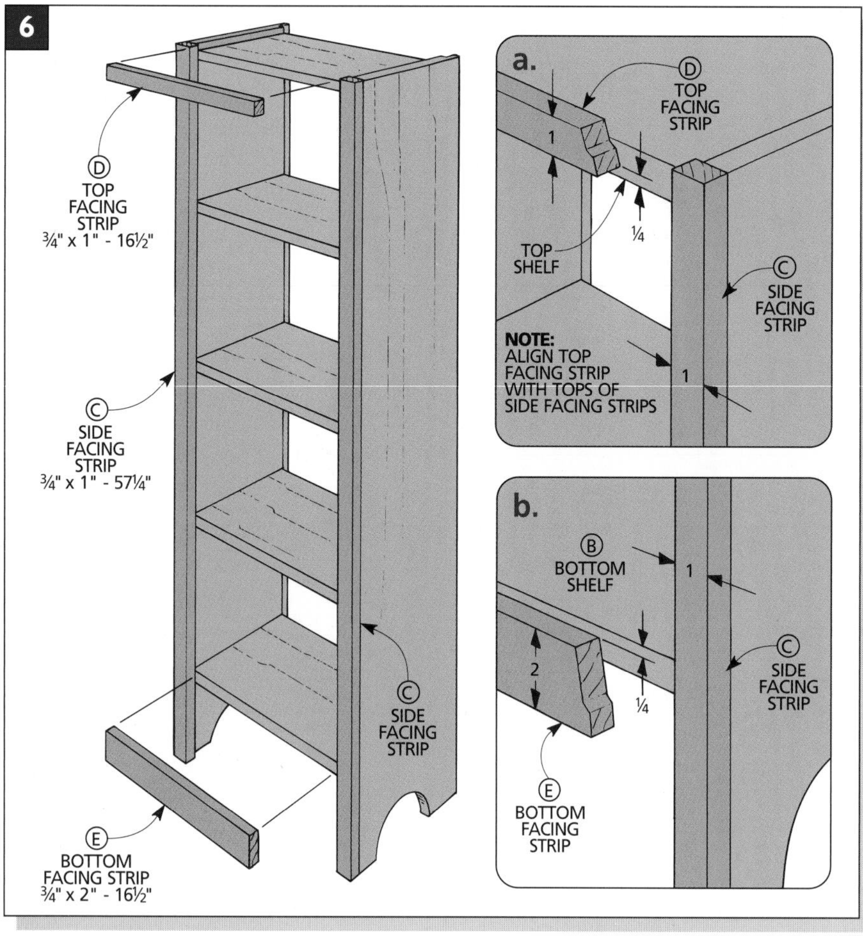
6
Ⓓ TOP FACING STRIP ¾" x 1" - 16½"
Ⓒ SIDE FACING STRIP ¾" x 1" - 57¼"
Ⓔ BOTTOM FACING STRIP ¾" x 2" - 16½"
Ⓒ SIDE FACING STRIP
a.
Ⓓ TOP FACING STRIP
1
¼
TOP SHELF
Ⓒ SIDE FACING STRIP
NOTE: ALIGN TOP FACING STRIP WITH TOPS OF SIDE FACING STRIPS
1
b.
Ⓑ BOTTOM SHELF
1
2
¼
Ⓒ SIDE FACING STRIP
Ⓔ BOTTOM FACING STRIP

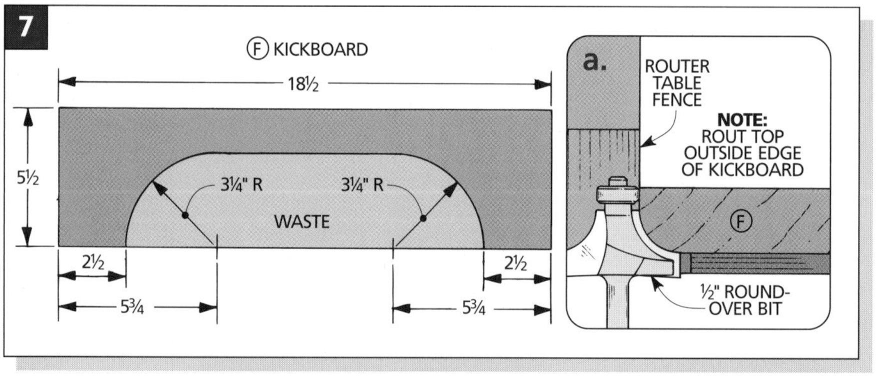
7
Ⓕ KICKBOARD
18½
5½
3¼" R
3¼" R
WASTE
2½
2½
5¾
5¾
a.
ROUTER TABLE FENCE
NOTE: ROUT TOP OUTSIDE EDGE OF KICKBOARD
Ⓕ
½" ROUND-OVER BIT

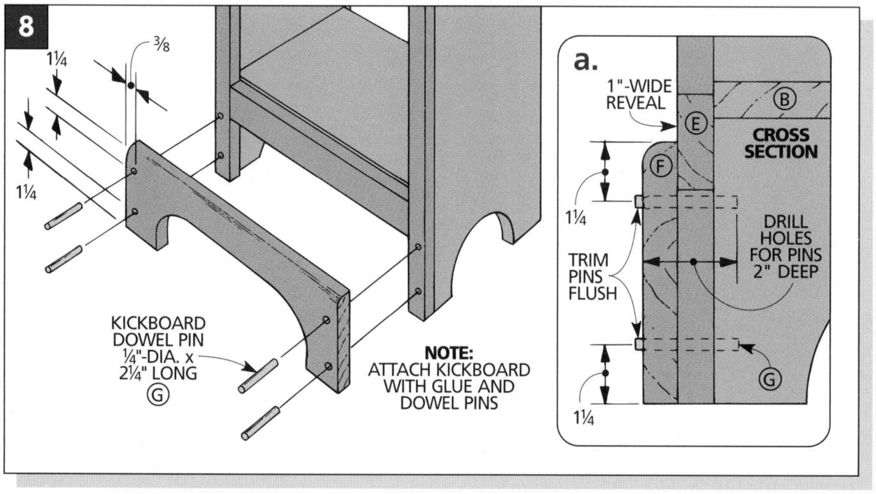
8
1¼
⅜
1¼
KICKBOARD DOWEL PIN ¼"-DIA. x 2¼" LONG Ⓖ
NOTE: ATTACH KICKBOARD WITH GLUE AND DOWEL PINS
a.
1"-WIDE REVEAL
Ⓔ
Ⓑ
CROSS SECTION
Ⓕ
1¼
DRILL HOLES FOR PINS 2" DEEP
TRIM PINS FLUSH
Ⓖ
1¼

FACING STRIPS

To create a frame that surrounds the door, facing strips are added next.

The facing strips are attached to the front edges of the cabinet sides and to the top and bottom shelves *(Fig. 6)*.

RIP TO WIDTH. First, I ripped two side facing strips (C) and one top facing strip (D) to a width of 1" *(Fig. 6)*.

SIDE STRIPS. Now cut the side strips to the same length as the cupboard sides. Then glue these to the sides, flush with the outside edges.

TOP AND BOTTOM STRIPS. Next, I ripped a 2"-wide piece for the bottom facing strip (E) *(Fig. 6)*.

Then the top and bottom facing strips (D, E) can be cut to length to fit snugly between the side strips.

ATTACH TO CASE. Before gluing on the top and bottom strips, make marks on the top and bottom shelves to indicate where the strips should be glued on *(Figs. 6a and 6b)*. By leaving 1/4" of each shelf edge exposed, a lip is created at the top and bottom of the door opening. These lips serve as stops for the door (attached later).

KICKBOARD

A kickboard at the bottom of the cupboard adds a decorative touch.

CUT TO SIZE. To make the kickboard (F), first rip a piece of 3/4"-thick stock to a width of 5 1/2" *(Fig. 7)*. Then cut it to length to match the width of the case.

ROUND OVER TOP EDGE. Next, to soften the transition between the kickboard and the lower facing strip, rout a 1/2" roundover along the top outside edge of the kickboard *(Fig. 7a)*.

TOE OPENING. To make a toe opening on the kickboard, I used my jig saw to cut out a profile along the bottom edge *(Fig. 7)*.

ATTACH TO CASE. Now the kickboard can be attached to the case. But I did this with dowel pins (G) *(Fig. 8)*. First, clamp the kickboard to the case and drill two 1/4"-dia. holes that go through the kickboard and facing strip into the cupboard side *(Fig. 8a)*.

Then cut four lengths of dowel to fit in the holes.

Note: Cut the dowels so they stand proud of the kickboard when they're tapped into the holes *(Fig. 8a)*. Then they can be trimmed and sanded flush after they're glued in place.

BACK & TOP

The back of the cupboard is made of individual slats to allow for plenty of expansion and contraction.

CUT TO SIZE. To make the back, start by ripping four back slats (H) from $3/4$"-thick stock to the same width *(Fig. 9)*. The finished width allows for a $1/16$" gap between the installed slats *(Fig. 9a)*.

Next, cut the slats to finished length so they extend from the top of the cabinet sides to the bottom of the lower shelf *(Fig. 9)*.

SHIP LAPS. The ship lap joint is really just overlapping rabbets. The rabbets are cut to a depth half the thickness of the pieces ($3/8$"), and to identical width.

Note: Cut rabbets on the *opposite* edges of the middle slats, but on just *one* edge of each outside slat *(Fig. 9a)*.

ATTACH SLATS. Now the back slats can be screwed to the cabinet, keeping the gaps between them equal *(Fig. 9a)*.

TOP. The top (I) is an edge-glued blank *(Fig. 10)*. Cut it to finished size to allow for a $3/4$" overhang at the front and sides *(Fig. 10a)* but *not* the back.

Next, rout $1/8$" roundovers on the edges of the top, and sand a $1/8$" radius on the corners. Now the top can be attached using woodscrews driven up from below *(Fig. 10a)*.

DOOR FRAME

The door of the cupboard is a frame and panel unit. Its construction is the same whether you use tin or wood panels.

DOOR FRAME. To make the door frame, start by ripping two door stiles (J) and two door rails (K) to finished width *(Fig. 11)*.

Then, to determine the length of the pieces, measure between the facing strips and subtract $1/8$" to allow for a $1/16$" gap all around the door. Cut the frame pieces to finished length *(Fig. 11)*.

END LAPS. Now cut the end lap joints half the thickness of each of the mating pieces *(Fig. 11a)*.

After the lap joints are cut, the frame can be glued and clamped together.

CORNER PINS. Next, I drilled two $1/4$"-dia. holes through each corner of the frame for the dowel pins (L) *(Fig. 11a)*. Then glue the pins into the holes and trim them flush with the frame.

RABBET. When the frame is assembled, rout a rabbet around the perimeter of the door opening in the back side *(Figs. 12 and 12a)*. This creates a lip for the door panels.

When the rabbet is cut, square up the corners with a chisel *(Fig. 12b)*.

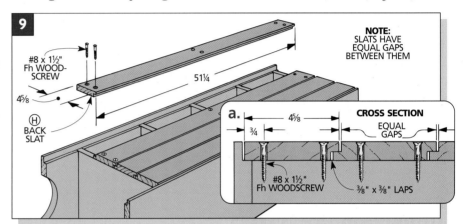

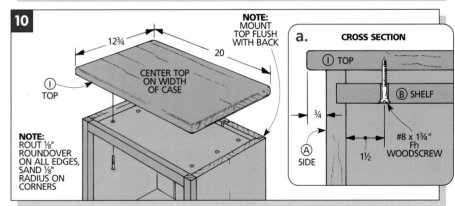

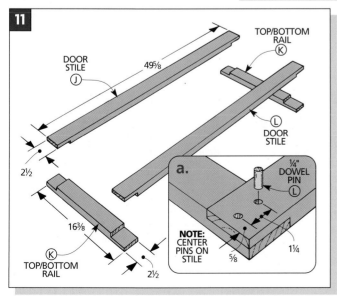

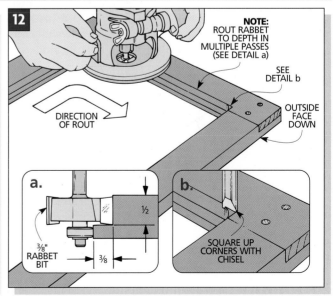

When the frame of the door is complete, the dividers (M) can be built. The purpose of the dividers is to separate — and support — the door panels.

CENTER DIVIDERS. Start by ripping three blanks to finished width *(Fig. 13)*. Then cut them to length to fit between the rabbets in the door frame.

TONGUES. The dividers are held in place by a short tongue on each end *(Fig. 13)*. I used a dado blade to cut the rabbets that form the tongues *(Fig. 14)*.

EDGE RABBETS. Now the dividers can fit flush down into the frame. But first, in order to completely support the panels, two more rabbets are needed on the edges of each divider *(Fig. 15a)*.

To cut these rabbets, I again used my dado blade *(Fig. 15)*. Cut these with the front of the divider facing up.

KEEPER STRIPS. Once the dividers are glued in place, work can begin on the keeper strips.

The panels are held in place by small quarter-round keeper strips (N) that are nailed to the door frame *(Fig. 13a)*. To make these keeper strips, first rout $^1/_4$" roundovers on both edges of a blank *(Fig. 16)*. Then set the rip fence $^1/_4$" from the blade and cut a $^3/_8$"-deep kerf on each edge. Finally, to separate a keeper strip from each edge, run the blank through the blade face down so the keeper strip falls to the waste side *(Fig. 17)*. This prevents kickback.

TIN PANELS. To make the tin panels, tape your pattern to the tin blank, then fasten the blank to a hardboard backing board. Punch the holes by striking an awl with a hammer. Use softer strikes for smaller holes, heavier strikes for larger holes. When each panel is finished, trim it to size and secure it in the door *(Fig. 13a)*.

MORTISES. After the panels are in place, the door is attached to the case. I used three 2"-long hinges and cut a

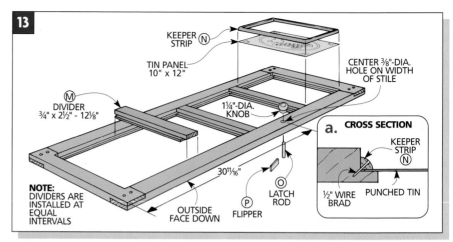

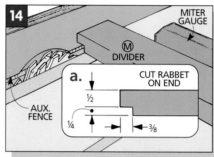

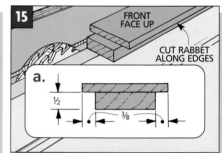

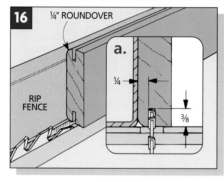

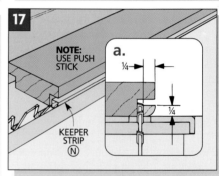

shallow mortise for each hinge in the door stile and the facing strip *(Fig. 18a and the Exploded View on page 107)*.

DOOR KNOB. Next, I built a knob and latch assembly. To start, drill a $^3/_8$"-dia. hole through the door stile *(Fig. 13)*. Then drill a hole in the wooden knob to accept a length of dowel (O) *(Fig. 19a)*.

A short "flipper" (P) fits in a slot in the end of the dowel *(Fig. 19)*. When the knob is turned, the flipper will catch the facing strip and prevent the door from swinging open (see photo).

FINISH. Now the cupboard can be stained and finished. Since pine can stain unevenly, use a sealer first. ∎

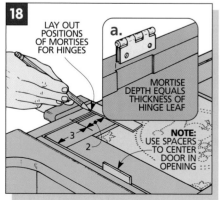

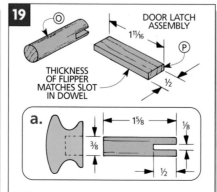

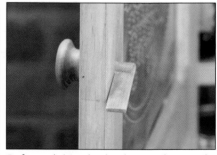

Before gluing the latch together, make sure it will rotate. If it doesn't, lightly sand the dowel until it does.

DESIGNER'S NOTEBOOK

Change the look of the cupboard just by using solid wood panels instead of punched tin. These raised panels can be made entirely on the table saw.

CONSTRUCTION NOTES:

■ To make the wood panels (Q), glue up four blanks from $3/4$"-thick stock.

■ Measure the rabbeted openings in the back of the door frame. Cut the panels $1/8$" less than these measurements to allow for a $1/16$" gap all around *(Fig. 2)*.

■ To steady the panels, fasten a tall auxiliary fence to the table saw rip fence *(Fig. 1)*. Then tilt the table saw blade 10° and raise the blade to $1^3/8$".

■ Cut the bevels in two passes, moving the rip fence slightly between passes. The first pass removes most of the waste. The second "skim" cut cleans up burn marks or blade swirls and creates the $1/16$"-wide shoulder *(Fig. 2)*.

Note: Before moving the rip fence for the second pass, cut the bevels on all the edges of all your panels.

Cut across the end grain edges first. Then any chipout will be removed when the cut is made on the face grain edges.

■ The tilted blade will slightly undercut the shoulder. To square it up, make a sanding block with a bevel on one edge that matches the bevel on the panels.

■ To make a tongue on the edge of the panel, cut a $3/4$"-wide rabbet $1/4$" deep on the back edges *(Fig. 2)*.

■ Now, fasten the panels in the door with keeper strips *(Fig. 2)*.

RAISED PANELS

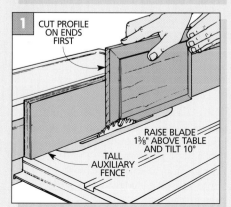

CUT PROFILE ON ENDS FIRST

RAISE BLADE $1^3/8$" ABOVE TABLE AND TILT 10°

TALL AUXILIARY FENCE

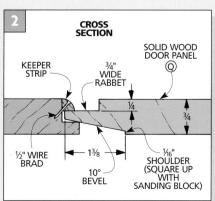

CROSS SECTION

KEEPER STRIP

$3/4$" WIDE RABBET

SOLID WOOD DOOR PANEL Q

$1/4$

$3/4$

$1/2$" WIRE BRAD

$1^3/8$

10° BEVEL

$1/16$" SHOULDER (SQUARE UP WITH SANDING BLOCK)

If a panel shrinks, an unfinished edge may be exposed. To prevent this, apply finish before mounting it in the frame.

Dovetail Chest

Hand-cut dovetails give this chest a traditional country look and also add strength to each corner. For a different look, try the frame and panel version. Both offer plenty of storage and a pull-out tray.

You don't want to rush hand-cut dovetails. They require careful, deliberate work. That doesn't mean they have to be perfect. After all, hand-cut dovetails aren't going to be machine-precise — especially when you're working with wide panels. But that fits the charm of this chest.

STEP-BY-STEP DOVETAILS. There was a time when I found the thought of cutting dovetails by hand rather intimidating. But that was before someone walked me through it step-by-step. So if you've never tried your hand at cutting this joint, we have complete, detailed instructions beginning on page 120.

FRAME AND PANEL OPTION. We also offer a frame and panel version of the chest. This style has a more formal appearance. Details on building this chest are in the Designer's Notebook on page 124.

TRAY. Both versions offer a lift-out tray. It rides on a couple of runners fastened to the front and back of the chest, so there's still storage below it.

The tray is built with a single wide tail at each corner. So even if you don't cut the dovetails for the chest, the tray offers a chance to try the technique on a smaller scale. It's sort of a "project within a project."

FINISH. I wanted a finish that would match the "antique" character of the chest. So I chose a finish that adds character to many antiques — shellac.

Shellac has been used on furniture a long time, and its color adds a natural warmth that's hard to get from an off-the-shelf stain.

Of course, many woodworkers think of shellac as a "delicate" finish. And while it may not match the durability of polyurethane, a lot of antiques finished with shellac have put up with years of wear. And it's not difficult to apply either. For step-by-step instructions, see the box on page 119.

EXPLODED VIEW

OVERALL DIMENSIONS:
$38\frac{1}{8}$W x $18\frac{1}{8}$D x $19\frac{9}{16}$H

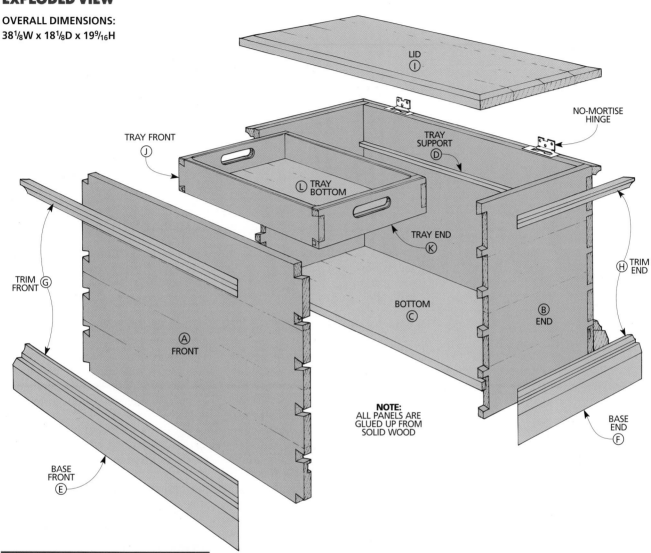

LID
(I)

NO-MORTISE
HINGE

TRAY FRONT
(J)

TRAY
SUPPORT
(D)

TRAY
BOTTOM
(L)

TRAY END
(K)

TRIM
FRONT (G)

TRIM
END
(H)

FRONT
(A)

BOTTOM
(C)

END
(B)

BASE
FRONT
(E)

BASE
END
(F)

NOTE:
ALL PANELS ARE
GLUED UP FROM
SOLID WOOD

MATERIALS LIST

WOOD

A	Front/Back (2)	$\frac{3}{4}$ x $18\frac{1}{2}$ - 36
B	Ends (2)	$\frac{3}{4}$ x $18\frac{1}{2}$ - 16
C	Bottom (1)	$\frac{3}{4}$ x $15\frac{1}{8}$ - $35\frac{1}{8}$
D	Tray Supports (2)	$\frac{3}{4}$ x $\frac{3}{8}$ - $34\frac{1}{2}$
E	Base Frt./Bk. (2)	$1\frac{1}{16}$ x 3 - 40 rough
F	Base Ends (2)	$1\frac{1}{16}$ x 3 - 20 rough
G	Trim Frt./Bk. (4)	$\frac{1}{2}$ x $\frac{3}{4}$ - 40 rough
H	Trim Ends (4)	$\frac{1}{2}$ x $\frac{3}{4}$ - 20 rough
I	Lid (1)	$1\frac{1}{16}$ x 18 - 38
J	Tray Frt./Bk. (2)	$\frac{3}{4}$ x $3\frac{1}{2}$ - 24
K	Tray Ends (2)	$\frac{3}{4}$ x $3\frac{1}{2}$ - $14\frac{3}{8}$
L	Tray Bottom (1)	$\frac{1}{2}$ x $13\frac{1}{2}$ - $23\frac{1}{8}$

HARDWARE SUPPLIES

(2) No. 8 x $\frac{5}{8}$" Rh brass screws
(1) 15" brass chain
(1 pr.) 3" no-mortise hinges w/ screws

CUTTING DIAGRAM

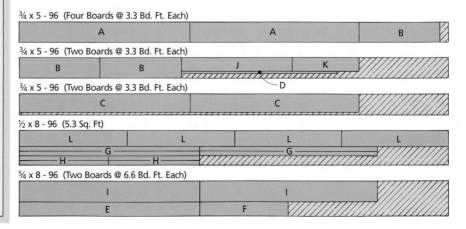

$\frac{3}{4}$ x 5 - 96 (Four Boards @ 3.3 Bd. Ft. Each)

A	A	B

$\frac{3}{4}$ x 5 - 96 (Two Boards @ 3.3 Bd. Ft. Each)

B	B	J	K

D

$\frac{3}{4}$ x 5 - 96 (Two Boards @ 3.3 Bd. Ft. Each)

C	C

$\frac{1}{2}$ x 8 - 96 (5.3 Sq. Ft)

L	L	L	L

G | G

H | H

$\frac{5}{4}$ x 8 - 96 (Two Boards @ 6.6 Bd. Ft. Each)

I	I
E	F

This dovetail chest starts out as you'd expect: gluing up oversized panels for each of the sides and for the bottom. There isn't anything unusual or difficult about these five ³⁄₄"-thick panels. The important thing is that they are flat and that the four side panels are all the same thickness. This will make it much easier when it comes time to cut the dovetails.

After the panels are glued up, the next step is to cut the front/back panels (A) and end panels (B) to finished size *(Fig. 1)*. (The bottom will be cut to size later.) I began by simply ripping each of these panels to width. But when crosscutting, the long panels require some extra support. To do this, I added a long auxiliary fence to the miter gauge. This way, it's much easier to get the ends of the panels square to the sides.

DOVETAILS. After the panels are cut to size, work can begin on the dovetails. The dovetails are laid out 3¹⁄₂" on center *(Fig. 2)*. This allows for 3"-wide tails and ¹⁄₂" pins.

Actually, not all the pins are ¹⁄₂". The top one is a little wider (1"). But the extra width is covered by some molding

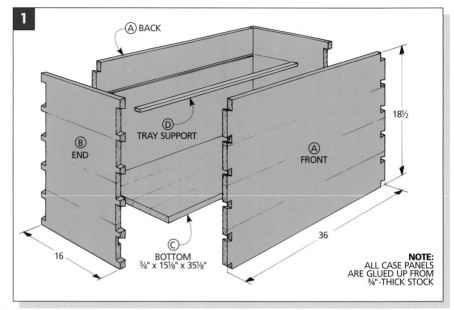

18½

NOTE:
ALL CASE PANELS
ARE GLUED UP FROM
³⁄₄"-THICK STOCK

added later, so once the chest is completed, it looks the same as the other pins *(Fig. 3)*.

With the layout finished, the pins and tails can now be cut.

Note: For step-by-step instructions on cutting dovetails by hand, see the Joinery article beginning on page 120.

GROOVES. When the dovetails are complete, there are some grooves to cut in the panels before you can assemble the case. I used a dado blade in the table saw to cut these.

The first two grooves are for the tray supports (added later). They are ³⁄₈" wide, ³⁄₈" deep, and cut on the inside faces of the front and back panels *only* *(Fig. 4)*. I centered these grooves in one of the pin openings. This way the pins on the end panels will hide the grooves when the case is assembled.

The other groove is for the bottom of the chest *(Fig. 5)*. It's ³⁄₄" wide, ³⁄₈" deep, and cut in all four pieces. This groove cuts through a tail, so it'll be visible from the outside when the case is

first assembled. But don't worry about this. Later, the groove will be covered by the molding that's fastened to the bottom of the case.

BOTTOM. Now it's time to begin work on the bottom panel (C). But to do this, first you need to dry-assemble the case. Then you can measure the case opening to determine the final size of the bottom *(Fig. 1)*. Remember to include the depth of both grooves in this measurement.

Because the bottom is a solid wood panel and not plywood, it needs enough room to expand and contract with changes in humidity. To allow for this movement, I cut the bottom (C) ¹⁄₈" smaller than each dimension *(Fig. 5a)*. (Mine was 15¹⁄₈" x 35¹⁄₈".)

CASE ASSEMBLY. After the bottom panel is ready, you can glue the case together *(Fig. 6)*. (But don't use glue on the bottom.) This takes quite a bit of time, so I used white glue. It sets up more slowly than yellow glue, so it gives you a little more time to work.

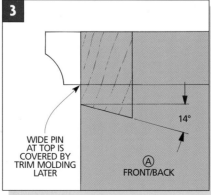

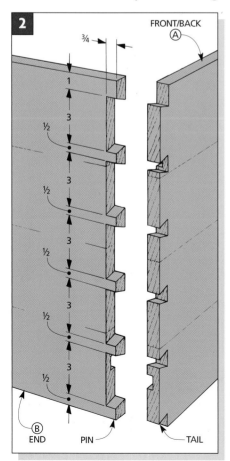

WIDE PIN
AT TOP IS
COVERED BY
TRIM MOLDING
LATER

14°

Ⓐ
FRONT/BACK

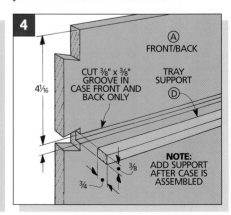

Ⓐ
FRONT/BACK

CUT ³⁄₈" x ³⁄₈"
GROOVE IN
CASE FRONT AND
BACK ONLY

TRAY
SUPPORT
Ⓓ

4¹⁄₁₆

³⁄₈

³⁄₄

NOTE:
ADD SUPPORT
AFTER CASE IS
ASSEMBLED

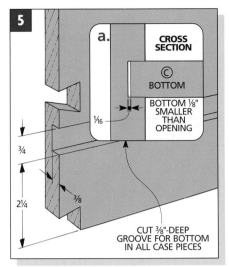

5

a. CROSS SECTION

© BOTTOM

BOTTOM ⅛" SMALLER THAN OPENING

1/16

¾

2¼

⅜

CUT ⅜"-DEEP GROOVE FOR BOTTOM IN ALL CASE PIECES

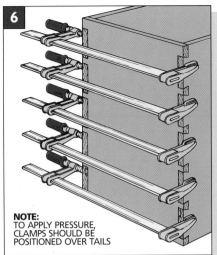

6

NOTE: TO APPLY PRESSURE, CLAMPS SHOULD BE POSITIONED OVER TAILS

First, glue both end panels (B) to the front panel (A). Then slide the bottom panel (C) into the groove before adding the back panel to the assembly.

TRAY SUPPORTS. While the glue is drying, cut two ¾"-wide tray supports (D) to fit in the grooves inside the case (*Fig. 4*). This time, I wanted the glue to set up fast, so I used yellow glue. That way, I didn't have to worry about using clamps. Applying a little hand pressure for a minute or two was all it took.

At this point, the case is essentially complete. But if there are pins or tails protruding, you'll need to sand them flush with the sides of the case (see the Shop Tip at right). If some pins or tails need more trimming than can be easily sanded, see the Shop Jig box below for one way to trim them down.

After the case is assembled and the corners are smoothed, all that's left to do is add the base molding, the trim molding, and the lid.

SHOP TIP
Sanding Flush

If the pins or tails (or both) stand proud of the side, one way to get them flush is to use a belt sander. However, it's easy to accidentally round over a corner. To prevent this, clamp a scrap piece across the end of the case flush with the panel the sander is riding on.

SHOP JIG . . . . Flush Trim Jig

With this jig, a straight bit will trim any over-long pins or tails perfectly flush with the sides.

This jig replaces the plastic base of the router. That's because the edge of a regular base will run into the pins or

tails before the bit can get near enough to trim them flush. To solve that problem, this auxiliary base raises the router above the case side.

The base is simply a ¾"-thick piece of stock with a wide rabbet cut on the bottom (*Step 1*).

To make the base stable, it's cut extra long (mine was 11"). And for added control, there's a block screwed and glued to one end for a handle. Use the plastic base from your router as a template to mark the mounting holes and the bit hole.

To use the jig, simply adjust the bit height so it trims the pins or tails flush (*Step 2*). To do this, set the jig on the case side. Then adjust the bit so it just barely grazes the side panel. Now, with the bit extended past the case, turn on the router. Move it onto the case and begin trimming. A slow feed rate will help prevent chipout.

HANDLE

1½

¾

¼

7

4

1½

BASE

6

3¾

1½" DIA.-HOLE

3

3

11

1 First, build an auxiliary base from ¾"-thick stock. A straight bit in the router trims the sides of the joint flush. The wide rabbet along the front of the jig provides clearance for the bit.

2 With the base on the case side, set the bit so it barely touches the case. Move the bit off the case, start the router, and trim the joint.

FEED THE ROUTER SLOWLY WHEN TRIMMING THE PINS OR TAILS

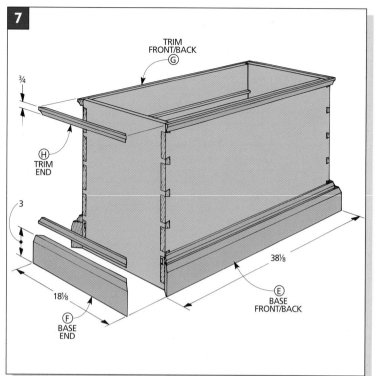

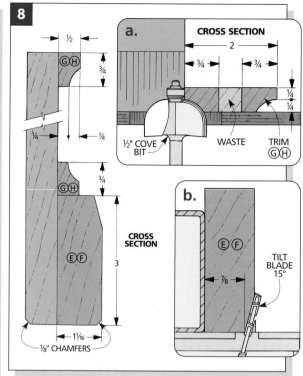

MOLDING

I've seen wide, thick base molding on some older chests, and I wanted the base on this chest to look the same. So instead of using 3/4"-thick stock, I cut the base pieces from 1 1/16"-thick stock.

BASE. The base front/back (E) and base ends (F) are first cut to rough length from 3"-wide blanks. Next, cut a decorative chamfer along the top edge *(Fig. 8b)*. I did this on the table saw with the blade angled 15°. Then to complete the base, miter the pieces to length and glue them to the case.

TRIM MOLDING. The next pieces to add are some strips of trim molding *(Fig. 7)*. Some of this trim will sit on top of the base molding. The rest will end up flush with the top of the case.

To make the trim front/back (G) and trim ends (H), start with blanks that are 1/2" thick and 2" wide *(Fig. 8a)*. Rout a 1/2" cove along two edges. Then two 3/4"-wide (tall) trim pieces can be ripped from each blank. Miter the pieces to length and glue them in place. (The cove profiles should face each other.)

Finally, to prevent chipping the edge if the chest gets dragged across the floor, rout 1/8" chamfers on the bottom edges of the case and molding *(Fig. 8)*.

LID

Now that the case is complete, I started work on the lid *(Fig. 9)*. This means you'll need to glue up another panel. But this panel is 1 1/16" thick.

Since you lift the lid from the edges, I wanted it to overhang the case a bit. So to determine the size of the lid (I), mea-

sure the case (including the trim) and cut the lid panel 1" longer and wider.

CHAMFER. I also wanted the lid to have the same chamfer that's around the base. But the panel is too long to stand on end on the table saw. So I used a block plane to cut this.

Before planing, lay out the edges of the chamfer *(Fig. 10)*. Then plane down to these lines, starting with the ends of the lid. To avoid chipout, skew the plane slightly so it shears off thin shavings.

HINGES. When the chamfer is cut, mount the lid to the case. To do this, I used a special "no-mortise hinge." It has an offset barrel and, as you'd expect,

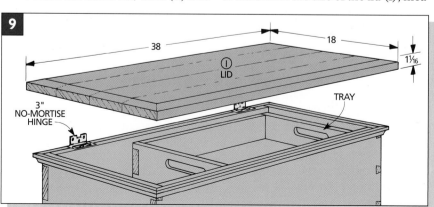

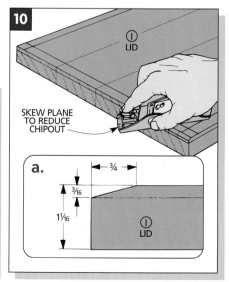

doesn't require a mortise *(Fig. 11)*. (See page 126 for sources of this hinge.)

To mount the hinges, first screw them to the case. Next, set the lid on top of the case and center it side-to-side and front-to-back. Then simply trace around the barrels of the hinges on the bottom of the lid. Now remove the lid and hinges. Then screw the hinges to the lid and reattach the hinges to the case.

LID SUPPORT CHAIN. The last thing to add is a 15"-long piece of brass chain to the inside of the case *(Fig. 11)*. This prevents the lid from dropping back.

Safety Note: If children will be opening and closing this lid, you should protect their fingers by installing a lid support. (For sources, see page 126.)

TRAY

With the lid attached, the last step is to build a tray that fits in the case and slides back and forth on tray supports.

First, the tray front/back (J) and tray ends (K) are cut to finished size. Then to join these pieces, I cut the dovetails by hand *(Figs. 12 and 13)*.

GROOVE AND BOTTOM. Next, I cut a $1/4$"-wide groove $3/8$" deep in each piece for the tray bottom *(Fig. 13)*.

The tray bottom (L) is a solid wood panel, glued up from $1/2$"-thick stock *(Fig. 12)*. After the glue dried, I cut the bottom to finished size. The panel should fit inside the tray (including the grooves) minus $1/8$". Of course, a $1/2$"-thick panel won't fit into a $1/4$" groove. So I cut a $3/8$"-wide rabbet along the bottom edge of the tray bottom to create a $1/4$"-thick tongue *(Fig. 13)*.

HANDLES. Next, I wanted to add some "handles" to the ends of the tray. These handles are simply slots drilled and cut in the end pieces *(Fig. 14)*. To do this, first drill 1"-dia. holes to establish the length of the handle slot. Then clean out the waste between the holes with a jig saw. Now sand the handles and rout small chamfers on both the inside and outside edges. When that's done, the tray can be glued together.

FINAL TOUCHES. There are just two steps left. First, you want to chamfer the inside and outside edges so there are no sharp corners *(Fig. 12)*. And finally, don't forget to plug the holes in the end pieces that were created by the grooves for the tray bottom *(Fig. 12)*. ∎

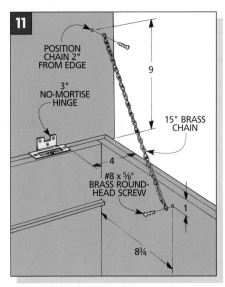

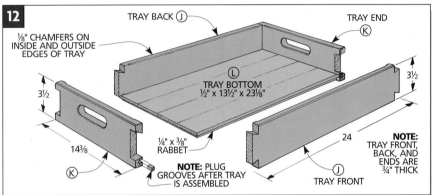

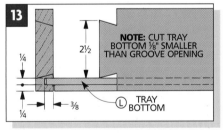

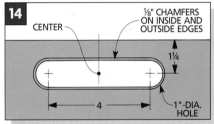

FINISHING TIP .... Shellac

To give the chest a warm, "aged" color, I used three coats of shellac.

The first coat was orange shellac. This gave the wood a nice, warm color — and it doesn't blotch like a pigment-based stain will.

Then to keep the color light, but still add more protection, I applied two coats of blonde shellac.

Shellac comes ready-to-use or in flakes that must be dissolved in alcohol. (See page 126 for sources.) Once dissolved, it begins to slowly deteriorate. So that I know it's

fresh, I mix my own from flakes.

Shellac is mixed in "pound cuts" — the number of pounds of flakes to a gallon of alcohol. I used a 2 lb. cut. But I only mixed up a pint at a time (which requires 4 oz. of shellac flakes). Don't worry about being precise. Just get it in the ballpark.

To apply shellac, I use a natural bristle brush. Don't work the finish too much with the brush. The shellac dries fast, so you can sand lightly after about three hours and apply another coat.

Which comes first, the pins or the tails? Frankly, you can cut them either way, but I like to start with the pins. There are some reasons for this, beyond the fact that it's how I was taught and how I've always cut them.

WHICH IS WHICH? But maybe I'm jumping the gun. After all, when you look at this joint, it can be hard to tell which is the tail and which is the pin.

The trick is to look at just the *face* of the board, not the ends *(Fig. 1)*. Looking at the face of the panel with the tails, you'll see the tails flare out — like a dove's tail. And from the face of the pin panel, the pins look straight, sort of like box joints. The pins slide in between the tails, but unlike box joints, they can only slide in one direction. The angled sides act as wedges, so you can't pull them apart any other way. This wedge is what makes a dovetail joint so strong.

PINS FIRST. So why do I cut the pins first? There are a couple reasons. First, I think the pins are easier to cut. But it's also easier to cut them accurately. And if they don't end up perfectly square to the baseline, it's easy to clean them up so they are. This is important because after the pins are cut, you'll use them to lay out the positions of the tails. (Laying out the tails from the pins is also easier than marking the pins from the tails.)

STOCK PREPARATION

Regardless of which panel you start with, your first step is always going to be the same: stock preparation.

FLAT AND SQUARE PANELS. Whether you're dealing with narrow boards or wide panels, each piece must be flat and smooth. In fact, all they should need is a little finish sanding. It's also important for the ends of the boards to be square to the edges.

ORIENTATION. When the panels are flat and square, the next thing to do is arrange the panels so the project will look its best when it's put together.

Once the panels are oriented, I label the outside and inside faces, as well as the top edges *(Fig. 2)*. Also, it's a good idea to label adjoining corners with a letter. When you transfer the pins to the mating tail panels later, these labels can save you a lot of head scratching.

BASELINE. Finally, I use a combination square and a pencil to mark baselines around the ends of each panel *(Fig. 3)*. The baselines show where to stop cutting and are drawn on both faces *(Fig. 2)*. (A razor knife can also be used to score the baseline into the panel.) Just set the adjustable square to the thickness of the panel. Then carefully run the square along the end of the panel while you mark the baseline.

Note: If you're working with small pieces, the easiest way to lay out the baseline is to use the boards themselves as a template. Stand up one board and place it against the end of the adjoining piece. Then simply trace around it.

Now that the panels are labeled and the baselines are drawn, you can begin work on the pins.

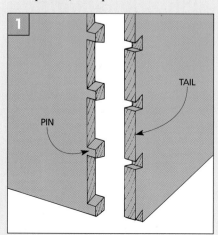

1

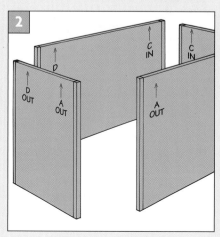

2

C IN / C IN
D
D OUT / A OUT / A OUT

TAIL

PIN

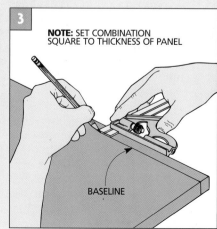

3

NOTE: SET COMBINATION SQUARE TO THICKNESS OF PANEL

BASELINE

When cutting the pins, there are three things to do: lay out the pins, make cuts on each side of them with a hand saw, and remove the waste between them.

LAY OUT. The first step is to lay out the position of each pin. (On the chest, the pins are on the end panels, B.) I start with the outside face of the panel toward me (the face with the narrowest part of the pins) *(Step 1)*.

Next, the layout can be drawn around to the inside face. To lay out the angles across the ends, I use a bevel gauge *(Step 2)*. (Since the chest was softwood, I used an angle of 14°. In hardwood, I'd use an angle of 9°.)

When the pins are laid out, I always mark the waste sections *(Step 3)*. This makes it harder for me to cut on the wrong side of the line.

CUTTING THE PINS. Now the pins can be cut *(Step 4)*. Here, it's important to keep the saw straight up and down so the pin ends up square to the baseline.

I keep the outside face of the panel toward me. This way, I can be extra careful with the good face. If I'm off the line a bit on the inside, it won't show.

REMOVING THE WASTE. When all the pins are cut, you can clean out the waste between them *(Steps 5-7)*.

Here, I do two things. To ensure a clean, straight baseline, I clamp a backing board to the panel. But this board can shift out of position. Especially when you start pounding on the chisel with a mallet. So to prevent this, I begin by removing tiny "bites."

Another thing I do is undercut the shoulder *(Step 6)*. That means after about 1/8" of waste is removed, I'll angle the top of the chisel slightly toward me when chopping out the waste. This way, it's easier to get a good, tight fit.

When all the waste is removed, you'll need to spend a little time cleaning up all the corners. And check that each pin is straight and square, making any adjustments if necessary *(Step 8)*.

1 *Secure the panel in a vise. Then, lay out the pins with the narrow part of the pin on the outside face of the panel.*

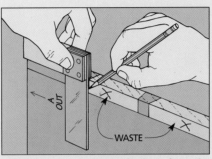

3 *Use a square to transfer lines from the ends down to the baseline. Do this on both sides of the panel. Then, before cutting, mark the waste sections.*

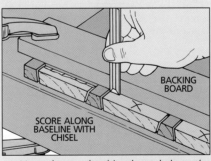

5 *Now clamp a backing board along the baseline. This will help keep your chisel straight up and down. Next, use a sharp chisel to establish the shoulder.*

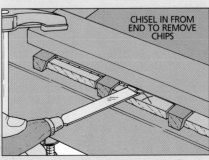

7 *When half the waste is gone, flip the panel over and reposition the backer board. Repeat the procedure to remove the rest of the waste.*

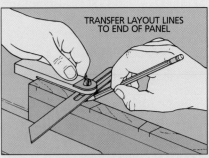

2 *To lay out the pin angle on the end of the panel, hold a pencil on the mark, then bring a bevel gauge up to it.*

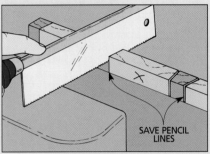

4 *Use a fine-tooth saw to cut to the waste side of all lines. Stop when the kerf has reached the baseline on both sides. Don't cut past the baseline.*

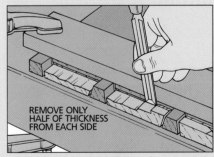

6 *To remove the waste, chop straight down. Then chip in from the end to remove tiny chips. After removing 1/8" of the thickness, start a slight undercut.*

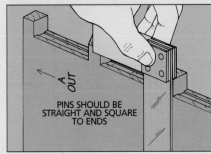

8 *After cleaning up the corners with a chisel, make sure each pin is straight and square to the end of the panel. Use a chisel to true up any out-of-square pins.*

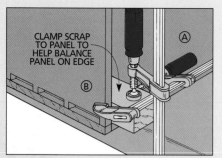

1 Lay out the tails from the pins. Set the tail panel inside-face up on the bench. Set the pin panel on top so edges align.

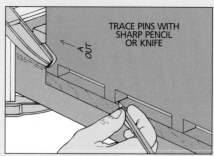

2 With the panels flush at both ends and the edges, trace the pins onto the tail panel. Use a sharp pencil.

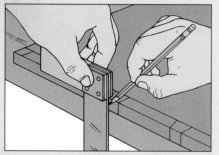

3 To extend the lines around the panel, draw parallel lines across the ends. To do this accurately, position the pencil, then slide the try square up to it.

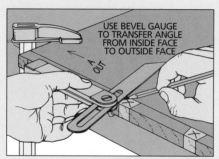

4 Transfer the angles on the inside face to the outside face. Adjust the bevel gauge to match the angle on the inside face. Then draw it on the outside face.

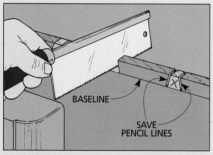

5 To form the sides of the tails, hold the saw at an angle and begin cutting, staying on the waste side of the line. Stop when the kerf reaches the baseline.

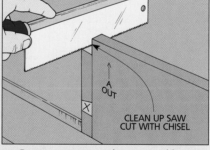

6 Remove waste at the top and bottom with a saw, cutting from the edges toward the first tail. Then clean up the cuts with a chisel.

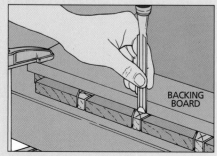

7 Use a chisel to remove the waste between the tails. As with the pins, clamp a backing board to the panel and score the shoulder.

8 Remove half the thickness of the waste from one side of the panel. Then flip the panel over and repeat the process. Finally, test fit the joint.

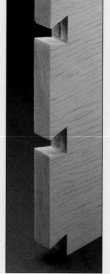

After the pins are complete, it's time to work on the tails. I mark the tails directly from the pins. This way, they will match them perfectly.

LAY OUT. To lay out the tails, first set the tail panel on the workbench, with the inside face up. Then stand the pin panel on top so the panels form a corner. These two panels should be flush at the ends and the edges, with both inside faces toward each other. (Here's where all that marking at the beginning helps.)

Note: To help the pin panel stand upright, I clamp a piece of scrap to it (Step 1). This also helps remove any slight cupping that may be in the panel.

Now that the tails are marked on the inside face, the lines can be transferred around the panel to the outside face (Steps 3-4). Drawing the straight lines across the ends of the panel is easy. But to transfer the angles to the outside face, you'll need to use the bevel gauge.

To be safe, I don't just draw the same angle I used to draw the pins. Instead, I check each angle on the inside face, adjust the bevel gauge if necessary, and then transfer this angle to the outside face. Then mark the waste areas.

CUTTING THE TAILS. When cutting the tails, the saw isn't straight up and down — it's angled (Step 5). This means starting the cut is a little trickier. The saw may tend to skate across the end, so I start more toward the waste side of the line. This leaves more clean-up, but the dovetails fit together better.

REMOVING THE WASTE. With all the kerfs cut, it's time to remove the waste.

But this time, use the saw to remove the waste sections for the pins at the top and bottom of the panel (Step 6). Then clean up the shoulders with a chisel.

Now you can clean out the rest of the waste between the tails using the same procedure used to clean between the pins (Steps 7-8).

Before the joint can be fully assembled, you'll likely have to do some fitting.

FITTING. To get the joint to fit, you'll probably need to remove a little material from either the tails or the pins. To see just where to remove this material, dry-assemble the joint as much as possible (see photo at right).

But don't force it. If you do, the pins at the top and bottom can split from the pressure. The goal is a final fit that can be dry-assembled with a few light taps.

With the joint dry-assembled as much as possible, you should be able to see where the joint is binding. And when you pull the joint apart, the tight spots will also be burnished slightly. To make these areas easier to see, I like to mark them with a pencil.

CHISEL. To remove a lot of waste, you can pare it away with a chisel *(Fig. 1)*. This removes the wood quickly, but it's

also easy to remove too much material.

SANDING STICK. So I often use a little sanding stick *(Fig. 2)*. I make one from a thin piece of scrap with some adhesive-backed sandpaper attached. I bevel the edges to match the angle of the tails so I can sand right into the corner.

ASSEMBLY. When all the joints fit, the case is ready to be assembled *(Fig. 3)*. I use white glue when assembling a large case. It has a longer setup time than yellow glue, which helps with all the small faces that need to be glued.

I usually apply glue just to the sides of the pins and tails. I don't bother gluing the baseline since it's end grain.

Clamping up dovetails usually takes a little preparation. To pull the joint tight, you only want to apply pressure to the tails (not the pins). You'll need a good number of clamps ready to go.

If you don't have many clamps, you

can distribute the clamping pressure evenly across the joint with a special clamping block *(Fig. 3)*.

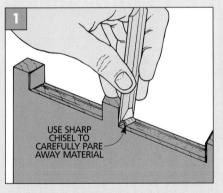

USE SHARP CHISEL TO CAREFULLY PARE AWAY MATERIAL

NOTE: SCRAP PIECE WITH ADHESIVE-BACKED SANDPAPER ON BOTTOM SIDE ONLY

a.
BEVEL EDGES TO FIT INTO CORNERS

SANDPAPER

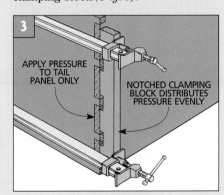

APPLY PRESSURE TO TAIL PANEL ONLY

NOTCHED CLAMPING BLOCK DISTRIBUTES PRESSURE EVENLY

TROUBLESHOOTING

Even after the joint fits together, there may still be some work to do.

PROTRUDING TAILS AND PINS. One common problem is when either the tails or pins stick out. But this is easily corrected with a little sanding or

routing. Refer to page 117 for some ways to do this.

GAPS BETWEEN DOVETAILS. Gaps between a tail and a pin can be fixed with your hand saw and a spline.

The idea is to cut an even kerf

through the gap *(Fig. 1)*. Then glue a spline in the kerf to "patch" it *(Fig. 1a)*.

GAPS AT BASELINE. You may find a gap along the baseline of the tails. Here the cut was too deep. The solution is to use wedges to fill the gaps *(Fig. 2)*.

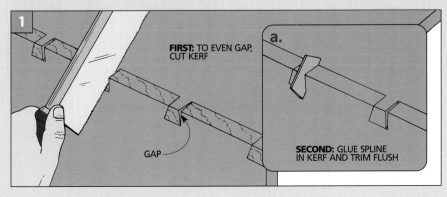

FIRST: TO EVEN GAP, CUT KERF

a.

GAP

SECOND: GLUE SPLINE IN KERF AND TRIM FLUSH

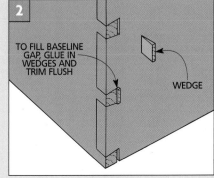

TO FILL BASELINE GAP, GLUE IN WEDGES AND TRIM FLUSH

WEDGE

DESIGNER'S NOTEBOOK

By using frame and panel construction for the sides, the chest takes on a more formal appearance. To complement this classic look, choose a hardwood such as oak, cherry, ash or walnut.

CONSTRUCTION NOTES:

■ Start by cutting all the rails and stiles (M, N, O, P, Q, R, S) to finished width and length *(Fig. 1)*.

■ To accept the panels added later, cut ¼"-wide grooves ½" deep centered on the thickness of each piece *(Fig. 1)*. Also cut grooves on *both* edges of the front/back short stiles (N).

■ Cut ½"-long tenons on the ends of the rails (O, P, R, S) to fit the grooves in the stiles *(Fig. 1)*. Also cut a tenon on each end of the front/back short stiles (N).

■ Use a dado blade in the table saw to cut a rabbet along one edge of each front/back long stile (M). This rabbet should be ⅜" deep and fit the thickness of the end stiles (Q) *(Figs. 1 and 3)*.

■ Now dry-assemble each set of rails and stiles, and measure for the six panels. (Make sure the short stiles are centered in the front/back assemblies.) Measure each opening, inside edge to inside edge, and add ¾" to each dimension. The assemblies for opposite sides should be the same width and length.

■ Glue up six ½"-thick blanks for the panels (T, U). Cut them to finished size after the glue dries.

■ To form the raised center on each panel, first fasten a tall auxiliary fence to the table saw rip fence. Raise the blade 1⅜" and tilt it 8°. Then position the rip fence ³⁄₁₆" from the blade with the blade tilted away from the fence.

■ Cut bevels on all four edges of all six panels *(Fig. 1)*. Cut the ends first, then the edges to clean up any tearout.

Safety Note: Use a zero clearance insert to help prevent the panel from tipping into the opening around the blade.

■ Use a beveled sanding block to remove blade marks and square up the shoulders of the raised panels.

■ Apply a finish before gluing the frame and panel assemblies together. Refer to the photo on page 113.

■ Now you can glue and clamp together the frame and panel assemblies. Do not use glue on the panels. Check that each assembly is flat and square.

■ Before gluing the chest together, two sets of grooves need to be cut. First, cut grooves on the inside faces of all four assemblies to fit the thickness of the bottom panel (C) *(Fig. 4)*. The bottom

MATERIALS LIST

CHANGED PARTS

D	Tray Supports (2)	¾ x ⅜ - 34½
K	Tray Ends (2)	¾ x 3½ - 13½
L	Tray Bottom (1)	½ x 12⅝ - 23⅛

NEW PARTS

M	Fr./Bk. Long Stiles (4)	¾ x 2 - 18½
N	Fr./Bk. Short Stiles (2)	¾ x 2 - 11
O	Fr./Bk. Top Rails (2)	¾ x 2¾ - 33
P	Fr./Bk. Btm. Rails (2)	¾ x 5¾ - 33
Q	End Stiles (4)	¾ x 1⅝ - 18½
R	End Top Rails (2)	¾ x 2¾ - 13
S	End Btm. Rails (2)	¾ x 5¾ - 13
T	Fr./Bk. Panels (4)	½ x 10¾ - 15¾
U	End Panels (2)	½ x 10¾ - 12¾
V	Tray Runners (2)	⅜ x ½ - 24

Note: Do not need parts A, B.

HARDWARE SUPPLIES

(8) #8 x ¾" Fh woodscrews

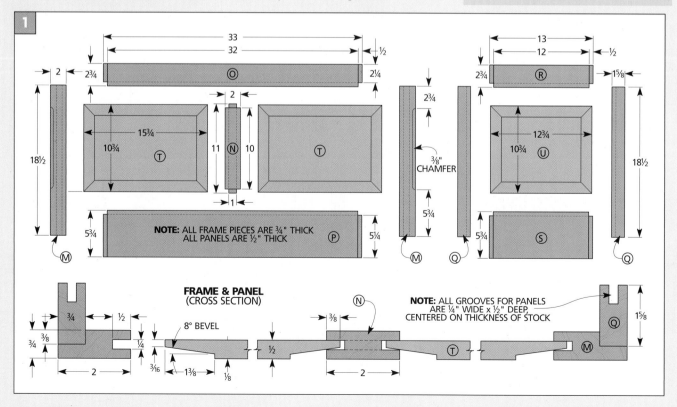

1

FRAME & PANEL (CROSS SECTION)

NOTE: ALL FRAME PIECES ARE ¾" THICK
ALL PANELS ARE ½" THICK

NOTE: ALL GROOVES FOR PANELS ARE ¼" WIDE x ½" DEEP, CENTERED ON THICKNESS OF STOCK

8° BEVEL

edge of each groove is $2^1/_4$" from the bottom edge of each assembly.

■ Now cut $^3/_8$"-wide grooves $^3/_8$" deep for the tray supports toward the top of the front/back assemblies *only (Figs. 4 and 6)*. The top edges of these grooves are $1^5/_8$" from the top edges of the front/back assemblies.

■ Next, dry-assemble the case and measure for the bottom panel. To do this, measure the opening, including the depth of the bottom grooves. Then subtract $^1/_8$" from the width *only* to allow for expansion. Glue up a panel and cut it to these dimensions.

■ To keep the corners aligned during glue up, two screws are driven at each corner *(Fig. 3)*. With the case dry-assembled, drill a pilot hole and a shank hole $^3/_8$" from the top and bottom edge on each front/back assembly. (These will be covered by trim later.) Drive screws in to pre-thread the holes, then remove them.

■ Now it's time to assemble the case with the four sides and bottom panel. Apply glue to each joint (but not to the bottom panel) and assemble the case with the screws. Use clamps as well.

■ Rout a $^3/_8$" stopped chamfer on the outside corner of each front/back long stile (M) *(Fig. 1)*.

■ Cut tray supports (D) to fit into the grooves in the front and back assemblies and between the end assemblies.

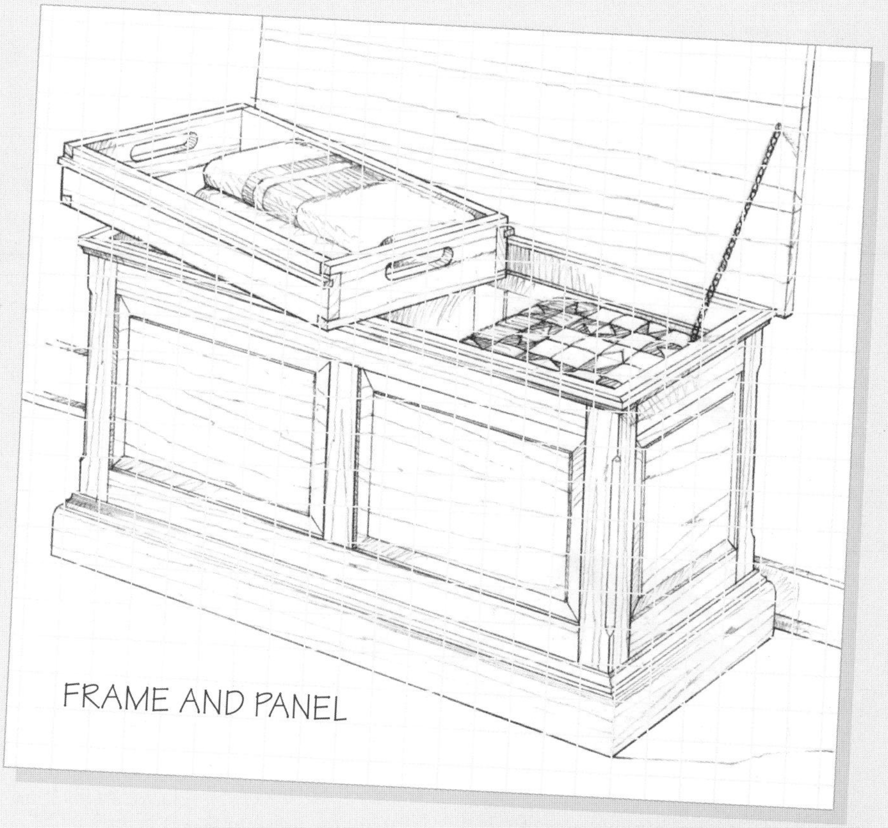
FRAME AND PANEL

Glue them in place *(Fig. 6)*.

■ The tray is built the same as for the dovetail chest, except the tray ends (K) are $13^1/_2$" long *(Fig. 5)*. Refer to page 119 for details on building the tray.

■ After the tray is assembled, cut grooves on the front and back (J) to hold tray runners *(Fig. 5)*. These grooves are $^3/_8$" wide and $^1/_8$" deep.

■ Cut tray runners (V) to fit the grooves and glue them in place *(Fig. 5)*.

■ To complete the chest, make and mount the trim and the lid the same as for the dovetail chest.

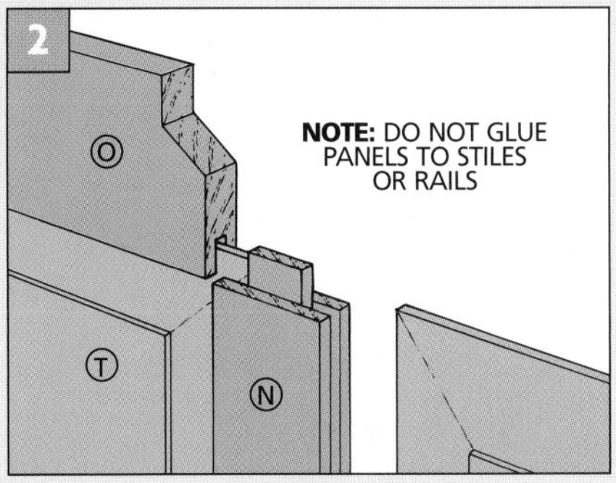
2
NOTE: DO NOT GLUE PANELS TO STILES OR RAILS
O
T
N

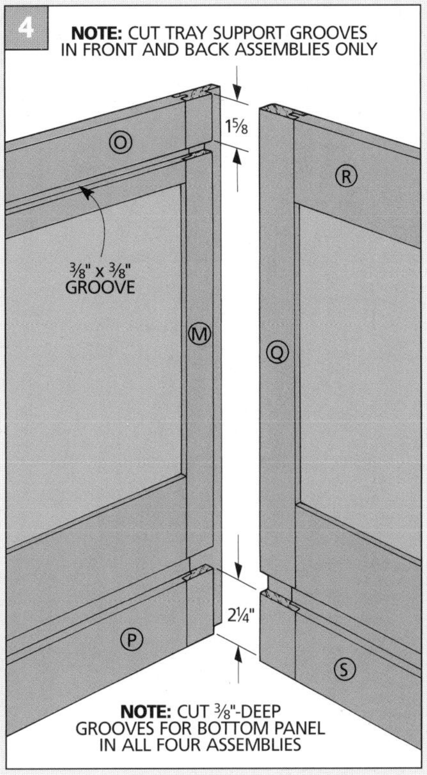
4
NOTE: CUT TRAY SUPPORT GROOVES IN FRONT AND BACK ASSEMBLIES ONLY
1⅝
O
R
⅜" x ⅜" GROOVE
M
Q
2¼"
P
S
NOTE: CUT ⅜"-DEEP GROOVES FOR BOTTOM PANEL IN ALL FOUR ASSEMBLIES

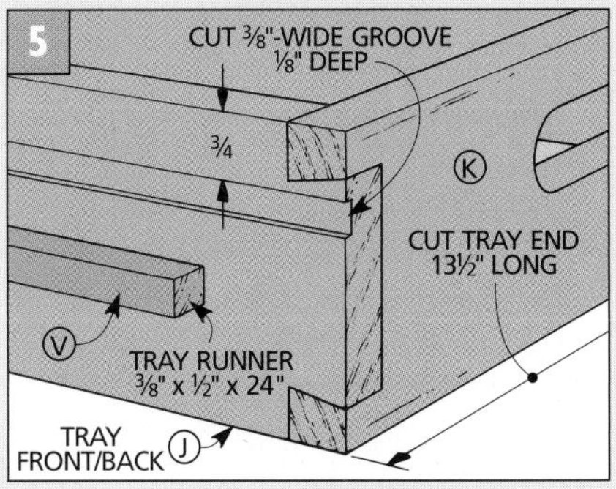
5
CUT ⅜"-WIDE GROOVE ⅛" DEEP
¾
K
CUT TRAY END 13½" LONG
V
TRAY RUNNER ⅜" x ½" x 24"
TRAY FRONT/BACK J

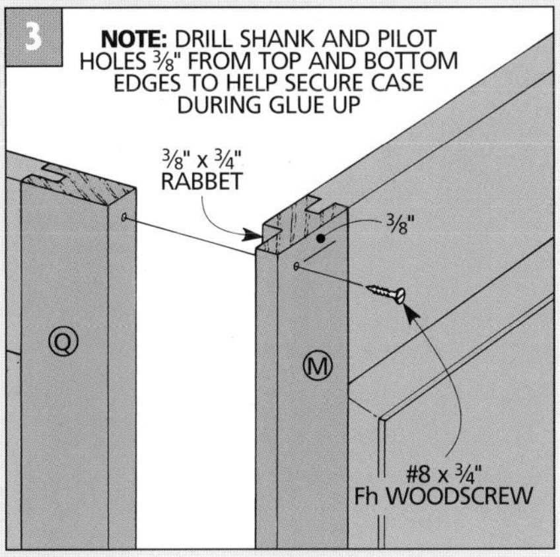
3
NOTE: DRILL SHANK AND PILOT HOLES ⅜" FROM TOP AND BOTTOM EDGES TO HELP SECURE CASE DURING GLUE UP
⅜" x ¾" RABBET
⅜"
Q
M
#8 x ¾" Fh WOODSCREW

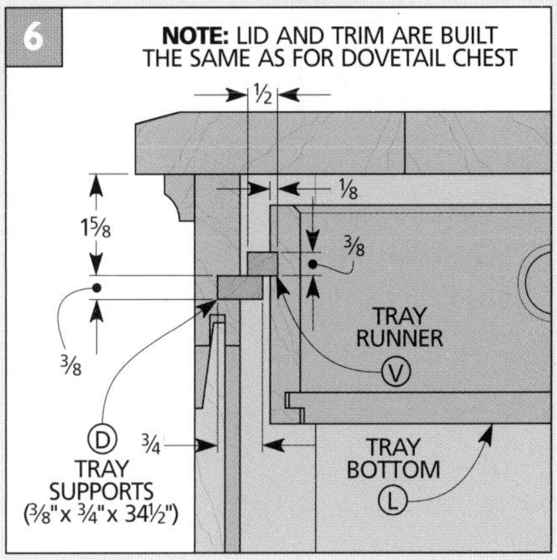
6
NOTE: LID AND TRIM ARE BUILT THE SAME AS FOR DOVETAIL CHEST
½
⅛
1⅝
⅜
⅜
TRAY RUNNER
V
D
¾
TRAY SUPPORTS (⅜" x ¾" x 34½")
TRAY BOTTOM
L

One of the first things we take into consideration when designing projects at *Woodsmith* is whether the hardware is commonly available. Most of the hardware and supplies for the projects in this book can be found at local hardware stores or home centers. Sometimes, though, you may have to order the hardware through the mail. If that's the case, we've tried to find reputable national mail order sources with toll-free phone numbers (see box at right).

In addition, *Woodsmith Project Supplies* offers hardware for some of the projects in this book (see below).

WOODSMITH PROJECT SUPPLIES

At the time of printing, the following project supply kits were available from *Woodsmith Project Supplies*. The kits include the items listed, but you must supply any lumber, plywood, or finish. For current prices and availability, call toll-free:

1-800-444-7527

Hall Tree
(pages 48-53) ....No. 8005-144
This kit provides full-size patterns for the hooks and feet.

Mission Bookcase
(pages 72-87) No.790-200
Includes the hinges, ball catches, screws, shelf supports and brads.

Coat and Glove Rack
(pages 90-95) ....No. 786-100
Includes full-size patterns for the back and sides, oak plugs, coat pegs, door knob, butt hinges and magnetic door catch.

Jelly Cupboard
(pages 106-113)
Hardware Kit...............No. 787-100
Screws, hinges, dowels for the pins and wooden door knob.

Tin Panel Kit................No. 787-110
Four blank tin panels ready to be punched with your choice of patterns (see page 107), plus instructions on punching and aging tin.

KEY: TL04

MAIL ORDER SOURCES

Some of the most important "tools" you can have in your shop are mail order catalogs. The ones listed below are filled with special hardware, tools, finishes, lumber, and supplies that can't be found at a local hardware store or home center. You should be able to find many of the supplies for the projects in this book in one or more of these catalogs.

It's amazing what you can learn about woodworking by looking through these catalogs. If they're not currently in your shop, you may want to have them sent to you.

Note: The information below was current when this book was printed. Time-Life Books and August Home Publishing do not guarantee these products will be available nor endorse any specific mail order company, catalog, or product.

THE WOODSMITH STORE

2625 Beaver Avenue
Des Moines, IA 50310
800–835–5084
Our own retail store filled with tools, jigs, hardware, books, and finishing supplies. Though we don't have a catalog, we do send out items mail order. Call for information.

WOODCRAFT

560 Airport Industrial Park
P.O. Box 1686
Parkersburg, WV 26102-1686
800–225–1153
www.woodcraft.com
Has all kinds of hardware including hinges, coat pegs, knobs and lid supports. They also carry a good selection of hand tools and accessories.

ROCKLER WOODWORKING & HARDWARE

4365 Willow Drive
Medina, MN 55340
800–279–4441
www.rockler.com
A great catalog of general hardware, specialty hardware, plus tool and shop accessories. It's also a good "idea-starter" for projects.

WOODWORKER'S SUPPLY

1108 North Glenn Road
Casper, WY 82601
800–645–9292
Z-shaped fasteners, power tools and accessories, hardware, shellac, milk paint and other finishing supplies, wood plugs and more.

CONSTANTINE'S

2050 Eastchester Road
Bronx, NY 10461
800–223–8087
www.constantines.com
One of the original woodworking mail order catalogs. Find cotton Shaker tape, hinges, tin panels, milk paint, and other finishing supplies.

TREND-LINES

135 American Legion Highway
Revere, MA 02151
800–767–9999
www.trend-lines.com
Another complete source for hinges, pegs, dowels, hardware, power tools and accessories.

MEISEL HARDWARE SPECIALTIES

P.O. Box 70
Mound, MN 55364
800–441–9870
In this plan-filled catalog, you'll also find pegs, lid supports, hinges, plus blank and pre-punched tin panels.

COUNTRY ACCENTS

P.O. Box 437
Montoursville, PA 17754
717–478–4127
A complete catalog of tin-punching supplies with pre-punched tin, punching tools, tin blanks and designs.

TREMONT NAIL COMPANY

P.O. Box 111
Wareham, MA 02571
800–842–0560
Over 175 years old and still making square nails the old-fashioned way.

INDEX

A B C

Bookcase
    Mission, 72-87
    Open, 87
Chair
    Rocking, 26-42
Chest
    Dovetail, 114-123
    Frame and panel, 124-125
Coat and Glove Rack, 90-95
Cotton Shaker tape, 38-41
Cutout patterns
    Diamond, 99
    Heart, 12, 99

D E F G

Doors, 81-82, 95, 111-112
    Panels, 112, 113
    Shop-built pulls, 83
Dovetail Chest, 114-125
Dovetails
    Cutting, 120-123
    Fitting, 123
    Troubleshooting, 123
Dowels
    Making, 37
    Notching, 35
    Pins, 110, 111
    Tenons, 31
Finishes
    Aging, 95, 105
    Danish oil, 9
    Milk paint, 104-105
    Shellac, 119
    Waxing, 72
Footstool, Shaker-Style, 43-45
Frame and panel, 75, 124-125
Frame and Panel Chest, 124-125
Glass
    Beveled, 68
    Doors, 82
Glass-Top Coffee Table, 62-71

H I J K

Hall Clothes Tree, 48-53
Hardware
    Chain, 119
    Door catches, 82, 112
    Hinges, 82, 95, 103, 112, 118
    Shelf pins, 83
    Sources, 126
    Square-cut nails, 109
    Tin panels, 112
    Z-shaped fasteners, 55, 60
High-Back Bench, 96-105
Jelly Cupboard, 106-113

Jigs
    Bevel, 61
    Chisel guide, 57
    Flush trim, 117
    Tapering, 22-23, 56, 64
Joinery
    End lap, 111
    Half-laps, 51
    Hand-cut dovetails, 10, 120-123
    Locked rabbet, 20
    Miter with spline, 68-69
    Mortise and tenon, 17, 57-58, 70, 76
    Pegged mortise and tenon, 79
    Tenons on dowels, 31
    Through mortise and tenon, 84-86, 99-100

L M N O

Lamp Table, 21
Milk paint, 95, 104-105
Mission Bookcase, 72-87
Mortises, 16, 57, 70
    Through mortise and tenon, 84-86, 99-100
Oak Sofa Table, 54-61

P Q R

Patterns
    Bench apron, 99
    Bench back, 99
    Bench side, 100
    Clothes hooks, 49
    Coat and Glove Rack back, 94
    Coat and Glove Rack sides, 92
    Diamond cutout, 99
    Foot, Hall Clothes Tree, 49
    Heart cutout, 12, 99
    Punched tin panels, 107
    Rockers, 36
    Rocker arms, 34
    Sources, 126
    Weaving, 42
Pegs
    Decorative, 79
    Shaker, 94
    Square, 92
Punched tin panels, 107, 112
    Sources, 126
Raised panels, 113, 124-125
Rocking Chair, 26-42

S

Shaker Hall Table, 14-25
Shaker Step Stool, 8-13
Shaker cotton tape, 38-41
Shaker-Style Footstool, 43

Shellac, 119
Shelves, 58, 60, 67, 83, 92-93, 109
Shop Tips
    Adding decorative pegs, 79
    Clamping with wedges, 109
    Drawing an arc, 65
    Filling gaps, 9
    Frame assembly, 75
    Hanging system, 94
    Mortises with a jig saw, 100
    Routing custom-fit dadoes, 108
    Sanding flush, 117
    Scraping and sanding corners, 78
    Shaping leg bottoms, 30
    Shop-built door pulls, 83
    Spacing slats, 98
    Special sanding block, 50
    Tight-fit shoulders, 17
Sources, 126
Step Stool, 8-13
    Country version, 12-13
Stools
    Country Step Stool, 12-13
    Shaker-Style Footstool, 43-45
    Shaker Step Stool, 8-13
Storage
    Coat and Glove Rack, 90-95
    Dovetail Chest, 114-125
    Hall Table, 14-25
    High-Back Bench, 102-103
    Jelly Cupboard, 106-113
    Mission Bookcase, 72-87
    Tray, 119
Square-cut nails, 109

T U V

Tables
    Coffee
        Glass-Top, 62-71
        Solid Wood Top, 71
    Hall, 14-25
    Lamp, 21
    Sofa, 54-61
Tapering legs
    Jigs, 22-23, 56, 64
    On a jointer, 24-25
Tin panels, 112
    Patterns, 107

W X Y Z

Weaving, 38-42

AUGUST HOME
PUBLISHING COMPANY

President & Publisher: Donald B. Peschke
Executive Editor: Douglas L. Hicks
Art Director: Steve Lueder
Creative Director: Ted Kralicek
Senior Graphic Designers: Chris Glowacki, Cheryl Simpson
Assistant Editors: Joseph E. Irwin, Craig Ruegsegger
Graphic Designer: Vu Nguyen
Design Intern: Katie VanDalsem

Designer's Notebook Illustrator: Mike Mittermeier
Photographer: Crayola England
Electronic Production: Douglas M. Lidster
Production: Troy Clark, Minniette Johnson, Susan Rueve
Project Designers: Ken Munkel, Kent Welsh, Kevin Boyle
Project Builders: Steve Curtis, Steve Johnson
Magazine Editors: Terry Strohman, Tim Robertson
Contributing Editors: Vincent S. Ancona, Tom Begnal, Jon Garbison,
Bryan Nelson
Magazine Art Directors: Todd Lambirth, Cary Christensen
Contributing Illustrators: Mark Higdon, David Kreyling, Erich Lage,
Roger Reiland, Kurt Schultz, Cinda Shambaugh, Dirk Ver Steeg

Controller: Robin Hutchinson
Production Director: George Chmielarz
Project Supplies: Bob Baker
New Media Manager: Gordon Gaippe

For subscription information about
Woodsmith and *ShopNotes* magazines, please write:
August Home Publishing Co.
2200 Grand Ave.
Des Moines, IA 50312
800-333-5075
www.augusthome.com/customwoodworking

Woodsmith® and *ShopNotes*® are registered trademarks of August Home
Publishing Co.

ISBN 0-7835-5953-4

TIME LIFE® BOOKS

Time-Life Books is a division of Time Life Inc.

TIME LIFE INC.
Chairman and Chief Executive Officer: Jim Nelson
President and Chief Operating Officer: Steven Janas
Senior Executive Vice President and Chief Operations Officer: Mary Davis Holt
Senior Vice President and Chief Financial Officer: Christopher Hearing

TIME-LIFE BOOKS
President: Joseph A. Kuna
Publisher/Managing Editor: Neil Kagan
Vice President, New Product Development: Amy Golden

CUSTOM WOODWORKING
American Style: Shaker, Mission & Country Projects
Editor: Glen B. Ruh
Assistant Art Director: Patricia Bray
Editorial Assistant: Patricia D. Whiteford
Cover Concept: Phil Unetic/3R1 Studios

MARKETING
Director: Wells P. Spence
Associate Marketing Manager: Jennifer C. Williams

Correspondents: Maria Vincenza Aloisi (Paris), Christine Hinze (London),
Christina Lieberman (New York)

Senior Vice President, Law & Business Affairs: Randolph H. Elkins
Vice President, Finance: Claudia Goldberg
Vice President, Book Production: Patricia Pascale
Vice President, Imaging: Marjann Caldwell
Director, Publishing Technology: Betsi McGrath
Director, Editorial Administration: Barbara Levitt
Director, Photography and Research: John Conrad Weiser
Director, Quality Assurance: James King
Manager, Technical Services: Anne Topp
Senior Production Manager: Ken Sabol
Chief Librarian: Louise D. Forstall

School and library distribution by Time-Life Education, P.O. Box 85026,
Richmond, Virginia 23285-5026.

Printed in U.S.A   R 10 9 8 7 6 5 4 3 2

X X X X X X X X X

The lighting you opt for will have a huge impact on the general ambience of the room. This is important if your kitchen is also a dining and meeting-up area, but you should never forget that it's also a work area. It pays to have a series of switches and dimmer switches so you can control your lighting independently – clean, bright lights for cooking; soothing ambient lighting for entertaining.

Things to consider

You need to plan your lighting right from the start of the project. It's not impossible to fit ceiling lights after you've finished installing your kitchen but it's much easier to do the 'first fixing' at the start of the project. This is especially true of any under-cabinet lighting – you can fit the lighting at the end, but you need to make sure the cabling etc. that this lighting will use is already in situ.

When planning your lighting, bear the following lighting 'types' in mind:

TASK LIGHTING

This is what you will be relying on when you're preparing and cooking in the kitchen. It needs to be bright and, ideally, have a sharper 'blue-white' light. Task lighting should be directly over the top of the work area. You don't want it coming from behind you,

as you'll end up casting your own shadow over your work area. Many cooker hoods come with task lights built into them.

AMBIENT LIGHTING

This is your mood lighting; important if your kitchen is also the main dining and entertaining area. It's a good idea to have a separate switching system that allows you to tone down the task lights and bring up the mood lighting as the evening progresses – dimmer switches are great for ambient lighting.

ACCENT LIGHTING

This is for when you want to draw attention to something, be it your lovely new cooker or a painting on the wall.

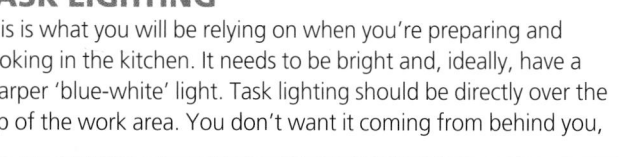

Types of light bulb

There's a lot of development in this area, so don't be too surprised if some of this information goes out of date quite quickly – see the blog that backs up this book if need be.

HALOGEN

Halogen bulbs can create a strong, bright white light that can be ideal over working areas. They can also be used with dimmers, which makes them suitable for both task and ambient lighting. With the demise of conventional bulbs, these tend to be the most popular option for the kitchen, either as recessed downlights or as track lights.

They use less electricity than conventional bulbs but aren't as efficient as LED and CFL lighting. They also get very, very hot, which can make them a hazard if using them under wall cabinets. Bear in mind they don't last that long and can work out as an expensive option.

LED

This is where most of the current development work is taking place. They are very energy efficient and, while expensive, last an absolute age. At the moment they aren't very good at generating a lot of bright light – the brighter they get the less efficient they become – but I dare say they'll get around this sooner rather than later.

LEDs are very good at producing colours, but white light is usually made by combining the LEDs together, which actually creates a very natural feel. You can buy these as tiny strip lights, which can look great along wall cabinets and on kickboards, but most standard light fittings, bayonet, screw thread, etc. are now available as LED.

Because LEDs are so energy efficient you can get a good life expectancy from battery-powered LEDs. If you managed to forget all about under-cabinet lighting when installing your kitchen this might be the easiest way for you to shed some light on the problem without ripping everything out again.

Another real boon for LEDs is that, because of the way they work, the light they produce tends not to attract insects, which is particularly handy in a kitchen.

You can buy 'dimmable' LEDs but you do need to state that these are what you need when you buy them.

CONVENTIONAL

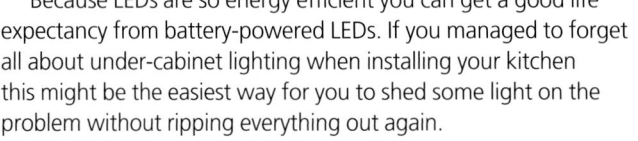

These are no longer available in Europe and will probably disappear altogether before too long. They are very cheap but very inefficient, so what you save on buying them you lose on running them.

COMPACT FLUORESCENT LIGHTS (CFL)

These used to be very slow to warm up and many people complained about headaches as a result of using them. On the upside, many of these defects have been dealt with, but they are still not suitable for dimmer switches, unless you buy ones specifically for that purpose. They don't get very hot so they are a popular option for under wall cabinets, but they are considered environmentally 'dirty' due to the amount of mercury they contain. In fairness it's a tiny amount, but it still isn't the best substance to be hanging over your dinner.

FLUORESCENT STRIP LIGHTS

In effect, these are what CFLs evolved from. Personally, I'd avoid them like the plague as a ceiling light as they can look quite awful. However, they're still useful as under-cabinet lighting and the modern ones tend to light up faster and don't emit that annoying hum. On the downside, many people claim they give them headaches and the light isn't very pleasing on the eye.

Types of lighting

CEILING LIGHTS

You should really use these for ambience only, as the light they cast will invariably come from behind the chef, casting a shadow over the work area. The obvious exception to this is if you have a kitchen island or peninsula, where downlights or a track light over the centre of the island can offer very effective task lighting. When used for task lighting halogen and LED bulbs are best, as these offer a white light that is very easy on the eye.

UNDER-CABINET LIGHTS

These are primarily task lights shining down onto the work surface. The cheapest option here are fluorescent strips but LED strips can give a better, albeit more expensive, effect. You can also use coloured LED lights to create an ambient effect by fitting them into the front of your cabinet plinths. If you can't get electricity to your cabinets, consider fitting battery-powered downlights (puck lights) instead, and use rechargeable batteries to keep the costs down.

KICKBOARD LIGHTING

This can be quite effective as an ambient light and can also be used as nighttime lighting. You can use small halogen lights but this form suits LEDs best, especially if you are going to leave them on at night, as LEDs use very little electricity. Kickboard lighting is usually easy to fit retrospectively, as you can use all the hidden space under the cabinets to run the electric cables you'll need.

11 FIXTURES AND APPLIANCES

Fitting out your kitchen with all its appliances can be a costly business, so let's just have a look at some of the pitfalls.

Kitchen sinks

Sink prices vary wildly, and more often than not this is a true reflection of the build quality. Other factors affecting price are the materials and how big the sink is.

There are three basic types of sink: 1 bowl, 1½ bowls and twin bowls. Personally, I'd always recommend getting a sink with at least 1½ bowls, no matter how good you think your dishwasher is. Sinks can come as 'one-tap-hole' for monobloc taps or as 'two-tap-hole' – see taps below for the options.

Sinks can be left- or right-handed, which relates to what side of the sink the drainer is situated. Most one-tap-hole sinks come, rather ironically, with two holes set opposite each other. The idea here is that you decide on which side you want the drainer, then fit a monobloc tap in one of the holes and blank the other off. For a 'two-tap-hole' sink, the orientation of the drainer is fixed, so make sure you know what you want before you buy.

Cheap steel sinks often use something that looks like a bit of tarmac on the base to give them some rigidity, but they're still very flimsy. If you're looking to buy a tall mixer-style tap, especially one with a retractable hose, then steer clear of anything but the most expensive steel sinks, as the base of the sink will not adequately support the tap.

If this advice has reached you too late you can try to alleviate the situation by fitting a 'top-hat' to the base of the tap. These

are either round or triangular and are just hard pieces of shaped plastic that spread the weight of the tap and provide a more secure base.

The golden rule of steel sinks is to go for the best you can afford and bear in mind that brushed or satin steel finishes tend to hide marks better. Other sink materials result in a far more rigid surface, which is ideal for more elaborate taps.

The old-fashioned clay or cast iron ceramic sinks provide a surface that is very easy to keep clean and is resistant to pretty much everything. On the downside, the ceramic can and does chip – although you can buy repair kits for them.

Composite sinks are made in much the same way as composite worktops – stone fragments or other material, mixed with resin and cast. As with the worktops, their durability is dictated by what particles are used to make it. Shell fragments, for example, might look nice but will dissolve if they come into contact with acids, such as vinegar and citrus juice.

Granite composites tend to be very robust; in fact, many people claim these are the most durable of all. I'd beg to differ, as my wife managed to destroy ours with the cunning deployment of paint stripper.

Kitchen taps

Taps come in a number of different 'styles' and are designed for specific water conditions:

HIGH/LOW PRESSURE TAPS

Most modern taps work on the idea that we all have high-pressure water in our homes; however, many of us don't. Most houses in the UK, until about the turn of this century, were designed with high-pressure cold water but low-pressure hot water. In this very common scenario, the cold water would be fed from a mains supply, which was then used to fill a cold-water storage tank in the loft. This tank would then supply water to the hot water cylinder below. The result can be a huge disparity in pressures, with the cold water having a pressure of 3–5bar (43–73psi), while the hot water languishes at a miserable 0.3bar (4psi).

This disparity in water pressure is no great issue if you have ordinary pillar taps (see overleaf), but it is an issue with mixer taps as the cold water just overwhelms the hot and the water doesn't mix properly as a result. High pressure can also be an issue if it's a bit too high – anything over 3bar (43psi) should be considered 'too high' – as water has a habit of shooting out of the tap, hitting the base of the sink and bouncing straight back out, soaking anyone within the vicinity.

So, check out how the water is delivered in your home and buy taps designed for the water pressures you have. If you have your heart set on mixer taps but have low-pressure hot water you might have to play around with check valves and pressure reducing valves to get good performance from the taps – see the Haynes *Home Plumbing Manual,* or ask a plumber.

MONOBLOC TAPS

A monobloc tap is designed for 'one-tap-hole' sinks. If you have a sink with two tap-holes you can either blank off one hole or mount

the tap into the actual worktop instead – a good idea if you have a flimsy steel sink and a bulky tap. The taps themselves can have two heads that you turn for hot and cold water or a single lever, but all monoblocs are mixer taps.

DECK MIXER

If you have a two-tap-hole sink this is a way of getting the benefits of a monobloc, without having to blank off one of the tap holes, which always looks a bit odd.

PILLAR TAPS

These are what everyone used to have. Two separate taps; one for hot and another for cold, where the water blends only when it fills the sink. Kitchen pillar taps are usually taller and are called 'high pillar taps'.

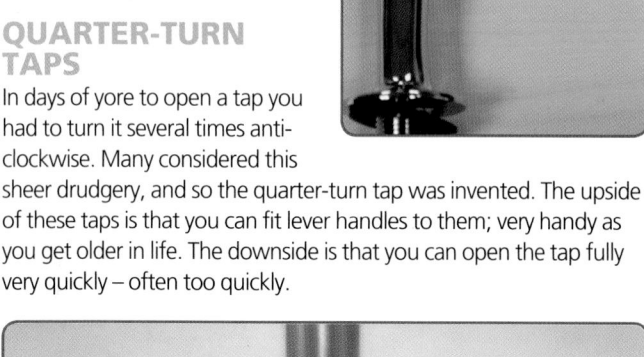

QUARTER-TURN TAPS

In days of yore to open a tap you had to turn it several times anti-clockwise. Many considered this sheer drudgery, and so the quarter-turn tap was invented. The upside of these taps is that you can fit lever handles to them; very handy as you get older in life. The downside is that you can open the tap fully very quickly – often too quickly.

Water filters and softeners

WATER FILTERS

A water filter is designed to remove impurities from the water, whether this is the fluoride that the water company has gone to a lot of trouble to introduce in the first place, or lead and other heavy metals picked up from very old pipework. You fit a water filter to the main tap that you intend to drink from.

The neatest way to fit a water filter is to buy a tri-tap, where you have a separate tap head or lever on your main kitchen tap that delivers filtered water. These are pretty expensive though, so many people opt for a separate filtered water tap. A more recent option are taps that deliver filtered and boiling water, so they can act as an alternative to a kettle as well as a filter. Alas, these often come with price tags that can leave your jaw resting on the floor. Most filtered taps can be installed quickly and simply enough by the homeowner. Boiling water taps are a different proposition, as heating water causes the water pressure

Below: Filtered water tap.
Right: Boiling tap.

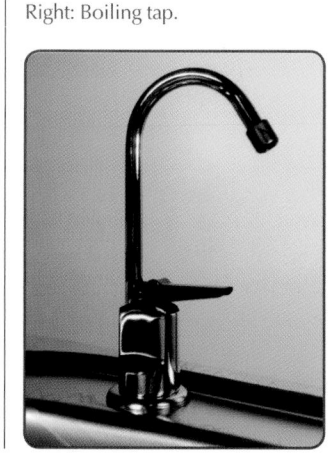

to rise, which can be dangerous. With this in mind, you'd be well advised to leave the installation of these to a professional.

TIP *A water filter improves your drinking water. A water softener protects your white appliances etc. As such they aren't an either/or and you ought to consider fitting both.*

WATER SOFTENERS

A water softener is designed to deal with 'hard water'. Hard water is where the water coming into your home contains a lot of minerals. These are a good thing in

Above: An Ion-exchange water softener.

many ways, certainly if you're planning on drinking the water, but when the water is heated, these minerals have a nasty habit of depositing as 'limescale'. Over time, this can ruin dishwashers, washing machines, taps and showers, as well as increasing the usage of soap.

The only way to actually 'soften water' is with an 'ion-exchange water softener'. These are fitted as close to the incoming cold water mains as is possible and are designed to soften all of the water in the house, with one exception; the tap you use to drink from.

Proper water softeners are both bulky and expensive and they also use salt to recharge themselves. Since this salt could – in theory at least – get into the softened water, you shouldn't drink it. If you do fit a water softener, you need to ensure that you have at least one tap that isn't connected to it that can be used for drinking water.

Because of the price and inconvenience of water softeners an entire industry has grown up offering cheap, small and simple-to-install alternatives. These cannot be called water softeners because they don't actually soften anything. Instead they are called water 'conditioners'. Some work by wrapping a wire around your incoming mains, some use zinc to alter the way the limescale forms and many use the mystic power of magnets. Personally, I think you'd be better off sacrificing a chicken to the God of Limescale.

Waste/garbage disposal units

In some countries people wouldn't dream of fitting a kitchen without installing a waste disposal unit; in other countries they are almost unheard of.

I've always regarded them with deep suspicion; they look to me like a really good way of destroying cutlery and losing the occasional finger. However, they are actually considered the 'green

alternative', in that, rather than your food waste just ending up in a landfill site, smelling strongly and releasing loads of methane gas, it can all be collected in your local water treatment plant and converted into handy things like fertiliser.

You can easily retrofit a waste disposal unit when you feel the need to use one. Almost all of these units use a standard-sized sink waste, so it's just a matter of unscrewing the one you currently have and fitting the one that came with your unit. At the base of this new waste there is usually a large rubber washer and the disposal unit fits to this washer, forming a waterproof seal either by twisting and locking the unit into place or by using three or four standard bolts.

The only thing you need now is an electrical connection and, since quite a few things close to your sink will require electricity, it's always a good idea to fit at least one double socket in the unit under the kitchen sink – making sure it's not going to get wet if the sink leaks in the future.

Dishwashers

A standard dishwasher is designed to go into a 600mm (24in) gap between units, so if you wish to maximise your choice of

dishwasher, make sure you use this gap in your kitchen design. If this isn't feasible, don't despair, as you can buy slimmer dishwashers. You can even buy tiny little ones that just sit on your kitchen worktop.

The easiest way to plumb in a dishwasher is to situate it close to the kitchen sink, which by happy chance is also the best place for a dishwasher. You can buy dishwasher/washing machine adapters that fit onto your existing kitchen sink trap or you can buy a new trap with the adapters built into it. If you have a sink waste trap that already has these adapters you need to be aware that these are usually blocked off when not in use. To use the adapter you either have to cut off the end using a junior hacksaw or unscrew the cap and remove the plastic insert from within the adapter.

If you're a fair distance from your kitchen sink you can buy hose extensions, but check with the manufacturer to see what maximum distance they allow. Alternatively, you can extend the waste pipework and fit a 'standpipe' behind, or just to one side of the dishwasher.

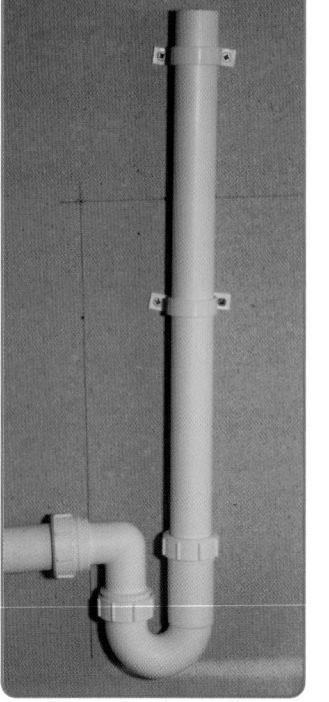

You can buy a dishwasher as a freestanding or 'built-in' unit. In the latter case you usually have to buy a cabinet specifically for the unit and you then fit a cupboard door to the face of the dishwasher. The attachments for fitting this door are slowly standardising, so it's not essential that you buy the dishwasher from the same people who supplied the kitchen.

Aside from an electric socket and connecting up the waste, the only other installation issue is getting the unit level. Most come with a little leg at each corner that can be wound up and down. It's usually easier to set the back legs first, push the unit into place and then adjust the front legs to get it level.

Washing machines

The issues involved with a washing machine are pretty much those associated with a dishwasher, so have a read of the section above. If you're really struggling for space in a galley-style kitchen you could look at buying a top-loading washing machine.

Ovens, cookers, hobs and microwaves

The oven is often the centrepiece of the kitchen and the options available are immense. As such, it really pays to put some thought into its purchase, ideally before you've built your new kitchen – the size of a cooker can vary from 500–1100mm (20–43in) and beyond.

In terms of options, you can have a cooker with the oven and hob combined, or separate them out. The former option is usually a more traditional 'range'-style cooker and can come with umpteen hob rings and more than one oven. If you opt for a separate oven and hob, consider fitting a high-level, built-in oven, especially if the main cook has back problems. If you go for a built-in oven, it makes sense to also go for a built-in microwave.

In terms of fuel options there is really only gas or electricity – although oil and LPG are available if you're not connected to the gas network. Dual fuel, where you have an electric oven with a gas hob, is a very popular option.

For hobs, there are a number of sub-options available, depending on the fuel you opt for. Your choice comes down to your budget, personal preference and, often, what you value the most: look or utility.

HOBS
ELECTRIC PLATE HOBS
Electric plate and coil hobs are how all electric hobs used to be. These days they tend to be the bargain

basement option, not because they don't work well but because the 'look' is fairly limited and a tad old-fashioned.

CERAMIC HOBS

The heating element is set under a ceramic glass top and as such these offer a neat, easy-clean surface. On the downside they don't respond as well as induction or gas hobs and the heat distribution isn't as good.

INDUCTION HOBS

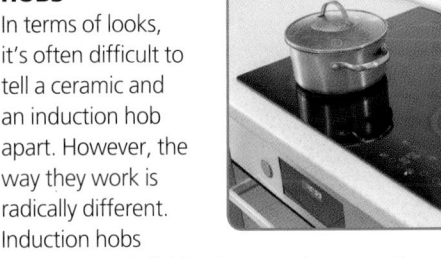

In terms of looks, it's often difficult to tell a ceramic and an induction hob apart. However, the way they work is radically different. Induction hobs use a magnetic field to heat up the pan without actually creating a hot surface. If you have small children and/or a cat these can be a godsend in terms of safety. They are usually more responsive than ceramic hobs and generate a more even heat. On the downside, you pay for this safety and they only work if your pans are magnetic.

GAS HOBS

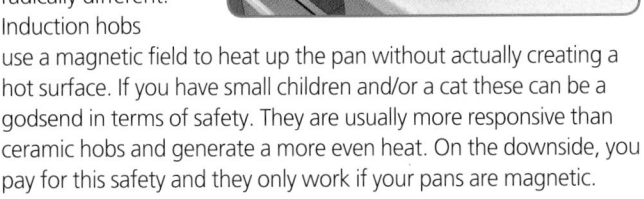

This is the most traditional option but it polarises views – people either love the look or hate it. Even if you love the look you will still have to spend far more time keeping the hob clean, which can dampen your enthusiasm. Gas gives very responsive hobs and it's easy to see exactly how much heat you're using.

GAS ON GLASS HOBS

This is a largely successful attempt to eliminate the main downside of gas hobs; namely keeping them clean. They are essentially gas hobs set onto a nice, smooth ceramic glass surface. The downside of these is that you pay for this easy-clean design.

OVENS

Gas ovens tend to be a thing of the past, although you can still buy them. The main advantage of electric ovens is that they can be fan-assisted.

If you have an electric oven then you can't just plug it into a standard electric socket and assume all will be well. The vast majority of ovens draw so much power that you run the very real risk of setting fire to your lovely new kitchen if you don't ensure it has been wired up properly, i.e. that it uses at least a 10mm electric cable that goes back directly to the main fuse box/consumer unit and feeds the oven only. This cable should always be tested for resistance to ensure it's safe to use.

If you go for a gas hob/oven you'll probably still need an electrical socket available for the ignition, although you can buy hobs that use a battery for the ignition process.

If you have a large range cooker you might need to use a larger gas pipe to ensure it works properly. It makes sense to get this checked at the start of the project and install a larger diameter pipe (22mm) if you're in any doubt.

MICROWAVES

I use microwaves to defrost peas and heat up milk, and that's it. As a result my needs are very simple, and I saved myself a lot of money by just buying a basic, cheap model. If your needs are greater than mine then you should consider the following:

SIZE

The physical dimensions of your microwave will affect how much you can cook at a time and how well it will fit into your kitchen, which can be critical if you're thinking of fitting it into a kitchen unit. Be aware that two microwaves with the same external dimensions might not have the same internal dimensions, so always check the internal size as well.

POWER

The wattage of your microwave will determine how quickly it will cook your food. In reality, the difference in cooking time is usually measured in seconds so, unless you're in a real hurry, it's rarely an issue. However, most packaged meals will list the timings based on the wattage, so you'll need to know your microwave's wattage even if it's not a factor when making your purchase.

LOCATION

The cheapest microwaves just sit on the worktop, which can take up valuable workspace. A microwave fitted into a kitchen unit frees up workspace, but costs a bit more and reduces storage space.

You can buy microwaves that are designed to be installed under kitchen units or over your cooker hob. These microwaves are supported by wall brackets so you'll need to ensure that the wall is strong enough. Check if the microwave requires an external vent. If it does, it will need to be on an external wall, you'll have to factor in the hassle of drilling the hole for the vent, and you'll need to make sure the vent isn't too close to your boiler flue. The downside of a microwave over your cooker is that this is where most cooker hoods go, so you might have to compromise on your kitchen air-extraction system.

CONTROLS

It's always worth going to a store and actually checking out the controls, as they have a huge influence on how easy it's going to be to use your microwave. Buttons can be quick to use but you can end up with so many of them that it just becomes confusing. Dials tend to be easier and more flexible, but aren't as accurate as buttons.

MICROWAVE GRILL AND COMBI MICROWAVES

The big downside of microwaves is that the cooked food can look very bland, soggy and unappetising. You can get around this by buying a microwave that also has a grill function. If you really want to push the boat out you can get a combi microwave, which also has a conventional oven function. These are ideal in small kitchens where you are cooking for only one or two people, as you can dispense with an oven entirely and just use your microwave. Alas, like many 'multi-functional' tools, you can end up with something that does everything but doesn't do any of them very well, so do your homework before you buy.

REVIEWS

There are literally thousands of microwaves on the market and the price and performance of them fluctuates enormously. It's always worth setting aside the time to read at least a few reviews from a number of different sources, especially if you're intending to rely on your microwave to provide most of your meals.

HOODS AND EXTRACTORS

These fall into two basic groups: extraction or recirculation. It's always best to go for an extractor, but this does rely on your cooker being close to an external wall, which isn't always the case. If your cooker is a distance from an outside wall you'll have to weigh up the benefit of better extraction versus the look of the vent pipe, although it's possible to hide the vent within cupboards or take it into the ceiling and run it between your joists to the outside. Another option is to go for a whole-kitchen extractor that can be placed away from the oven but close to an external wall.

The hood/extractor you go for will have to fit your cooker and your kitchen. If you've gone for a large, range-style cooker then you'll need a suitably wide extractor.

To calculate the extraction rate, you'll need to measure the volume of your kitchen in cubic metres (length x breadth x height) and then multiply this value by 12 for 12 changes of air per hour – you can go as low as 10, but 12 is best. For example, if your kitchen is 5m long, 3m wide and has a ceiling height of 2.3m, you'll have an extraction rate of: $(5 \times 3 \times 2.3) \times 12 = 414m^3$ per hour. In countries that don't follow metric, these measurements tend to be in CFM (cubic feet per minute). In this instance, work out all your measurements in feet and then divide by 5, e.g. $(16.4 \times 9.8 \times 7.5) / 5 = 241$ f^3/m.

Be aware that to save on energy many regions (the EU for example) have set a maximum extraction rate. In the EU this is 650 m^3/h. You can go beyond this as a 'boost' function but for no more than ten minutes.

The ideal place for lighting when using a cooker is directly overhead, which is usually where the hood is. With this is mind check the quality of the lighting that the hood comes with, if it comes with any.

CHIMNEY COOKER HOODS

These need to back onto a wall and are designed together with your cooker to make a statement. If you like the look, all you need

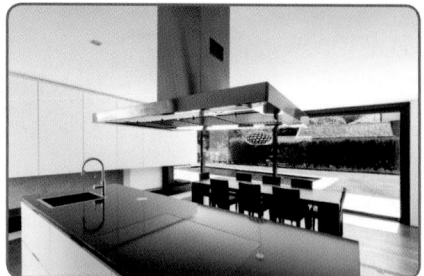

to consider is the extraction power and the quality of the lighting underneath.

ISLAND COOKER HOODS

These are like chimney hoods but are attached to the ceiling rather than the wall. As such, you need to make sure your ceiling is capable of supporting the weight. These are generally more suitable for larger cookers, but come with a hefty price tag.

INTEGRATED/CANOPY HOODS

In terms of design, these are the antithesis of the chimney hood in that they are designed to be hidden from view rather than draw attention to themselves. You may struggle to buy one of these suitable for a larger cooker.

Integrated hoods tend to look like canopy hoods when not being used – i.e. they are hidden in a unit, but when you want to cook, you pull the hood open and away they go.

DOWNDRAFT EXTRACTORS

These are quite neat. They are usually fitted behind your cooker and when not in use they are hidden below the worktop. When you want to use them you press a button, the extractor pops up from behind your cooker, extracts away and then disappears again when you've finished.

These can be very handy if you want an island cooker with a minimalist look, although to extract from an island you'd either need a vent going up to the ceiling – which rather spoils the minimalist look – or you need to run ducting under the floor, which can be an expensive business all by itself. The downside of these is the price.

Fridges and icemakers

A standard fridge used to be designed to fit in a worktop gap of 600mm (24in). Alas, times change and fridges are now getting bigger and bigger by the day.

If you go for a standard fridge all you need to worry about is having a plug available. If you go for an 'American-style' fridge-freezer with integrated filtered water and ice-maker then there are a few more things to ponder.

The first issue is the size. These fridges tend to be deeper than a standard worktop so they invariably stand proud of the rest of the kitchen, which can be no bad thing. However, the reason they stand proud is because the doors need to swing open, so you need to consider not only the actual width of the fridge but also its width when the doors are wide open – which units will be blocked off, how to stop the doors banging into cabinets, etc.

If you have a fridge with a water and/or icemaking facility you'll need to get a water supply to it, although some fridges use a water store that you just top up by hand every few days. As a general rule these fridges use a 6mm plastic pipe, with an isolation valve so that you can disconnect the water supply if need be, and a check valve, to ensure that the water can only go in one direction. The isolation valve is often exactly the same as those used for dishwashers and washing machines and all the connections are usually push-fit, so it's not something you have to bring in the professionals for.

Be aware that 6mm is not a standard pipe size in the plumbing industry but it is used a lot in the hydraulic and air-conditioning sectors, so if you need more pipe try these companies first.

Entertainment

In days of yore, kitchen entertainment was largely restricted to watching people like me try to cook. For better or worse, the sight of a guy cooking dinner, oblivious to the fact that the tea towel in his back pocket has just burst into flames, is no longer deemed enough when it comes to kitchen entertainment.

KITCHEN TV

With the advent of flat-screen technology the TV was no longer considered too bulky to fit into the average kitchen, so these days you can cook along with the TV chefs.

At its simplest you can just affix the kitchen TV to the wall using a standard wall bracket but, if you want to go a little more stylish, you can fit a flip-down TV bracket that allows you to hide the TV under a wall cabinet when it's not in use.

The only downside to this is that, if you have a worktop under the wall cabinet then the maximum size of your TV is going to be limited to 24in or 32in at a push. If you have fitted a plinth underneath your cabinets then you might have to play around with the position of the bracket to make sure it clears the plinth.

A more expensive option is to buy an integrated TV. These are designed so that instead of a cabinet door you have a door that

Courtesy of reflectv.co.uk

is a TV. When they're not being used they just look like a built-in oven. There are also ones that function as a mirror when they aren't turned on or can be part of the splashback as shown above.

Another option is a ceiling-mounted TV. These can either be permanently hung from the ceiling or can fold away into the ceiling when not in use. The latter is something you'd have to look into very early on in the kitchen design process; it's also expensive and isn't suitable for all ceilings.

Depending on where you're thinking of siting the TV you might want to consider buying one that is waterproof. I would shy away from fitting any electrical appliance too close to a sink, but if you're planning this at least ask the manufacturer for advice beforehand.

SOUND SYSTEMS

These days it's usually easier to use your phone to store and play your music collection. The only issue for the kitchen is mounting the speakers and the most popular place in a kitchen is on or in the ceiling, the wall cabinet pelmets or the base unit kickboards. If you're feeling really flash you might consider a pop-up countertop-mounted speaker system – one press and you suddenly have a speaker on your worktop.

You can buy radios that are designed to be built into cabinets or set onto kitchen walls, and if you opt for Bluetooth you can avoid having to hide a network of wires.

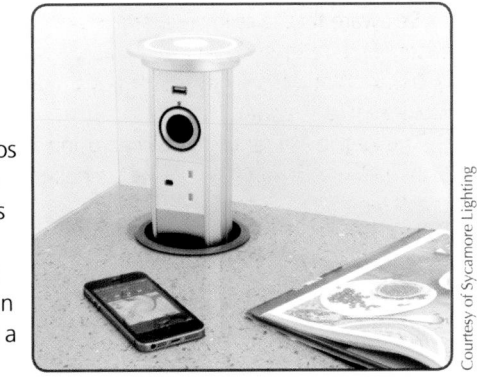

Courtesy of Sycamore Lighting

Index

accent lighting 13, 175
alcoves 13
ambient lighting 13, 175
appliances 9
Apron sinks 12
asbestos 35
augers 50
   cutting around pipes and cables 115–16

base units 9
   fitting 109–12
   sorting screws 109
batons, fixing 130–1
   fitting to drylined wall (dot and dab) 131
Belfast sinks 12
blind base units 10
   blind base corner base units 105
boiler flues 27
bradawls 38
breakfast bars 16
breakfront 13
brick walls 44
budgets 17
   how much are you going to change? 17
   how much do you have? 17
   new kitchen or refurbishment? 17
   second-hand kitchens 17
   what are you going to do for yourself? 17–18
Butler sinks 12

cabinets 12, 105
   cabinet construction 16
   cabinet refacing and refinishing 16
   childproofing 83–4
   corner units 105–6
   cornices 128–9
   cutting around pipes and cables 115–16
   fitting base units 109–12
   fitting batons into stud walls 130–1
   fitting door and drawer handles 124
   fitting doors and drawers 121–4
   fitting filler pieces, corner pieces and end
     panels 116–21
   fitting kickboards (plinths) 125–7
   fitting to wall 107
   fitting wall units 112–14
   framed and frameless cabinets 55
   pelmets 128–9
   plinth drawers 106
   pull-out shelves and drawers 106
   removing base cabinets 94–5
   removing wall cabinets 91–2
   setting the height 107–8

cables, cutting around 115–16
carpenter's awls 38
cartridge guns 43
ceiling lights 177
ceiling repairs 101–2
   reboarding the ceiling 102–3
ceramic hobs 183
chair rails 13
chemicals 85
childproofing your kitchen 83–4
   safety considerations 85
chimney cooker hoods 184
chopping boards, fitting 156–8
clamps 43
claw hammers 43
clearance space 13, 25–6
compact florescent light (CFL) bulbs 176
composite countertops 133–4
conventional light bulbs 176
cooker hoods 10, 184
cookers 27, 182
   cooker clearance areas 26
   fitting cooker hob 156
   hobs 182–3
corbels 13
cordless hammer drills 39–40
Corian countertops 133
corner pieces, fitting 119
corner strips 150–1
corner units 10, 105–6
cornices 10
   fitting 128–9
counter-sink drill bits 50
countertops 12, 72, 133
   concrete countertops 75–8
   do-it-yourself option 136
   epoxy resin countertops 78–9
   fitting a countersunk chopping board 156–8
   fitting corner and edging strips 150–3
   fitting the cooker hob 156
   fitting the sink 154–6
   installing solid wood 159
   mitred corners 140–8
   mitred rounded worktop edges and
     curves 150
   mitred straight connections 148–9
   renovating and adapting 79–81
   repairing damaged countertops 159
   tiled countertops 72–4
   types 72–9, 133–6
   see also worktops
craft knives 38
cuts 34

dado rails 13
deck mixers 180
design 20
   adding to basic design principles 27
   clearances and design distances 25–6
   common layouts 23–4
   creating your design 28–31
   design ergonomics 22–3
   drawing up a plan 20–2
   islands and peninsulas 24–5
   using kitchen planners 31
diagonal corner units 10, 106
dining areas 25
dishwashers 181–2
dismantling old kitchen 87
   demolition process 87–8
   planning ahead 87
   plumbing 95–6
   removing base cabinets 94–5
   removing existing worktop 92–4
   removing hob 96
   removing old doors and drawers 89–91
   removing old flooring 97
   removing wall cabinets 91–2
do-it-yourself 17, 36
   basic tools 38–43
   bits and screws 49–50
   building work 17
   decorating 18
   electrical work 17–18, 37
   fitting kitchen units 36
   furnishings 18
   gas work 18, 37
   heating 18
   lighting 37
   plastering 36
   plumbing work 18, 36–7
   tiling 18, 36
   using silicon sealant 51–3
   wall and floor coverings 36
   walls and wall plugs 44–7
doors 55
   adjusting doors with modern hinges 122–3
   changing door handles 67
   fitting door handles 65, 124
   fitting inset doors onto face-framed
     cabinets 63–5
   fitting new doors 57, 121–2
   fitting overlay doors onto face-framed
     cabinets 63
   fitting overlay doors onto frameless
     cabinets 59–62
   fitting soft-close doors 62

making a template 57–8
marking hinge and handle positions 58
measuring 55–6
painting 67–70
refacing 71
removing frameless doors with quick-release hinges 89
removing frameless doors with sliding hinges 89
removing handles 91
removing overlay and inset doors on framed cabinets 90
renovating existing doors 66
staining 70–1
varnishing 70
dot and dab 131
downdraft extractors 184
draw frontage 16
drawerline units 9
drawers 55
  childproofing 83–4
  fitting drawer handles 65, 124
  fitting drawers 57–65, 124
  fitting soft-close drawers 62
  levelling drawer fronts 124
  measuring 55–6
  painting 67–70
  plinth drawers 106
  pull-out shelves and drawers 106
  refacing 71
  removing 90
  removing drawer fronts 91
  removing handles 91
  renovating existing drawers 66
  staining 70–1
  varnishing 70
drill bits 49
  drill bit diameters 48
drills 39–40
drylined walls 44
  dryline wall plugs 47
  fitting batons (dot and dab) 131
dust protection 34

ear protection 35
edging strips 151–3
electric plate hobs 182–3
electric screwdrivers 38–9
electrical work 17–18, 37
  moving electrical outlets and changing lighting 100–1
  removing hob 96
electricity safety 85
elevation plan/drawing 14
end panels 10–11, 112
  fitting end panels 120–1
ergonomics 22–3
extractors 10, 184
  boiler flues 27
eye protection 34

Farmhouse sinks 12
Fein saws 42
filler pieces 11, 116
  making and fitting 117–18
fitted appliances 9
floor plan/drawing 14
flooring 36
  alternative flooring 173
  comfort 169
  coping with impacts 169
  coping with water 169
  fitting laminate flooring 171–3
  removing laminate flooring 97
  removing old floor tiles 97
  removing vinyl tiles 97
  tiling floor 169–70
florescent strip lights 176
footprint 14
freestanding appliances 9
fridges 185

garbage disposal units 181
gas cooker safety 27
gas hobs 183
gas on glass hobs 183
gas work 18, 37
  moving the gas services 99
  removing hob 96
glass countertops 136
gloves 35
granite countertops 135–6
  painting 80–1
  repairing damage 80

halogen light bulbs 176
hammer drills 39–40
hand screwdrivers 39
handle ties and straps 84
heat safety 85
heating 18, 19
hex screws 49
hexalobular screws 49
high pressure taps 179
highline units 9
hobs 182–3
  fitting 156
  removing 96
hole cutters 165
holesaws 50

icemakers 185
impact drivers 39
induction hobs 183
injuries 33–4
inset sinks 11
installation 99
  moving electrical outlets and changing lighting 100–1
  moving gas services 99
  moving plumbing 99–100

planning work schedule 99
  reboarding and repairing holes in walls and ceilings 101–2
  reboarding ceiling 102–3
integrated/canopy hoods 184
islands 11, 24–5
  island cooker hoods 184

jigs 141
jigsaws 40–1
  down-stroke laminate blades 41
  scroll/tight curve blades 41
  tile blades 41

kickboards 12
  fitting kickboards 125–7
  kickboard heaters 19
  kickboard lighting 177
kitchens 4
  fitted kitchens 14
  freestanding kitchens 14–15
  galley kitchens 23–4
  L-shaped kitchens 23–4
  one-wall kitchens 23
  U-shaped kitchens 23–4
knee protection 34

laminate countertops 133
  installing 137–9
  painting 80–1
  repairing damage 79–80
laminate edging strips 152–3
laminate flooring 171–3
laminate splashbacks 166
  fitting laminate splashback 166–7
  removing 81
layouts 23–4
Lazy Susans 10, 106
LED light bulbs 176
levels 38
lighting 37, 175
  changing lighting 100–1
  types of light bulb 176
  types of lighting 177
locks 84
low pressure taps 179

magnetic locks 84
mantles 15
marker pens 38
masonry drill bits 49
metal corner strips 150–1
metal countertops 136
metal drill bits (HSS) 49
metal edging strips 151
metal joining strips 151
microwaves 183–4
  microwave grill and combi microwaves 184
  reviews 184
mitre saws 42

mitred corners 140–1
  cutting a mitred corner 142–8
  worktop template (jig) 141
mitred rounded worktop edges and curves 150
mitred straight connections 148–9
monobloc taps 179–80
multiple rectangles 22–3

non-standard construction walls 44

oblique projection drawings 15
ovens 182, 183
  clearance areas 26

painting countertops 81
painting doors and drawers 67–70
pelmets 12
  fitting 128–9
pencils 38
peninsulas 15, 24–5
perspective drawings 15
Phillips screws 49
picture rails 13
pilasters 15
pillar taps 180
pipes, cutting around 115–16
plans 14
  creating your design 28–31
  drawing up a plan of your kitchen 20–2
  using kitchen planners 31
plasterboard repairs 101–2
plastering 36
plinths 12
  fitting plinths 125–7
  plinth drawers 106
plumbing work 18, 36–7
  disconnecting the sink 96
  moving the plumbing 99–100
  turning off the water 95–6
pocket doors 15
Pozidriv screws 49
preparation areas 25
professional help 87

quarter-turn taps 180
quick-release hinges 122

radiators 19
radius feature ends 16
reciprocating saws 41–2
refrigerator landing areas 26
refurbishment see renovation
renovation 17
  changing countertops 72–81
  changing doors and drawers 55–6
  changing splashbacks 81–2
  fitting new doors and drawers 57–65
  moving cabinets 71
  renovating existing doors and
    drawers 66–71
resin-based fixing kits 47

rip saws 41
router and template 42–3
rubber mallets 43

safety considerations 33–4
  childproofing your kitchen 83–5
  safety equipment 34–5, 87
saws 41–2
  multitools 42
sconces 16
screwdrivers 38–9
screws 49
  screw bits 49
  screw gauges 48
  screw lengths 48
  sorting screws 109
SDS chisels 50
SDS drill bits 49
SDS hammer drills 39
self-drill plasterboard fixings 45–6
Shaker style 16
shelf frontage 16
silicon sealants 51
  applying silicon sealant 52–3
  buying the right sealant 51
  removing old sealant 52
sinks 11–12, 179
  disconnecting the sink 96
  fitting 154–6
  sink areas 25
sit-on sinks 11
slide-on hinges 122
slipped disc 33
slotted screws 49
snack bars 16
soft-close hinges 124
solid surface countertops 133
sound systems 185
splashbacks 12, 161–7
  changing splashbacks 81–2
  removing existing splashbacks 81–2
  using a tile hole cutter 165
spring toggles 46
spring-release locks 84
staining doors and drawers 70–1
staining wooden countertops 81
stone countertops 135–6
storage calculations 26
stud detectors 43
stud walls 44
  fitting batons into stud walls 130–1
  fixings for stud walls 45–7

tape measures 38, 56
taps 179–80
task lighting 175
tennis elbow 33
tenon saws 42
terminology 7–12
  design terminology 13–16
  regional terminology 48

thermal block fixings 47
thermal units 19
Thermalite 47
three 3D elevation drawings 15
tile drill bits 49–50
tiled splashbacks 161–3
  fitting a tiled splashback 163–5
  removing 82
tiling 18, 36
  tiling floor 169–70
toe kicks 16
tools 38–43, 87
  drill batteries 40
  fitting laminate countertop 137, 140
  fitting laminate flooring 171
  fitting laminate splashback 166
  fitting new cabinets 107
  fitting tiled splashback 162–3
  manufacturers' deals 39
  units of power 41
torx screws 49
traffic patterns 16
TV 185

under-cabinet lights 177
under floor central heating (UFCH) 19
undermount sinks 11–12
unit construction 16
unit refacing and refinishing 16
upstands 12
utility knives 38

varnishing doors and drawers 70

walkways 25
wall units 12
  fitting 112–14
walls 44
  fitting batons 130–1
  fitting new cabinets 107
  reboarding and repairing holes 101–2
  securing to low-density Thermalite 47
  wall plugs 44–7
washing machines 182
waste disposal units 181
water filters 180–1
water softeners 181
wood drill bits 49
wooden countertops 134–5
  installing 159
  staining or painting 81
work aisles 16, 25
work areas 25
work centres 22–3
work triangle 16, 22
work zones 22–3
workbenches 35
worktops 12
  removing existing worktop 92–4
  worktop area 26
  see also countertops